QUANTITATIVE INVESTMENT ANALYSIS

T0293049

Fourth Edition

Richard A. DeFusco, CFA

Dennis W. McLeavey, CFA

Jerald E. Pinto, CFA

David E. Runkle, CFA

WILEY

CONTENTS

LEARNING OBJECTIVES, SUMMARY OVERVIEW, AND PROBLEMS

Part 1

LEARNING OBJECTIVES,
SUMMARY OVERVIEW,
AND PROBLEMS

CHAPTER 1

THE TIME VALUE OF MONEY

LEARNING OUTCOMES

The candidate should be able to:

- interpret interest rates as required rates of return, discount rates, or opportunity costs;
- explain an interest rate as the sum of a real risk-free rate and premiums that compensate investors for bearing distinct types of risk;
- calculate and interpret the effective annual rate, given the stated annual interest rate and the frequency of compounding;
- solve time value of money problems for different frequencies of compounding;
- calculate and interpret the future value (FV) and present value (PV) of a single sum of money, an ordinary annuity, an annuity due, a perpetuity (PV only), and a series of unequal cash flows;
- demonstrate the use of a time line in modeling and solving time value of money problems.

SUMMARY

In this chapter, we have explored a foundation topic in investment mathematics, the time value of money. We have developed and reviewed the following concepts for use in financial applications:

- The interest rate, r, is the required rate of return; r is also called the discount rate or opportunity cost.
- An interest rate can be viewed as the sum of the real risk-free interest rate and a set of premiums that compensate lenders for risk: an inflation premium, a default risk premium, a liquidity premium, and a maturity premium.
- The future value, FV, is the present value, PV, times the future value factor, $(1 + r)^N$.
- The interest rate, r, makes current and future currency amounts equivalent based on their time value.
- The stated annual interest rate is a quoted interest rate that does not account for compounding within the year.

- The periodic rate is the quoted interest rate per period; it equals the stated annual interest rate divided by the number of compounding periods per year.
- The effective annual rate is the amount by which a unit of currency will grow in a year with interest on interest included.
- An annuity is a finite set of level sequential cash flows.
- There are two types of annuities, the annuity due and the ordinary annuity. The annuity due has a first cash flow that occurs immediately; the ordinary annuity has a first cash flow that occurs one period from the present (indexed at $t = 1$).
- On a time line, we can index the present as 0 and then display equally spaced hash marks to represent a number of periods into the future. This representation allows us to index how many periods away each cash flow will be paid.
- Annuities may be handled in a similar approach as single payments if we use annuity factors rather than single-payment factors.
- The present value, PV, is the future value, FV, times the present value factor, $(1 + r)^{-N}$.
- The present value of a perpetuity is A/r, where A is the periodic payment to be received forever.
- It is possible to calculate an unknown variable, given the other relevant variables in time value of money problems.
- The cash flow additivity principle can be used to solve problems with uneven cash flows by combining single payments and annuities.

PRACTICE PROBLEMS

1. The table below gives current information on the interest rates for two two-year and two eight-year maturity investments. The table also gives the maturity, liquidity, and default risk characteristics of a new investment possibility (Investment 3). All investments promise only a single payment (a payment at maturity). Assume that premiums relating to inflation, liquidity, and default risk are constant across all time horizons.

Investment	Maturity (in Years)	Liquidity	Default Risk	Interest Rate (%)
1	2	High	Low	2.0
2	2	Low	Low	2.5
3	7	Low	Low	r_3
4	8	High	Low	4.0
5	8	Low	High	6.5

Based on the information in the above table, address the following:
A. Explain the difference between the interest rates on Investment 1 and Investment 2.
B. Estimate the default risk premium.
C. Calculate upper and lower limits for the interest rate on Investment 3, r_3.

2. A couple plans to set aside $20,000 per year in a conservative portfolio projected to earn 7 percent a year. If they make their first savings contribution one year from now, how much will they have at the end of 20 years?

3. Two years from now, a client will receive the first of three annual payments of $20,000 from a small business project. If she can earn 9 percent annually on her investments and

plans to retire in six years, how much will the three business project payments be worth at the time of her retirement?

4. To cover the first year's total college tuition payments for his two children, a father will make a $75,000 payment five years from now. How much will he need to invest today to meet his first tuition goal if the investment earns 6 percent annually?

5. A client can choose between receiving 10 annual $100,000 retirement payments, starting one year from today, or receiving a lump sum today. Knowing that he can invest at a rate of 5 percent annually, he has decided to take the lump sum. What lump sum today will be equivalent to the future annual payments?

6. You are considering investing in two different instruments. The first instrument will pay nothing for three years, but then it will pay $20,000 per year for four years. The second instrument will pay $20,000 for three years and $30,000 in the fourth year. All payments are made at year-end. If your required rate of return on these investments is 8 percent annually, what should you be willing to pay for:
    A. The first instrument?
    B. The second instrument (use the formula for a four-year annuity)?

7. Suppose you plan to send your daughter to college in three years. You expect her to earn two-thirds of her tuition payment in scholarship money, so you estimate that your payments will be $10,000 a year for four years. To estimate whether you have set aside enough money, you ignore possible inflation in tuition payments and assume that you can earn 8 percent annually on your investments. How much should you set aside now to cover these payments?

8. A client plans to send a child to college for four years starting 18 years from now. Having set aside money for tuition, she decides to plan for room and board also. She estimates these costs at $20,000 per year, payable at the beginning of each year, by the time her child goes to college. If she starts next year and makes 17 payments into a savings account paying 5 percent annually, what annual payments must she make?

9. A couple plans to pay their childs college tuition for 4 years starting 18 years from now. The current annual cost of college is C$7,000, and they expect this cost to rise at an annual rate of 5 percent. In their planning, they assume that they can earn 6 percent annually. How much must they put aside each year, starting next year, if they plan to make 17 equal payments?

10. The nominal risk-free rate is *best* described as the sum of the real risk-free rate and a premium for:
    A. maturity.
    B. liquidity.
    C. expected inflation.

11. Which of the following risk premiums is most relevant in explaining the difference in yields between 30-year bonds issued by the US Treasury and 30-year bonds issued by a small private issuer?
    A. Inflation
    B. Maturity
    C. Liquidity

12. A bank quotes a stated annual interest rate of 4.00%. If that rate is equal to an effective annual rate of 4.08%, then the bank is compounding interest:
    A. daily.
    B. quarterly.
    C. semiannually.

13. The value in six years of $75,000 invested today at a stated annual interest rate of 7% compounded quarterly is *closest* to:
    A. $112,555.
    B. $113,330.
    C. $113,733.

14. A client requires £100,000 one year from now. If the stated annual rate is 2.50% compounded weekly, the deposit needed today is *closest* to:
    A. £97,500.
    B. £97,532.
    C. £97,561.

15. For a lump sum investment of ¥250,000 invested at a stated annual rate of 3% compounded daily, the number of months needed to grow the sum to ¥1,000,000 is *closest* to:
    A. 555.
    B. 563.
    C. 576.

16. Given a €1,000,000 investment for four years with a stated annual rate of 3% compounded continuously, the difference in its interest earnings compared with the same investment compounded daily is *closest* to:
    A. €1.
    B. €6.
    C. €455.

17. An investment pays €300 annually for five years, with the first payment occurring today. The present value (PV) of the investment discounted at a 4% annual rate is *closest* to:
    A. €1,336.
    B. €1,389.
    C. €1,625.

18. A perpetual preferred stock makes its first quarterly dividend payment of $2.00 in five quarters. If the required annual rate of return is 6% compounded quarterly, the stock's present value is *closest* to:
    A. $31.
    B. $126.
    C. $133.

19. A saver deposits the following amounts in an account paying a stated annual rate of 4%, compounded semiannually:

Year	End-of-Year Deposits ($)
1	4,000
2	8,000
3	7,000
4	10,000

At the end of Year 4, the value of the account is *closest* to:
A. $30,432
B. $30,447
C. $31,677

20.   An investment of €500,000 today that grows to €800,000 after six years has a stated annual interest rate *closest* to:
A.   7.5% compounded continuously.
B.   7.7% compounded daily.
C.   8.0% compounded semiannually.

21.   A sweepstakes winner may select either a perpetuity of £2,000 a month beginning with the first payment in one month or an immediate lump sum payment of £350,000. If the annual discount rate is 6% compounded monthly, the present value of the perpetuity is:
A.   less than the lump sum.
B.   equal to the lump sum.
C.   greater than the lump sum.

22.   At a 5% interest rate per year compounded annually, the present value (PV) of a 10-year ordinary annuity with annual payments of $2,000 is $15,443.47. The PV of a 10-year annuity due with the same interest rate and payments is *closest* to:
A. $14,708.
B. $16,216.
C. $17,443.

23.   Grandparents are funding a newborn's future university tuition costs, estimated at $50,000/year for four years, with the first payment due as a lump sum in 18 years. Assuming a 6% effective annual rate, the required deposit today is *closest* to:
A. $60,699.
B. $64,341.
C. $68,201.

24.   The present value (PV) of an investment with the following year-end cash flows (CF) and a 12% required annual rate of return is *closest* to:

Year	Cash Flow (€)
1	100,000
2	150,000
5	−10,000

A.   €201,747.
B.   €203,191.
C.   €227,573.

25.   A sports car, purchased for £200,000, is financed for five years at an annual rate of 6% compounded monthly. If the first payment is due in one month, the monthly payment is *closest* to:
A.   £3,847.
B.   £3,867.
C.   £3,957.

26. Given a stated annual interest rate of 6% compounded quarterly, the level amount that, deposited quarterly, will grow to £25,000 at the end of 10 years is *closest* to:
    A. £461.
    B. £474.
    C. £836.

27. Given the following time line and a discount rate of 4% a year compounded annually, the present value (PV), as of the end of Year 5 (PV_5), of the cash flow received at the end of Year 20 is *closest* to:
    A. $22,819.
    B. $27,763.
    C. $28,873.

28. A client invests €20,000 in a four-year certificate of deposit (CD) that annually pays interest of 3.5%. The annual CD interest payments are automatically reinvested in a separate savings account at a stated annual interest rate of 2% compounded monthly. At maturity, the value of the combined asset is *closest* to:
    A. €21,670.
    B. €22,890.
    C. €22,950.

CHAPTER 2

ORGANIZING, VISUALIZING, AND DESCRIBING DATA

LEARNING OUTCOMES

The candidate should be able to:

- Identify and compare data types;
- Describe how data are organized for quantitative analysis;
- Interpret frequency and related distributions;
- Interpret a contingency table;
- Describe ways that data may be visualized and evaluate uses of specific visualizations;
- Describe how to select among visualization types;
- Calculate and interpret measures of central tendency;
- Select among alternative definitions of mean to address an investment problem;
- Calculate quantiles and interpret related visualizations;
- Calculate and interpret measures of dispersion;
- Calculate and interpret target downside deviation;
- Interpret skewness;
- Interpret kurtosis;
- Interpret correlation between two variables.

SUMMARY

In this chapter, we have presented tools and techniques for organizing, visualizing, and describing data that permit us to convert raw data into useful information for investment analysis.

- Data can be defined as a collection of numbers, characters, words, and text—as well as images, audio, and video—in a raw or organized format to represent facts or information.

9

- From a statistical perspective, data can be classified as numerical data and categorical data. Numerical data (also called quantitative data) are values that represent measured or counted quantities as a number. Categorical data (also called qualitative data) are values that describe a quality or characteristic of a group of observations and usually take only a limited number of values that are mutually exclusive.
- Numerical data can be further split into two types: continuous data and discrete data. Continuous data can be measured and can take on any numerical value in a specified range of values. Discrete data are numerical values that result from a counting process and therefore are limited to a finite number of values.
- Categorical data can be further classified into two types: nominal data and ordinal data. Nominal data are categorical values that are not amenable to being organized in a logical order, while ordinal data are categorical values that can be logically ordered or ranked.
- Based on how they are collected, data can be categorized into three types: cross-sectional, time series, and panel. Time-series data are a sequence of observations for a single observational unit on a specific variable collected over time and at discrete and typically equally spaced intervals of time. Cross-sectional data are a list of the observations of a specific variable from multiple observational units at a given point in time. Panel data are a mix of time-series and cross-sectional data that consists of observations through time on one or more variables for multiple observational units.
- Based on whether or not data are in a highly organized form, they can be classified into structured and unstructured types. Structured data are highly organized in a pre-defined manner, usually with repeating patterns. Unstructured data do not follow any conventionally organized forms; they are typically alternative data as they are usually collected from unconventional sources.
- Raw data are typically organized into either a one-dimensional array or a two-dimensional rectangular array (also called a data table) for quantitative analysis.
- A frequency distribution is a tabular display of data constructed either by counting the observations of a variable by distinct values or groups or by tallying the values of a numerical variable into a set of numerically ordered bins. Frequency distributions permit us to evaluate how data are distributed.
- The relative frequency of observations in a bin (interval or bucket) is the number of observations in the bin divided by the total number of observations. The cumulative relative frequency cumulates (adds up) the relative frequencies as we move from the first bin to the last, thus giving the fraction of the observations that are less than the upper limit of each bin.
- A contingency table is a tabular format that displays the frequency distributions of two or more categorical variables simultaneously. One application of contingency tables is for evaluating the performance of a classification model (using a confusion matrix). Another application of contingency tables is to investigate a potential association between two categorical variables by performing a chi-square test of independence.
- Visualization is the presentation of data in a pictorial or graphical format for the purpose of increasing understanding and for gaining insights into the data.
- A histogram is a bar chart of data that have been grouped into a frequency distribution. A frequency polygon is a graph of frequency distributions obtained by drawing straight lines joining successive midpoints of bars representing the class frequencies.

- A bar chart is used to plot the frequency distribution of categorical data, with each bar representing a distinct category and the bar's height (or length) proportional to the frequency of the corresponding category. Grouped bar charts or stacked bar charts can present the frequency distribution of multiple categorical variables simultaneously.
- A tree-map is a graphical tool to display categorical data. It consists of a set of colored rectangles to represent distinct groups, and the area of each rectangle is proportional to the value of the corresponding group. Additional dimensions of categorical data can be displayed by nested rectangles.
- A word cloud is a visual device for representing textual data, with the size of each distinct word being proportional to the frequency with which it appears in the given text.
- A line chart is a type of graph used to visualize ordered observations and often to display the change of data series over time. A bubble line chart is a special type of line chart that uses varying-sized bubbles as data points to represent an additional dimension of data.
- A scatter plot is a type of graph for visualizing the joint variation in two numerical variables. It is constructed by drawing dots to indicate the values of the two variables plotted against the corresponding axes. A scatter plot matrix organizes scatter plots between pairs of variables into a matrix format to inspect all pairwise relationships between more than two variables in one combined visual.
- A heat map is a type of graphic that organizes and summarizes data in a tabular format and represents it using a color spectrum. It is often used in displaying frequency distributions or visualizing the degree of correlation among different variables.
- The key consideration when selecting among chart types is the intended purpose of visualizing data (i.e., whether it is for exploring/presenting distributions or relationships or for making comparisons).
- A population is defined as all members of a specified group. A sample is a subset of a population.
- A parameter is any descriptive measure of a population. A sample statistic (statistic, for short) is a quantity computed from or used to describe a sample.
- Sample statistics—such as measures of central tendency, measures of dispersion, skewness, and kurtosis—help with investment analysis, particularly in making probabilistic statements about returns.
- Measures of central tendency specify where data are centered and include the mean, median, and mode (i.e., the most frequently occurring value).
- The arithmetic mean is the sum of the observations divided by the number of observations. It is the most frequently used measure of central tendency.
- The median is the value of the middle item (or the mean of the values of the two middle items) when the items in a set are sorted into ascending or descending order. The median is not influenced by extreme values and is most useful in the case of skewed distributions.
- The mode is the most frequently observed value and is the only measure of central tendency that can be used with nominal data. A distribution may be unimodal (one mode), bimodal (two modes), trimodal (three modes), or have even more modes.
- A portfolio's return is a weighted mean return computed from the returns on the individual assets, where the weight applied to each asset's return is the fraction of the portfolio invested in that asset.

- The geometric mean, $\overline{X}_G$, of a set of observations $X_1, X_2, ..., X_n$, is $\overline{X}_G = \sqrt[n]{X_1 X_2 X_3 ... X_n}$, with $X_i \geq 0$ for $i = 1, 2, ..., n$. The geometric mean is especially important in reporting compound growth rates for time-series data. The geometric mean will always be less than an arithmetic mean whenever there is variance in the observations.
- The harmonic mean, $\overline{X}_H$, is a type of weighted mean in which an observation's weight is inversely proportional to its magnitude.
- Quantiles—such as the median, quartiles, quintiles, deciles, and percentiles—are location parameters that divide a distribution into halves, quarters, fifths, tenths, and hundredths, respectively.
- A box and whiskers plot illustrates the interquartile range (the "box") as well as a range outside of the box that is based on the interquartile range, indicated by the "whiskers."
- Dispersion measures—such as the range, mean absolute deviation (MAD), variance, standard deviation, target downside deviation, and coefficient of variation—describe the variability of outcomes around the arithmetic mean.
- The range is the difference between the maximum value and the minimum value of the dataset. The range has only a limited usefulness because it uses information from only two observations.
- The MAD for a sample is the average of the absolute deviations of observations from the mean, $\dfrac{\sum_{i=1}^{n} |X_i - \overline{X}|}{n}$, where $\overline{X}$ is the sample mean and n is the number of observations in the sample.
- The variance is the average of the squared deviations around the mean, and the standard deviation is the positive square root of variance. In computing sample variance (s^2) and sample standard deviation (s), the average squared deviation is computed using a divisor equal to the sample size minus 1.
- The target downside deviation, or target semideviation, is a measure of the risk of being below a given target. It is calculated as the square root of the average squared deviations from the target, but it includes only those observations below the target (B), or $$\sqrt{\sum_{\text{for all } X_i \leq B}^{n} \frac{(X_i - B)^2}{n - 1}}.$$
- The coefficient of variation, CV, is the ratio of the standard deviation of a set of observations to their mean value. By expressing the magnitude of variation among observations relative to their average size, the CV permits direct comparisons of dispersion across different datasets. Reflecting the correction for scale, the CV is a scale-free measure (i.e., it has no units of measurement).
- Skew or skewness describes the degree to which a distribution is asymmetric about its mean. A return distribution with positive skewness has frequent small losses and a few extreme gains compared to a normal distribution. A return distribution with negative skewness has frequent small gains and a few extreme losses compared to a normal distribution. Zero skewness indicates a symmetric distribution of returns.
- Kurtosis measures the combined weight of the tails of a distribution relative to the rest of the distribution. A distribution with fatter tails than the normal distribution is referred to as fat-tailed (leptokurtic); a distribution with thinner tails than the normal distribution is referred to as thin-tailed (platykurtic). Excess kurtosis is kurtosis minus 3, since 3 is the value of kurtosis for all normal distributions.

- The correlation coefficient is a statistic that measures the association between two variables. It is the ratio of covariance to the product of the two variables' standard deviations. A positive correlation coefficient indicates that the two variables tend to move together, whereas a negative coefficient indicates that the two variables tend to move in opposite directions. Correlation does not imply causation, simply association. Issues that arise in evaluating correlation include the presence of outliers and spurious correlation.

PRACTICE PROBLEMS

1. Published ratings on stocks ranging from 1 (strong sell) to 5 (strong buy) are examples of which measurement scale?
   A. Ordinal
   B. Continuous
   C. Nominal

2. Data values that are categorical and not amenable to being organized in a logical order are *most likely* to be characterized as:
   A. ordinal data.
   B. discrete data.
   C. nominal data.

3. Which of the following data types would be classified as being categorical?
   A. Discrete
   B. Nominal
   C. Continuous

4. A fixed-income analyst uses a proprietary model to estimate bankruptcy probabilities for a group of firms. The model generates probabilities that can take any value between 0 and 1. The resulting set of estimated probabilities would *most likely* be characterized as:
   A. ordinal data.
   B. discrete data.
   C. continuous data.

5. An analyst uses a software program to analyze unstructured data—specifically, management's earnings call transcript for one of the companies in her research coverage. The program scans the words in each sentence of the transcript and then classifies the sentences as having negative, neutral, or positive sentiment. The resulting set of sentiment data would *most likely* be characterized as:
   A. ordinal data.
   B. discrete data.
   C. nominal data.

Use the following information to answer Questions 6 and 7.

An equity analyst gathers total returns for three country equity indexes over the past four years. The data are presented below.

Time Period	Index A	Index B	Index C
Year t–3	15.56%	11.84%	–4.34%
Year t–2	–4.12%	–6.96%	9.32%
Year t–1	11.19%	10.29%	–12.72%
Year t	8.98%	6.32%	21.44%

6. Each individual column of data in the table can be *best* characterized as:
   A. panel data.
   B. time-series data.
   C. cross-sectional data.

7. Each individual row of data in the table can be *best* characterized as:
   A. panel data.
   B. time-series data.
   C. cross-sectional data.

8. A two-dimensional rectangular array would be most suitable for organizing a collection of raw:
   A. panel data.
   B. time-series data.
   C. cross-sectional data.

9. In a frequency distribution, the absolute frequency measure:
   A. represents the percentages of each unique value of the variable.
   B. represents the actual number of observations counted for each unique value of the variable.
   C. allows for comparisons between datasets with different numbers of total observations.

10. An investment fund has the return frequency distribution shown in the following exhibit.

Return Interval (%)	Absolute Frequency
–10.0 to –7.0	3
–7.0 to –4.0	7
–4.0 to –1.0	10
–1.0 to +2.0	12
+2.0 to +5.0	23
+5.0 to +8.0	5

Which of the following statements is correct?
A. The relative frequency of the bin "–1.0 to +2.0" is 20%.
B. The relative frequency of the bin "+2.0 to +5.0" is 23%.
C. The cumulative relative frequency of the bin "+5.0 to +8.0" is 91.7%.

11. An analyst is using the data in the following exhibit to prepare a statistical report.

Portfolio's Deviations from Benchmark Return for a 12-Year Period (%)

Year 1	2.48	Year 7	-9.19
Year 2	-2.59	Year 8	-5.11
Year 3	9.47	Year 9	1.33
Year 4	-0.55	Year 10	6.84
Year 5	-1.69	Year 11	3.04
Year 6	-0.89	Year 12	4.72

The cumulative relative frequency for the bin $-1.71\% \le x < 2.03\%$ is *closest* to:
A. 0.250.
B. 0.333.
C. 0.583.

Use the following information to answer Questions 12 and 13.

A fixed-income portfolio manager creates a contingency table of the number of bonds held in her portfolio by sector and bond rating. The contingency table is presented here:

	Bond Rating		
Sector	A	AA	AAA
Communication Services	25	32	27
Consumer Staples	30	25	25
Energy	100	85	30
Health Care	200	100	63
Utilities	22	28	14

12. The marginal frequency of energy sector bonds is *closest* to:
A. 27.
B. 85.
C. 215.

13. The relative frequency of AA rated energy bonds, based on the total count, is *closest* to:
A. 10.5%.
B. 31.5%.
C. 39.5%.

The following information relates to Questions 14–15

The following histogram shows a distribution of the S&P 500 Index annual returns for a 50-year period:

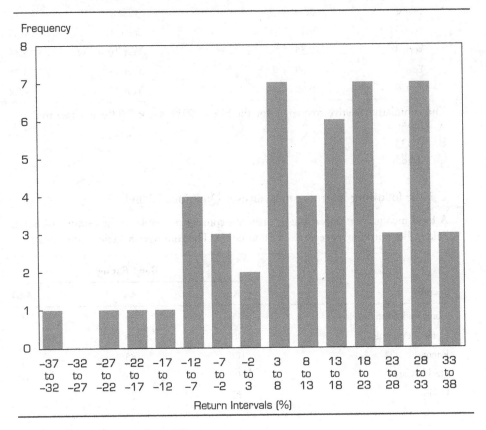

14. The bin containing the median return is:
    A. 3% to 8%.
    B. 8% to 13%.
    C. 13% to 18%.

15. Based on the previous histogram, the distribution is *best* described as being:
    A. unimodal.
    B. bimodal.
    C. trimodal.

16. The following is a frequency polygon of monthly exchange rate changes in the US dollar/Japanese yen spot exchange rate for a four-year period. A positive change represents yen appreciation (the yen buys more dollars), and a negative change represents yen depreciation (the yen buys fewer dollars).

Monthly Changes in the US Dollar/Japanese Yen Spot Exchange Rate

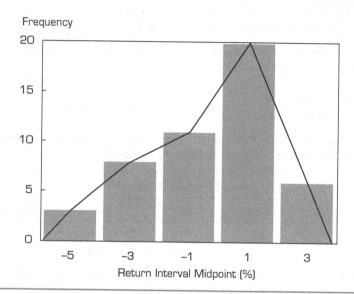

Based on the chart, yen appreciation:
A. occurred more than 50% of the time.
B. was less frequent than yen depreciation.
C. in the 0.0 to 2.0 interval occurred 20% of the time.

17. A bar chart that orders categories by frequency in descending order and includes a line
     displaying cumulative relative frequency is referred to as a:
     A. Pareto Chart.
     B. grouped bar chart.
     C. frequency polygon.

18. Which visualization tool works *best* to represent unstructured, textual data?
     A. Tree-Map
     B. Scatter plot
     C. Word cloud

19. A tree-map is best suited to illustrate:
     A. underlying trends over time.
     B. joint variations in two variables.
     C. value differences of categorical groups.

20. A line chart with two variables—for example, revenues and earnings per share—is best
     suited for visualizing:
     A. the joint variation in the variables.
     B. underlying trends in the variables over time.
     C. the degree of correlation between the variables.

21. A heat map is best suited for visualizing the:
    A. frequency of textual data.
    B. degree of correlation between different variables.
    C. shape, center, and spread of the distribution of numerical data.

22. Which valuation tool is recommended to be used if the goal is to make comparisons of three or more variables over time?
    A. Heat map
    B. Bubble line chart
    C. Scatter plot matrix

23. The annual returns for three portfolios are shown in the following exhibit. Portfolios P and R were created in Year 1, Portfolio Q in Year 2.

	Annual Portfolio Returns (%)				
	Year 1	Year 2	Year 3	Year 4	Year 5
Portfolio P	−3.0	4.0	5.0	3.0	7.0
Portfolio Q		−3.0	6.0	4.0	8.0
Portfolio R	1.0	−1.0	4.0	4.0	3.0

The median annual return from portfolio creation to Year 5 for:
    A. Portfolio P is 4.5%.
    B. Portfolio Q is 4.0%.
    C. Portfolio R is higher than its arithmetic mean annual return.

24. At the beginning of Year X, an investor allocated his retirement savings in the asset classes shown in the following exhibit and earned a return for Year X as also shown.

Asset Class	Asset Allocation (%)	Asset Class Return for Year X (%)
Large-cap US equities	20.0	8.0
Small-cap US equities	40.0	12.0
Emerging market equities	25.0	−3.0
High-yield bonds	15.0	4.0

The portfolio return for Year X is *closest to*:
    A. 5.1%.
    B. 5.3%.
    C. 6.3%.

25. The following exhibit shows the annual returns for Fund Y.

	Fund Y (%)
Year 1	19.5
Year 2	−1.9
Year 3	19.7
Year 4	35.0
Year 5	5.7

The geometric mean return for Fund Y is *closest* to:
A.   14.9%.
B.   15.6%.
C.   19.5%.

26. A portfolio manager invests €5,000 annually in a security for four years at the prices shown in the following exhibit.

	Purchase Price of Security (€ per unit)
Year 1	62.00
Year 2	76.00
Year 3	84.00
Year 4	90.00

The average price is *best* represented as the:
A.   harmonic mean of €76.48.
B.   geometric mean of €77.26.
C.   arithmetic average of €78.00.

The following information relates to Questions 27–28.

The following exhibit shows the annual MSCI World Index total returns for a 10-year period.

Year 1	15.25%	Year 6	30.79%
Year 2	10.02%	Year 7	12.34%
Year 3	20.65%	Year 8	-5.02%
Year 4	9.57%	Year 9	16.54%
Year 5	-40.33%	Year 10	27.37%

27. The fourth quintile return for the MSCI World Index is *closest* to:
A.   20.65%.
B.   26.03%.
C.   27.37%.

28. For Year 6–Year 10, the mean absolute deviation of the MSCI World Index total returns is *closest* to:
A.   10.20%.
B.   12.74%.
C.   16.40%.

29. Annual returns and summary statistics for three funds are listed in the following exhibit:

	Annual Returns (%)		
Year	Fund ABC	Fund XYZ	Fund PQR
Year 1	−20.0	−33.0	−14.0
Year 2	23.0	−12.0	−18.0
Year 3	−14.0	−12.0	6.0
Year 4	5.0	−8.0	−2.0
Year 5	−14.0	11.0	3.0
Mean	−4.0	−10.8	−5.0
Standard deviation	17.8	15.6	10.5

The fund with the highest absolute dispersion is:
A. Fund PQR if the measure of dispersion is the range.
B. Fund XYZ if the measure of dispersion is the variance.
C. Fund ABC if the measure of dispersion is the mean absolute deviation.

30. The mean monthly return and the standard deviation for three industry sectors are shown in the following exhibit.

Sector	Mean Monthly Return (%)	Standard Deviation of Return (%)
Utilities (UTIL)	2.10	1.23
Materials (MATR)	1.25	1.35
Industrials (INDU)	3.01	1.52

Based on the coefficient of variation, the riskiest sector is:
A. utilities.
B. materials.
C. industrials.

31. The average return for Portfolio A over the past twelve months is 3%, with a standard deviation of 4%. The average return for Portfolio B over this same period is also 3%, but with a standard deviation of 6%. The geometric mean return of Portfolio A is 2.85%. The geometric mean return of Portfolio B is:
A. less than 2.85%.
B. equal to 2.85%.
C. greater than 2.85%.

32. An analyst calculated the excess kurtosis of a stock's returns as −0.75. From this information, we conclude that the distribution of returns is:
A. normally distributed.
B. thin-tailed compared to the normal distribution.
C. fat-tailed compared to the normal distribution.

33. When analyzing investment returns, which of the following statements is correct?
    A. The geometric mean will exceed the arithmetic mean for a series with non-zero variance.
    B. The geometric mean measures an investment's compound rate of growth over multiple periods.
    C. The arithmetic mean measures an investment's terminal value over multiple periods.

The following information relates to Questions 34–38

A fund had the following experience over the past 10 years:

Year	Return
1	4.5%
2	6.0%
3	1.5%
4	–2.0%
5	0.0%
6	4.5%
7	3.5%
8	2.5%
9	5.5%
10	4.0%

34. The arithmetic mean return over the 10 years is *closest* to:
    A. 2.97%.
    B. 3.00%.
    C. 3.33%.

35. The geometric mean return over the 10 years is *closest* to:
    A. 2.94%.
    B. 2.97%.
    C. 3.00%.

36. The harmonic mean return over the 10 years is *closest* to:
    A. 2.94%.
    B. 2.97%.
    C. 3.00%.

37. The standard deviation of the 10 years of returns is *closest* to:
    A. 2.40%.
    B. 2.53%.
    C. 7.58%.

38. The target semideviation of the returns over the 10 years if the target is 2% is *closest* to:
    A. 1.42%.
    B. 1.50%.
    C. 2.01%.

39. A correlation of 0.34 between two variables, X and Y, is *best* described as:
    A. changes in X causing changes in Y.
    B. a positive association between X and Y.
    C. a curvilinear relationship between X and Y.

40. Which of the following is a potential problem with interpreting a correlation coefficient?
    A. Outliers
    B. Spurious correlation
    C. Both outliers and spurious correlation

The following relates to Questions 41 and 42

An analyst is evaluating the tendency of returns on the portfolio of stocks she manages to move along with bond and real estate indexes. She gathered monthly data on returns and the indexes:

	Returns (%)		
	Portfolio Returns	Bond Index Returns	Real Estate Index Returns
Arithmetic average	5.5	3.2	7.8
Standard deviation	8.2	3.4	10.3

	Portfolio Returns and Bond Index Returns	Portfolio Returns and Real Estate Index Returns
Covariance	18.9	–55.9

41. Without calculating the correlation coefficient, the correlation of the portfolio returns and the bond index returns is:
    A. negative.
    B. zero.
    C. positive.

42. Without calculating the correlation coefficient, the correlation of the portfolio returns and the real estate index returns is:
    A. negative.
    B. zero.
    C. positive.

43. Consider two variables, A and B. If variable A has a mean of –0.56, variable B has a mean of 0.23, and the covariance between the two variables is positive, the correlation between these two variables is:
    A.   negative.
    B.   zero.
    C.   positive.

The following information relates to Questions 44–45.

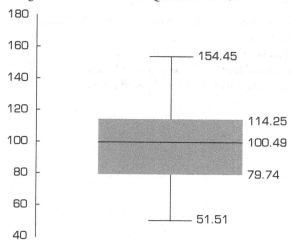

44. The median is *closest* to:
    A.   34.51.
    B.   100.49.
    C.   102.98.

45. The interquartile range is *closest* to:
    A.   13.76.
    B.   25.74.
    C.   34.51.

The following information relates to Questions 46–48

An analyst examined a cross-section of annual returns for 252 stocks and calculated the following statistics:

Arithmetic Average	9.986%
Geometric Mean	9.909%
Variance	0.001723
Skewness	0.704
Excess Kurtosis	0.503

46. The coefficient of variation is closest to:
    A. 0.02.
    B. 0.42.
    C. 2.41.

47. This distribution is best described as:
    A. negatively skewed.
    B. having no skewness.
    C. positively skewed.

48. Compared to the normal distribution, this sample's distribution is best described as having tails of the distribution with:
    A. less probability than the normal distribution.
    B. the same probability as the normal distribution.
    C. more probability than the normal distribution.

CHAPTER 3

PROBABILITY CONCEPTS

LEARNING OUTCOMES

The candidate should be able to:

- define a random variable, an outcome, an event, mutually exclusive events, and exhaustive events;
- state the two defining properties of probability and distinguish among empirical, subjective, and a priori probabilities;
- state the probability of an event in terms of odds for and against the event;
- distinguish between unconditional and conditional probabilities;
- explain the multiplication, addition, and total probability rules;
- calculate and interpret 1) the joint probability of two events, 2) the probability that at least one of two events will occur, given the probability of each and the joint probability of the two events, and 3) a joint probability of any number of independent events;
- distinguish between dependent and independent events;
- calculate and interpret an unconditional probability using the total probability rule;
- explain the use of conditional expectation in investment applications;
- explain the use of a tree diagram to represent an investment problem;
- calculate and interpret covariance and correlation;
- calculate and interpret the expected value, variance, and standard deviation of a random variable and of returns on a portfolio;
- calculate and interpret covariance given a joint probability function;
- calculate and interpret an updated probability using Bayes' formula;
- identify the most appropriate method to solve a particular counting problem and solve counting problems using factorial, combination, and permutation concepts.

SUMMARY

In this chapter, we have discussed the essential concepts and tools of probability. We have applied probability, expected value, and variance to a range of investment problems.

- A random variable is a quantity whose outcome is uncertain.
- Probability is a number between 0 and 1 that describes the chance that a stated event will occur.
- An event is a specified set of outcomes of a random variable.
- Mutually exclusive events can occur only one at a time. Exhaustive events cover or contain all possible outcomes.
- The two defining properties of a probability are, first, that $0 \leq P(E) \leq 1$ (where $P(E)$ denotes the probability of an event E), and second, that the sum of the probabilities of any set of mutually exclusive and exhaustive events equals 1.
- A probability estimated from data as a relative frequency of occurrence is an empirical probability. A probability drawing on personal or subjective judgment is a subjective probability. A probability obtained based on logical analysis is an a priori probability.
- A probability of an event E, $P(E)$, can be stated as odds for $E = P(E)/[1 - P(E)]$ or odds against $E = [1 - P(E)]/P(E)$.
- Probabilities that are inconsistent create profit opportunities, according to the Dutch Book Theorem.
- A probability of an event *not* conditioned on another event is an unconditional probability. The unconditional probability of an event A is denoted $P(A)$. Unconditional probabilities are also called marginal probabilities.
- A probability of an event given (conditioned on) another event is a conditional probability. The probability of an event A given an event B is denoted $P(A \mid B)$.
- The probability of both A and B occurring is the joint probability of A and B, denoted $P(AB)$.
- $P(A \mid B) = P(AB)/P(B)$, $P(B) \neq 0$.
- The multiplication rule for probabilities is $P(AB) = P(A \mid B)P(B)$.
- The probability that A or B occurs, or both occur, is denoted by $P(A \text{ or } B)$.
- The addition rule for probabilities is $P(A \text{ or } B) = P(A) + P(B) - P(AB)$.
- When events are independent, the occurrence of one event does not affect the probability of occurrence of the other event. Otherwise, the events are dependent.
- The multiplication rule for independent events states that if A and B are independent events, $P(AB) = P(A)P(B)$. The rule generalizes in similar fashion to more than two events.
- According to the total probability rule, if S_1, S_2, ..., S_n are mutually exclusive and exhaustive scenarios or events, then $P(A) = P(A \mid S_1)P(S_1) + P(A \mid S_2)P(S_2) + ... + P(A \mid S_n)P(S_n)$.
- The expected value of a random variable is a probability-weighted average of the possible outcomes of the random variable. For a random variable X, the expected value of X is denoted $E(X)$.
- The total probability rule for expected value states that $E(X) = E(X \mid S_1)P(S_1) + E(X \mid S_2)P(S_2) + ... + E(X \mid S_n)P(S_n)$, where S_1, S_2, ..., S_n are mutually exclusive and exhaustive scenarios or events.
- The variance of a random variable is the expected value (the probability-weighted average) of squared deviations from the random variable's expected value $E(X)$: $\sigma^2(X) = E\{[X - E(X)]^2\}$, where $\sigma^2(X)$ stands for the variance of X.
- Variance is a measure of dispersion about the mean. Increasing variance indicates increasing dispersion. Variance is measured in squared units of the original variable.

- Standard deviation is the positive square root of variance. Standard deviation measures dispersion (as does variance), but it is measured in the same units as the variable.
- Covariance is a measure of the co-movement between random variables.
- The covariance between two random variables R_i and R_j in a forward-looking sense is the expected value of the cross-product of the deviations of the two random variables from their respective means: $\text{Cov}(R_i,R_j) = E\{[R_i - E(R_i)][R_j - E(R_j)]\}$. The covariance of a random variable with itself is its own variance.
- The historical or sample covariance between two random variables R_i and R_j based on a sample of past data of size n is the average value of the product of the deviations of observations on two random variables from their sample means:

$$\text{Cov}(R_i,R_j) = \sum_{i=1}^{n}(R_{i,t} - \overline{R}_i)(R_{j,t} - \overline{R}_j)/(n-1)$$

- Correlation is a number between -1 and $+1$ that measures the co-movement (linear association) between two random variables: $\rho(R_i,R_j) = \text{Cov}(R_i,R_j)/[\sigma(R_i)\ \sigma(R_j)]$.
- If two variables have a very strong linear relation, then the absolute value of their correlation will be close to 1. If two variables have a weak linear relation, then the absolute value of their correlation will be close to 0.
- If the correlation coefficient is positive, the two variables are directly related; if the correlation coefficient is negative, the two variables are inversely related.
- To calculate the variance of return on a portfolio of n assets, the inputs needed are the n expected returns on the individual assets, n variances of return on the individual assets, and $n(n-1)/2$ distinct covariances.
- Portfolio variance of return is $\sigma^2(R_p) = \sum_{i=1}^{n}\sum_{j=1}^{n}w_i w_j \text{Cov}(R_i,R_j)$.
- The calculation of covariance in a forward-looking sense requires the specification of a joint probability function, which gives the probability of joint occurrences of values of the two random variables.
- When two random variables are independent, the joint probability function is the product of the individual probability functions of the random variables.
- Bayes' formula is a method for updating probabilities based on new information.
- Bayes' formula is expressed as follows: Updated probability of event given the new information = [(Probability of the new information given event)/(Unconditional probability of the new information)] × Prior probability of event.
- The multiplication rule of counting says, for example, that if the first step in a process can be done in 10 ways, the second step, given the first, can be done in 5 ways, and the third step, given the first two, can be done in 7 ways, then the steps can be carried out in $(10)(5)(7) = 350$ ways.
- The number of ways to assign every member of a group of size n to n slots is $n! = n\,(n-1)(n-2)(n-3)\ldots 1$. (By convention, $0! = 1$.)
- The number of ways that n objects can be labeled with k different labels, with n_1 of the first type, n_2 of the second type, and so on, with $n_1 + n_2 + \ldots + n_k = n$, is given by $n!/(n_1!n_2! \ldots n_k!)$. This expression is the multinomial formula.
- A special case of the multinomial formula is the combination formula. The number of ways to choose r objects from a total of n objects, when the order in which the r objects are listed does not matter, is

$$_nC_r = \binom{n}{r} = \frac{n!}{(n-r)!r!}$$

- The number of ways to choose r objects from a total of n objects, when the order in which the r objects are listed does matter, is

$$_nP_r = \frac{n!}{(n-r)!}$$

This expression is the permutation formula.

PRACTICE PROBLEMS

1. Suppose that 5 percent of the stocks meeting your stock-selection criteria are in the telecommunications (telecom) industry. Also, dividend-paying telecom stocks are 1 percent of the total number of stocks meeting your selection criteria. What is the probability that a stock is dividend paying, given that it is a telecom stock that has met your stock selection criteria?

2. You are using the following three criteria to screen potential acquisition targets from a list of 500 companies:

Criterion	Fraction of the 500 Companies Meeting the Criterion
Product lines compatible	0.20
Company will increase combined sales growth rate	0.45
Balance sheet impact manageable	0.78

If the criteria are independent, how many companies will pass the screen?

3. You apply both valuation criteria and financial strength criteria in choosing stocks. The probability that a randomly selected stock (from your investment universe) meets your valuation criteria is 0.25. Given that a stock meets your valuation criteria, the probability that the stock meets your financial strength criteria is 0.40. What is the probability that a stock meets both your valuation and financial strength criteria?

4. Suppose the prospects for recovering principal for a defaulted bond issue depend on which of two economic scenarios prevails. Scenario 1 has probability 0.75 and will result in recovery of $0.90 per $1 principal value with probability 0.45, or in recovery of $0.80 per $1 principal value with probability 0.55. Scenario 2 has probability 0.25 and will result in recovery of $0.50 per $1 principal value with probability 0.85, or in recovery of $0.40 per $1 principal value with probability 0.15.

   A. Compute the probability of each of the four possible recovery amounts: $0.90, $0.80, $0.50, and $0.40.
   B. Compute the expected recovery, given the first scenario.
   C. Compute the expected recovery, given the second scenario.
   D. Compute the expected recovery.
   E. Graph the information in a tree diagram.

5. You have developed a set of criteria for evaluating distressed credits. Companies that do not receive a passing score are classed as likely to go bankrupt within 12 months. You gathered the following information when validating the criteria:
   - Forty percent of the companies to which the test is administered will go bankrupt within 12 months: P(*nonsurvivor*) = 0.40.
   - Fifty-five percent of the companies to which the test is administered pass it: P(*pass test*) = 0.55.
   - The probability that a company will pass the test given that it will subsequently survive 12 months, is 0.85: P(*pass test* | *survivor*) = 0.85.

   A. What is P(*pass test* | *nonsurvivor*)?
   B. Using Bayes' formula, calculate the probability that a company is a survivor, given that it passes the test; that is, calculate P(survivor | pass test).
   C. What is the probability that a company is a *nonsurvivor*, given that it fails the test?
   D. Is the test effective?

6. In probability theory, exhaustive events are *best* described as events:
   A. with a probability of zero.
   B. that are mutually exclusive.
   C. that include all potential outcomes.

7. Which probability estimate *most likely* varies greatly between people?
   A. An *a priori* probability
   B. An empirical probability
   C. A subjective probability

8. If the probability that Zolaf Company sales exceed last year's sales is 0.167, the odds for exceeding sales are *closest* to:
   A. 1 to 5.
   B. 1 to 6.
   C. 5 to 1.

9. The probability of an event given that another event has occurred is a:
   A. joint probability.
   B. marginal probability.
   C. conditional probability.

10. After estimating the probability that an investment manager will exceed his benchmark return in each of the next two quarters, an analyst wants to forecast the probability that the investment manager will exceed his benchmark return over the two-quarter period in total. Assuming that each quarter's performance is independent of the other, which probability rule should the analyst select?
    A. Addition rule
    B. Multiplication rule
    C. Total probability rule

11. Which of the following is a property of two dependent events?
    A. The two events must occur simultaneously.
    B. The probability of one event influences the probability of the other event.
    C. The probability of the two events occurring is the product of each event's probability.

12. Which of the following *best* describes how an analyst would estimate the expected value of a firm under the scenarios of bankruptcy and survivorship? The analyst would use:
   A. the addition rule.
   B. conditional expected values.
   C. the total probability rule for expected value.

13. An analyst developed two scenarios with respect to the recovery of $100,000 principal from defaulted loans:

Scenario	Probability of Scenario (%)	Amount Recovered ($)	Probability of Amount (%)
1	40	50,000	60
		30,000	40
2	60	80,000	90
		60,000	10

The amount of the expected recovery is *closest* to:
   A. $36,400.
   B. $63,600.
   C. $81,600.

14. US and Spanish bonds have return standard deviations of 0.64 and 0.56, respectively. If the correlation between the two bonds is 0.24, the covariance of returns is *closest* to:
   A. 0.086.
   B. 0.670.
   C. 0.781.

15. The covariance of returns is positive when the returns on two assets tend to:
   A. have the same expected values.
   B. be above their expected value at different times.
   C. be on the same side of their expected value at the same time.

16. Which of the following correlation coefficients indicates the weakest linear relationship between two variables?
   A. −0.67
   B. −0.24
   C. 0.33

17. An analyst develops the following covariance matrix of returns:

	Hedge Fund	Market Index
Hedge Fund	256	110
Market Index	110	81

The correlation of returns between the hedge fund and the market index is *closest* to:
   A. 0.005.
   B. 0.073.
   C. 0.764.

18. All else being equal, as the correlation between two assets approaches +1.0, the diversification benefits:
    A. decrease.
    B. stay the same.
    C. increase.

19. Given a portfolio of five stocks, how many unique covariance terms, excluding variances, are required to calculate the portfolio return variance?
    A. 10
    B. 20
    C. 25

20. The probability distribution for a company's sales is:

Probability	Sales ($ millions)
0.05	70
0.70	40
0.25	25

The standard deviation of sales is *closest* to:
    A. $9.81 million.
    B. $12.20 million.
    C. $32.40 million.

21. Which of the following statements is *most* accurate? If the covariance of returns between two assets is 0.0023, then:
    A. the assets' risk is near zero.
    B. the asset returns are unrelated.
    C. the asset returns have a positive relationship.

22. An analyst produces the following joint probability function for a foreign index (FI) and a domestic index (DI).

	$R_{DI} = 30\%$	$R_{DI} = 25\%$	$R_{DI} = 15\%$
$R_{FI} = 25\%$	0.25		
$R_{FI} = 15\%$		0.50	
$R_{FI} = 10\%$			0.25

The covariance of returns on the foreign index and the returns on the domestic index is *closest* to:
    A. 26.39.
    B. 26.56.
    C. 28.12.

23. A manager will select 20 bonds out of his universe of 100 bonds to construct a portfolio. Which formula provides the number of possible portfolios?
    A. Permutation formula
    B. Multinomial formula
    C. Combination formula

24. A firm will select two of four vice presidents to be added to the investment committee. How many different groups of two are possible?
    A. 6
    B. 12
    C. 24

25. From an approved list of 25 funds, a portfolio manager wants to rank 4 mutual funds from most recommended to least recommended. Which formula is *most* appropriate to calculate the number of possible ways the funds could be ranked?
    A. Permutation formula
    B. Multinomial formula
    C. Combination formula

CHAPTER 4

COMMON PROBABILITY DISTRIBUTIONS

LEARNING OUTCOMES

The candidate should be able to:

- define a probability distribution and distinguish between discrete and continuous random variables and their probability functions;
- describe the set of possible outcomes of a specified discrete random variable;
- interpret a cumulative distribution function;
- calculate and interpret probabilities for a random variable, given its cumulative distribution function;
- define a discrete uniform random variable, a Bernoulli random variable, and a binomial random variable;
- calculate and interpret probabilities given the discrete uniform and the binomial distribution functions;
- construct a binomial tree to describe stock price movement;
- define the continuous uniform distribution and calculate and interpret probabilities, given a continuous uniform distribution;
- explain the key properties of the normal distribution;
- distinguish between a univariate and a multivariate distribution and explain the role of correlation in the multivariate normal distribution;
- determine the probability that a normally distributed random variable lies inside a given interval;
- define the standard normal distribution, explain how to standardize a random variable, and calculate and interpret probabilities using the standard normal distribution;
- define shortfall risk, calculate the safety-first ratio, and select an optimal portfolio using Roy's safety-first criterion;
- explain the relationship between normal and lognormal distributions and why the lognormal distribution is used to model asset prices;

- distinguish between discretely and continuously compounded rates of return and calculate and interpret a continuously compounded rate of return, given a specific holding period return;
- describe Monte Carlo simulation.

SUMMARY

In this chapter, we have presented the most frequently used probability distributions in investment analysis and the Monte Carlo simulation.

- A probability distribution specifies the probabilities of the possible outcomes of a random variable.
- The two basic types of random variables are discrete random variables and continuous random variables. Discrete random variables take on at most a countable number of possible outcomes that we can list as $x_1, x_2, \ldots$ In contrast, we cannot describe the possible outcomes of a continuous random variable Z with a list $z_1, z_2, \ldots$ because the outcome $(z_1 + z_2)/2$, not in the list, would always be possible.
- The probability function specifies the probability that the random variable will take on a specific value. The probability function is denoted $p(x)$ for a discrete random variable and $f(x)$ for a continuous random variable. For any probability function $p(x)$, $0 \leq p(x) \leq 1$, and the sum of $p(x)$ over all values of X equals 1.
- The cumulative distribution function, denoted $F(x)$ for both continuous and discrete random variables, gives the probability that the random variable is less than or equal to x.
- The discrete uniform and the continuous uniform distributions are the distributions of equally likely outcomes.
- The binomial random variable is defined as the number of successes in n Bernoulli trials, where the probability of success, p, is constant for all trials and the trials are independent. A Bernoulli trial is an experiment with two outcomes, which can represent success or failure, an up move or a down move, or another binary (two-fold) outcome.
- A binomial random variable has an expected value or mean equal to np and variance equal to $np(1 - p)$.
- A binomial tree is the graphical representation of a model of asset price dynamics in which, at each period, the asset moves up with probability p or down with probability $(1 - p)$. The binomial tree is a flexible method for modeling asset price movement and is widely used in pricing options.
- The normal distribution is a continuous symmetric probability distribution that is completely described by two parameters: its mean, μ, and its variance, σ^2.
- A univariate distribution specifies the probabilities for a single random variable. A multivariate distribution specifies the probabilities for a group of related random variables.
- To specify the normal distribution for a portfolio when its component securities are normally distributed, we need the means, standard deviations, and all the distinct pairwise correlations of the securities. When we have those statistics, we have also specified a multivariate normal distribution for the securities.
- For a normal random variable, approximately 68 percent of all possible outcomes are within a one standard deviation interval about the mean, approximately 95 percent are

within a two standard deviation interval about the mean, and approximately 99 percent are within a three standard deviation interval about the mean.

- A normal random variable, X, is standardized using the expression $Z = (X - \mu)/\sigma$, where μ and σ are the mean and standard deviation of X. Generally, we use the sample mean $\bar{X}$ as an estimate of μ and the sample standard deviation s as an estimate of σ in this expression.

- The standard normal random variable, denoted Z, has a mean equal to 0 and variance equal to 1. All questions about any normal random variable can be answered by referring to the cumulative distribution function of a standard normal random variable, denoted $N(x)$ or $N(z)$.

- Shortfall risk is the risk that portfolio value will fall below some minimum acceptable level over some time horizon.

- Roy's safety-first criterion, addressing shortfall risk, asserts that the optimal portfolio is the one that minimizes the probability that portfolio return falls below a threshold level. According to Roy's safety-first criterion, if returns are normally distributed, the safety-first optimal portfolio P is the one that maximizes the quantity $[E(R_P) - R_L]/\sigma_P$, where R_L is the minimum acceptable level of return.

- A random variable follows a lognormal distribution if the natural logarithm of the random variable is normally distributed. The lognormal distribution is defined in terms of the mean and variance of its associated normal distribution. The lognormal distribution is bounded below by 0 and skewed to the right (it has a long right tail).

- The lognormal distribution is frequently used to model the probability distribution of asset prices because it is bounded below by zero.

- Continuous compounding views time as essentially continuous or unbroken; discrete compounding views time as advancing in discrete finite intervals.

- The continuously compounded return associated with a holding period is the natural log of 1 plus the holding period return, or equivalently, the natural log of ending price over beginning price.

- If continuously compounded returns are normally distributed, asset prices are lognormally distributed. This relationship is used to move back and forth between the distributions for return and price. Because of the central limit theorem, continuously compounded returns need not be normally distributed for asset prices to be reasonably well described by a lognormal distribution.

- Monte Carlo simulation involves the use of a computer to represent the operation of a complex financial system. A characteristic feature of Monte Carlo simulation is the generation of a large number of random samples from specified probability distribution(s) to represent the operation of risk in the system. Monte Carlo simulation is used in planning, in financial risk management, and in valuing complex securities. Monte Carlo simulation is a complement to analytical methods but provides only statistical estimates, not exact results.

PRACTICE PROBLEMS

1. A European put option on stock conveys the right to sell the stock at a prespecified price, called the exercise price, at the maturity date of the option. The value of this put at maturity is (exercise price − stock price) or $0, whichever is greater. Suppose the exercise price is $100 and the underlying stock trades in ticks of $0.01. At any time before maturity, the terminal value of the put is a random variable.

A. Describe the distinct possible outcomes for terminal put value. (Think of the put's maximum and minimum values and its minimum price increments.)

B. Is terminal put value, at a time before maturity, a discrete or continuous random variable?

C. Letting Y stand for terminal put value, express in standard notation the probability that terminal put value is less than or equal to $24. No calculations or formulas are necessary.

2. Define the term "binomial random variable." Describe the types of problems for which the binomial distribution is used.

3. The value of the cumulative distribution function $F(x)$, where x is a particular outcome, for a discrete uniform distribution:
    A. sums to 1.
    B. lies between 0 and 1.
    C. decreases as x increases.

4. For a binomial random variable with five trials, and a probability of success on each trial of 0.50, the distribution will be:
    A. skewed.
    B. uniform.
    C. symmetric.

5. In a discrete uniform distribution with 20 potential outcomes of integers 1 to 20, the probability that X is greater than or equal to 3 but less than 6, $P(3 \leq X < 6)$, is:
    A. 0.10.
    B. 0.15.
    C. 0.20.

6. Over the last 10 years, a company's annual earnings increased year over year seven times and decreased year over year three times. You decide to model the number of earnings increases for the next decade as a binomial random variable.
    A. What is your estimate of the probability of success, defined as an increase in annual earnings?

    For Parts B, C, and D of this problem, assume the estimated probability is the actual probability for the next decade.

    B. What is the probability that earnings will increase in exactly 5 of the next 10 years?
    C. Calculate the expected number of yearly earnings increases during the next 10 years.
    D. Calculate the variance and standard deviation of the number of yearly earnings increases during the next 10 years.
    E. The expression for the probability function of a binomial random variable depends on two major assumptions. In the context of this problem, what must you assume about annual earnings increases to apply the binomial distribution in Part B? What reservations might you have about the validity of these assumptions?

7. A portfolio manager annually outperforms her benchmark 60 percent of the time. Assuming independent annual trials, what is the probability that she will outperform her benchmark four or more times over the next five years?
    A. 0.26
    B. 0.34
    C. 0.48

8. You are examining the record of an investment newsletter writer who claims a 70 percent success rate in making investment recommendations that are profitable over a one-year time horizon. You have the one-year record of the newsletter's seven most recent recommendations. Four of those recommendations were profitable. If all the recommendations are independent and the newsletter writer's skill is as claimed, what is the probability of observing four or fewer profitable recommendations out of seven in total?

9. You are forecasting sales for a company in the fourth quarter of its fiscal year. Your low-end estimate of sales is €14 million, and your high-end estimate is €15 million. You decide to treat all outcomes for sales between these two values as equally likely, using a continuous uniform distribution.

    A. What is the expected value of sales for the fourth quarter?

    B. What is the probability that fourth-quarter sales will be less than or equal to €14,125,000?

10. State the approximate probability that a normal random variable will fall within the following intervals:

    A. Mean plus or minus one standard deviation.

    B. Mean plus or minus two standard deviations.

    C. Mean plus or minus three standard deviations.

11. Find the area under the normal curve up to $z = 0.36$; that is, find $P(Z \leq 0.36)$. Interpret this value.

12. If the probability that a portfolio outperforms its benchmark in any quarter is 0.75, the probability that the portfolio outperforms its benchmark in three or fewer quarters over the course of a year is *closest* to:

    A. 0.26

    B. 0.42

    C. 0.68

13. In futures markets, profits or losses on contracts are settled at the end of each trading day. This procedure is called marking to market or daily resettlement. By preventing a trader's losses from accumulating over many days, marking to market reduces the risk that traders will default on their obligations. A futures markets trader needs a liquidity pool to meet the daily mark to market. If liquidity is exhausted, the trader may be forced to unwind his position at an unfavorable time.

    Suppose you are using financial futures contracts to hedge a risk in your portfolio. You have a liquidity pool (cash and cash equivalents) of λ dollars per contract and a time horizon of T trading days. For a given size liquidity pool, λ, Kolb, Gay, and Hunter (1985) developed an expression for the probability stating that you will exhaust your liquidity pool within a T-day horizon as a result of the daily mark to market. Kolb et al. assumed that the expected change in futures price is 0 and that futures price changes are normally distributed. With σ representing the standard deviation of daily futures price changes, the standard deviation of price changes over a time horizon to day T is $\sigma\sqrt{T}$, given continuous compounding. With that background, the Kolb et al. expression is

    $$\text{Probability of exhausting liquidity pool} = 2[1 - N(x)]$$

where $x = \lambda/(\sigma\sqrt{T})$. Here x is a standardized value of λ. $N(x)$ is the standard normal cumulative distribution function. For some intuition about $1 - N(x)$ in the expression, note that the liquidity pool is exhausted if losses exceed the size of the liquidity pool at any time up to and including T; the probability of that event happening can be shown to be proportional to an area in the right tail of a standard normal distribution, $1 - N(x)$. Using the Kolb et al. expression, answer the following questions:

A. Your hedging horizon is five days, and your liquidity pool is $2,000 per contract. You estimate that the standard deviation of daily price changes for the contract is $450. What is the probability that you will exhaust your liquidity pool in the five-day period?

B. Suppose your hedging horizon is 20 days, but all the other facts given in Part A remain the same. What is the probability that you will exhaust your liquidity pool in the 20-day period?

14. Which of the following is characteristic of the normal distribution?
   A. Asymmetry
   B. Kurtosis of 3
   C. Definitive limits or boundaries

15. Which of the following assets *most likely* requires the use of a multivariate distribution for modeling returns?
   A. A call option on a bond
   B. A portfolio of technology stocks
   C. A stock in a market index

16. The total number of parameters that fully characterizes a multivariate normal distribution for the returns on two stocks is:
   A. 3.
   B. 4.
   C. 5.

17. A client has a portfolio of common stocks and fixed-income instruments with a current value of £1,350,000. She intends to liquidate £50,000 from the portfolio at the end of the year to purchase a partnership share in a business. Furthermore, the client would like to be able to withdraw the £50,000 without reducing the initial capital of £1,350,000. The following table shows four alternative asset allocations.

Mean and Standard Deviation for Four Allocations (in Percent)

	A	B	C	D
Expected annual return	16	12	10	9
Standard deviation of return	24	17	12	11

Address the following questions (assume normality for Parts B and C):

A. Given the client's desire not to invade the £1,350,000 principal, what is the shortfall level, R_L? Use this shortfall level to answer Part B.

B. According to the safety-first criterion, which of the allocations is the best?

C. What is the probability that the return on the safety-first optimal portfolio will be less than the shortfall level, R_L?

Please refer to Exhibit 1 for Questions 18 and 19.

EXHIBIT 1.   Z-Table Values, $P(Z \le z) = N(z)$ for $z \ge 0$

Z	0.00	0.01	0.02	0.03	0.04	0.05	0.06	0.07	0.08	0.09
0.00	0.5000	0.5040	0.5080	0.5120	0.5160	0.5199	0.5239	0.5279	0.5319	0.5359
0.1	0.5398	0.5438	0.5478	0.5517	0.5557	0.5596	0.5636	0.5675	0.5714	0.5753
0.2	0.5793	0.5832	0.5871	0.5910	0.5948	0.5987	0.6026	0.6064	0.6103	0.6141
0.3	0.6179	0.6217	0.6255	0.6293	0.6331	0.6368	0.6406	0.6443	0.6480	0.6517
0.4	0.6554	0.6591	0.6628	0.6664	0.6700	0.6736	0.6772	0.6808	0.6844	0.6879
0.5	0.6915	0.6950	0.6985	0.7019	0.7054	0.7088	0.7123	0.7157	0.7190	0.7224

18. A portfolio has an expected mean return of 8 percent and standard deviation of 14 percent. The probability that its return falls between 8 and 11 percent is *closest* to:
    A.   8.3%
    B.   14.8%.
    C.   58.3%.

19. A portfolio has an expected return of 7% with a standard deviation of 13%. For an investor with a minimum annual return target of 4%, the probability that the portfolio return will fail to meet the target is *closest* to:
    A.   33%.
    B.   41%.
    C.   59%.

20. A.   Define Monte Carlo simulation and explain its use in finance.
    B.   Compared with analytical methods, what are the strengths and weaknesses of Monte Carlo simulation for use in valuing securities?

21. Which of the following is a continuous random variable?
    A.   The value of a futures contract quoted in increments of $0.05
    B.   The total number of heads recorded in 1 million tosses of a coin
    C.   The rate of return on a diversified portfolio of stocks over a three-month period

22. *X* is a discrete random variable with possible outcomes $X = \{1,2,3,4\}$. Three functions $f(x)$, $g(x)$, and $h(x)$ are proposed to describe the probabilities of the outcomes in *X*.

	Probability Function		
$X = x$	$f(x) = P(X = x)$	$g(x) = P(X = x)$	$h(x) = P(X = x)$
1	−0.25	0.20	0.20
2	0.25	0.25	0.25
3	0.50	0.50	0.30
4	0.25	0.05	0.35

The conditions for a probability function are satisfied by:
A. $f(x)$.
B. $g(x)$.
C. $h(x)$.

23. The cumulative distribution function for a discrete random variable is shown in the following table.

$X = x$	Cumulative Distribution Function $F(x) = P(X \leq x)$
1	0.15
2	0.25
3	0.50
4	0.60
5	0.95
6	1.00

The probability that X will take on a value of either 2 or 4 is *closest* to:
A. 0.20.
B. 0.35.
C. 0.85.

24. Which of the following events can be represented as a Bernoulli trial?
A. The flip of a coin
B. The closing price of a stock
C. The picking of a random integer between 1 and 10

25. The weekly closing prices of Mordice Corporation shares are as follows:

Date	Closing Price (€)
1 August	112
8 August	160
15 August	120

The continuously compounded return of Mordice Corporation shares for the period August 1 to August 15 is *closest to*:
A. 6.90%
B. 7.14%
C. 8.95%

26. A stock is priced at $100.00 and follows a one-period binomial process with an up move that equals 1.05 and a down move that equals 0.97. If 1 million Bernoulli trials are conducted, and the average terminal stock price is $102.00, the probability of an up move (p) is *closest* to:
A. 0.375.
B. 0.500.
C. 0.625.

27. A call option on a stock index is valued using a three-step binomial tree with an up move that equals 1.05 and a down move that equals 0.95. The current level of the index is $190, and the option exercise price is $200. If the option value is positive when the stock price exceeds the exercise price at expiration and $0 otherwise, the number of terminal nodes with a positive payoff is:
    A.   one.
    B.   two.
    C.   three.

28. A random number between zero and one is generated according to a continuous uniform distribution. What is the probability that the first number generated will have a value of exactly 0.30?
    A.   0%
    B.   30%
    C.   70%

29. A Monte Carlo simulation can be used to:
    A.   directly provide precise valuations of call options.
    B.   simulate a process from historical records of returns.
    C.   test the sensitivity of a model to changes in assumptions.

30. A limitation of Monte Carlo simulation is:
    A.   its failure to do "what if" analysis.
    B.   that it requires historical records of returns.
    C.   its inability to independently specify cause-and-effect relationships.

31. Which parameter equals zero in a normal distribution?
    A.   Kurtosis
    B.   Skewness
    C.   Standard deviation

32. An analyst develops the following capital market projections.

	Stocks	Bonds
Mean Return	10%	2%
Standard Deviation	15%	5%

Assuming the returns of the asset classes are described by normal distributions, which of the following statements is correct?
    A.   Bonds have a higher probability of a negative return than stocks.
    B.   On average, 99 percent of stock returns will fall within two standard deviations of the mean.
    C.   The probability of a bond return less than or equal to 3 percent is determined using a *Z*-score of 0.25.

33. A client holding a £2,000,000 portfolio wants to withdraw £90,000 in one year without invading the principal. According to Roy's safety-first criterion, which of the following portfolio allocations is optimal?

	Allocation A	Allocation B	Allocation C
Expected annual return	6.5%	7.5%	8.5%
Standard deviation of returns	8.35%	10.21%	14.34%

   A. Allocation A
   B. Allocation B
   C. Allocation C

34. In contrast to normal distributions, lognormal distributions:
   A. are skewed to the left.
   B. have outcomes that cannot be negative.
   C. are more suitable for describing asset returns than asset prices.

35. The lognormal distribution is a more accurate model for the distribution of stock prices than the normal distribution because stock prices are:
   A. symmetrical.
   B. unbounded.
   C. non-negative.

36. The price of a stock at $t = 0$ is $208.25 and at $t = 1$ is $186.75. The continuously compounded rate of return for the stock from $t = 0$ to $t = 1$ is *closest* to:
   A. −10.90%.
   B. −10.32%.
   C. 11.51%.

CHAPTER 5

SAMPLING AND ESTIMATION

LEARNING OUTCOMES

The candidate should be able to:

- define simple random sampling and a sampling distribution;
- explain sampling error;
- distinguish between simple random and stratified random sampling;
- distinguish between time-series and cross-sectional data;
- explain the central limit theorem and its importance;
- calculate and interpret the standard error of the sample mean;
- identify and describe desirable properties of an estimator;
- distinguish between a point estimate and a confidence interval estimate of a population parameter;
- describe properties of Student's *t*-distribution and calculate and interpret its degrees of freedom;
- calculate and interpret a confidence interval for a population mean, given a normal distribution with 1) a known population variance, 2) an unknown population variance, or 3) an unknown population variance and a large sample size;
- describe the issues regarding selection of the appropriate sample size, data-mining bias, sample selection bias, survivorship bias, look-ahead bias, and time-period bias.

SUMMARY

In this chapter, we have presented basic concepts and results in sampling and estimation. We have also emphasized the challenges faced by analysts in appropriately using and interpreting financial data. As analysts, we should always use a critical eye when evaluating the results from any study. The quality of the sample is of the utmost importance: If the sample is biased, the conclusions drawn from the sample will be in error.

- To draw valid inferences from a sample, the sample should be random.
- In simple random sampling, each observation has an equal chance of being selected. In stratified random sampling, the population is divided into subpopulations, called strata or cells, based on one or more classification criteria; simple random samples are then drawn from each stratum.
- Stratified random sampling ensures that population subdivisions of interest are represented in the sample. Stratified random sampling also produces more-precise parameter estimates than simple random sampling.
- Time-series data are a collection of observations at equally spaced intervals of time. Cross-sectional data are observations that represent individuals, groups, geographical regions, or companies at a single point in time.
- The central limit theorem states that for large sample sizes, for any underlying distribution for a random variable, the sampling distribution of the sample mean for that variable will be approximately normal, with mean equal to the population mean for that random variable and variance equal to the population variance of the variable divided by sample size.
- Based on the central limit theorem, when the sample size is large, we can compute confidence intervals for the population mean based on the normal distribution regardless of the distribution of the underlying population. In general, a sample size of 30 or larger can be considered large.
- An estimator is a formula for estimating a parameter. An estimate is a particular value that we calculate from a sample by using an estimator.
- Because an estimator or statistic is a random variable, it is described by some probability distribution. We refer to the distribution of an estimator as its sampling distribution. The standard deviation of the sampling distribution of the sample mean is called the standard error of the sample mean.
- The desirable properties of an estimator are *unbiasedness* (the expected value of the estimator equals the population parameter), *efficiency* (the estimator has the smallest variance), and *consistency* (the probability of accurate estimates increases as sample size increases).
- The two types of estimates of a parameter are point estimates and interval estimates. A point estimate is a single number that we use to estimate a parameter. An interval estimate is a range of values that brackets the population parameter with some probability.
- A confidence interval is an interval for which we can assert with a given probability $1 - \alpha$, called the degree of confidence, that it will contain the parameter it is intended to estimate. This measure is often referred to as the $100(1 - \alpha)\%$ confidence interval for the parameter.
- A $100(1 - \alpha)\%$ confidence interval for a parameter has the following structure: Point estimate $\pm$ Reliability factor $\times$ Standard error, where the reliability factor is a number based on the assumed distribution of the point estimate and the degree of confidence ($1 - \alpha$) for the confidence interval and where standard error is the standard error of the sample statistic providing the point estimate.
- A $100(1 - \alpha)\%$ confidence interval for population mean μ when sampling from a normal distribution with known variance σ^2 is given by $\bar{X} \pm z_{\alpha/2} \frac{\sigma}{\sqrt{n}}$, where $z_{\alpha/2}$ is the point of the standard normal distribution such that $\alpha/2$ remains in the right tail.
- Student's t-distribution is a family of symmetrical distributions defined by a single parameter, degrees of freedom.

- A random sample of size n is said to have $n - 1$ degrees of freedom for estimating the population variance, in the sense that there are only $n - 1$ independent deviations from the mean on which to base the estimate.
- The degrees of freedom number for use with the t-distribution is also $n - 1$.
- The t-distribution has fatter tails than the standard normal distribution but converges to the standard normal distribution as degrees of freedom go to infinity.
- A $100(1 - \alpha)\%$ confidence interval for the population mean μ when sampling from a normal distribution with unknown variance (a t-distribution confidence interval) is given by $\bar{X} \pm t_{\alpha/2}(s/\sqrt{n})$, where $t_{\alpha/2}$ is the point of the t-distribution such that $\alpha/2$ remains in the right tail and s is the sample standard deviation. This confidence interval can also be used, because of the central limit theorem, when dealing with a large sample from a population with unknown variance that may not be normal.
- We may use the confidence interval $\bar{X} \pm z_{\alpha/2}(s/\sqrt{n})$ as an alternative to the t-distribution confidence interval for the population mean when using a large sample from a population with unknown variance. The confidence interval based on the z-statistic is less conservative (narrower) than the corresponding confidence interval based on a t-distribution.
- Three issues in the selection of sample size are the need for precision, the risk of sampling from more than one population, and the expenses of different sample sizes.
- Sample data in investments can have a variety of problems. *Survivorship bias* occurs if companies are excluded from the analysis because they have gone out of business or because of reasons related to poor performance. *Data-mining bias* comes from finding models by repeatedly searching through databases for patterns. *Look-ahead bias* exists if the model uses data not available to market participants at the time the market participants act in the model. Finally, time-period bias is present if the time period used makes the results time-period specific or if the time period used includes a point of structural change.

PRACTICE PROBLEMS

1. Peter Biggs wants to know how growth managers performed last year. Biggs assumes that the population cross-sectional standard deviation of growth manager returns is 6 percent and that the returns are independent across managers.
   A. How large a random sample does Biggs need if he wants the standard deviation of the sample means to be 1 percent?
   B. How large a random sample does Biggs need if he wants the standard deviation of the sample means to be 0.25 percent?

2. Petra Munzi wants to know how value managers performed last year. Munzi estimates that the population cross-sectional standard deviation of value manager returns is 4 percent and assumes that the returns are independent across managers.
   A. Munzi wants to build a 95 percent confidence interval for the mean return. How large a random sample does Munzi need if she wants the 95 percent confidence interval to have a total width of 1 percent?
   B. Munzi expects a cost of about $10 to collect each observation. If she has a $1,000 budget, will she be able to construct the confidence interval she wants?

3. Assume that the equity risk premium is normally distributed with a population mean of 6 percent and a population standard deviation of 18 percent. Over the last four years,

equity returns (relative to the risk-free rate) have averaged −2.0 percent. You have a large client who is very upset and claims that results this poor should *never* occur. Evaluate your client's concerns.

A. Construct a 95 percent confidence interval around the population mean for a sample of four-year returns.

B. What is the probability of a −2.0 percent or lower average return over a four-year period?

4. Compare the standard normal distribution and Student's *t*-distribution.

5. Find the reliability factors based on the *t*-distribution for the following confidence intervals for the population mean (DF = degrees of freedom, n = sample size):

A. A 99 percent confidence interval, DF = 20.

B. A 90 percent confidence interval, DF = 20.

C. A 95 percent confidence interval, n = 25.

D. A 95 percent confidence interval, n = 16.

6. Assume that monthly returns are normally distributed with a mean of 1 percent and a sample standard deviation of 4 percent. The population standard deviation is unknown. Construct a 95 percent confidence interval for the sample mean of monthly returns if the sample size is 24.

7. Ten analysts have given the following fiscal year earnings forecasts for a stock:

Forecast (X_i)	Number of Analysts (n_i)
1.40	1
1.43	1
1.44	3
1.45	2
1.47	1
1.48	1
1.50	1

Because the sample is a small fraction of the number of analysts who follow this stock, assume that we can ignore the finite population correction factor. Assume that the analyst forecasts are normally distributed.

A. What are the mean forecast and standard deviation of forecasts?

B. Provide a 95 percent confidence interval for the population mean of the forecasts.

8. Thirteen analysts have given the following fiscal-year earnings forecasts for a stock:

Forecast (X_i)	Number of Analysts (n_i)
0.70	2
0.72	4
0.74	1
0.75	3
0.76	1
0.77	1
0.82	1

Because the sample is a small fraction of the number of analysts who follow this stock, assume that we can ignore the finite population correction factor.

A. What are the mean forecast and standard deviation of forecasts?

B. What aspect of the data makes us uncomfortable about using *t*-tables to construct confidence intervals for the population mean forecast?

9. Explain the differences between constructing a confidence interval when sampling from a normal population with a known population variance and sampling from a normal population with an unknown variance.

10. An exchange rate has a given expected future value and standard deviation.

A. Assuming that the exchange rate is normally distributed, what are the probabilities that the exchange rate will be at least 2 or 3 standard deviations away from its mean?

B. Assume that you do not know the distribution of exchange rates. Use Chebyshev's inequality (that at least $1 - 1/k^2$ proportion of the observations will be within k standard deviations of the mean for any positive integer k greater than 1) to calculate the maximum probabilities that the exchange rate will be at least 2 or 3 standard deviations away from its mean.

11. Although he knows security returns are not independent, a colleague makes the claim that because of the central limit theorem, if we diversify across a large number of investments, the portfolio standard deviation will eventually approach zero as n becomes large. Is he correct?

12. Why is the central limit theorem important?

13. What is wrong with the following statement of the central limit theorem?

Central Limit Theorem. "If the random variables X_1, X_2, X_3, ..., X_n are a random sample of size n from any distribution with finite mean μ and variance σ^2, then the distribution of $\bar{X}$ will be approximately normal, with a standard deviation of $\sigma/\sqrt{n}$."

14. Suppose we take a random sample of 30 companies in an industry with 200 companies. We calculate the sample mean of the ratio of cash flow to total debt for the prior year. We find that this ratio is 23 percent. Subsequently, we learn that the population cash flow to total debt ratio (taking account of all 200 companies) is 26 percent. What is the explanation for the discrepancy between the sample mean of 23 percent and the population mean of 26 percent?
    A. Sampling error.
    B. Bias.
    C. A lack of consistency.

15. Alcorn Mutual Funds is placing large advertisements in several financial publications. The advertisements prominently display the returns of 5 of Alcorn's 30 funds for the past 1-, 3-, 5-, and 10-year periods. The results are indeed impressive, with all of the funds beating the major market indexes and a few beating them by a large margin. Is the Alcorn family of funds superior to its competitors?

16. Julius Spence has tested several predictive models in order to identify undervalued stocks. Spence used about 30 company-specific variables and 10 market-related variables to predict returns for about 5,000 North American and European stocks. He found that a final model using eight variables applied to telecommunications and computer stocks yields spectacular results. Spence wants you to use the model to select investments. Should you? What steps would you take to evaluate the model?

17. The *best* approach for creating a stratified random sample of a population involves:
    A. drawing an equal number of simple random samples from each subpopulation.
    B. selecting every *k*th member of the population until the desired sample size is reached.
    C. drawing simple random samples from each subpopulation in sizes proportional to the relative size of each subpopulation.

18. A population has a non-normal distribution with mean E and variance σ^2. The sampling distribution of the sample mean computed from samples of large size from that population will have:
    A. the same distribution as the population distribution.
    B. its mean approximately equal to the population mean.
    C. its variance approximately equal to the population variance.

19. A sample mean is computed from a population with a variance of 2.45. The sample size is 40. The standard error of the sample mean is *closest* to:
    A. 0.039.
    B. 0.247.
    C. 0.387.

20. An estimator with an expected value equal to the parameter that it is intended to estimate is described as:
    A. efficient.
    B. unbiased.
    C. consistent.

21. If an estimator is consistent, an increase in sample size will increase the:
    A. accuracy of estimates.
    B. efficiency of the estimator.
    C. unbiasedness of the estimator.

22. For a two-sided confidence interval, an increase in the degree of confidence will result in:
    A. a wider confidence interval.
    B. a narrower confidence interval.
    C. no change in the width of the confidence interval.

23. As the *t*-distribution's degrees of freedom decrease, the *t*-distribution *most likely*:
    A. exhibits tails that become fatter.
    B. approaches a standard normal distribution.
    C. becomes asymmetrically distributed around its mean value.

24. For a sample size of 17, with a mean of 116.23 and a variance of 245.55, the width of a 90 percent confidence interval using the appropriate *t*-distribution is *closest to*:
    A. 13.23.
    B. 13.27.
    C. 13.68.

25. For a sample size of 65 with a mean of 31 taken from a normally distributed population with a variance of 529, a 99 percent confidence interval for the population mean will have a lower limit *closest* to:
    A. 23.64.
    B. 25.41.
    C. 30.09.

26. An increase in sample size is *most likely* to result in a:
    A. wider confidence interval.
    B. decrease in the standard error of the sample mean.
    C. lower likelihood of sampling from more than one population.

27. A report on long-term stock returns focused exclusively on all currently publicly traded firms in an industry is *most likely* susceptible to:
    A. look-ahead bias.
    B. survivorship bias.
    C. intergenerational data mining.

28. Which sampling bias is *most likely* investigated with an out-of-sample test?
    A. Look-ahead bias
    B. Data-mining bias
    C. Sample selection bias

29. Which of the following characteristics of an investment study *most likely* indicates time-period bias?
    A. The study is based on a short time-series.
    B. Information not available on the test date is used.
    C. A structural change occurred prior to the start of the study's time series.

CHAPTER 6

HYPOTHESIS TESTING

LEARNING OUTCOMES

The candidate should be able to:

- define a hypothesis, describe the steps of hypothesis testing, and describe and interpret the choice of the null and alternative hypotheses;
- distinguish between one-tailed and two-tailed tests of hypotheses;
- explain a test statistic, Type I and Type II errors, a significance level, and how significance levels are used in hypothesis testing;
- explain a decision rule, the power of a test, and the relation between confidence intervals and hypothesis tests;
- distinguish between a statistical result and an economically meaningful result;
- explain and interpret the *p*-value as it relates to hypothesis testing;
- identify the appropriate test statistic and interpret the results for a hypothesis test concerning the population mean of both large and small samples when the population is normally or approximately normally distributed and the variance is 1) known or 2) unknown;
- identify the appropriate test statistic and interpret the results for a hypothesis test concerning the equality of the population means of two at least approximately normally distributed populations, based on independent random samples with 1) equal or 2) unequal assumed variances;
- identify the appropriate test statistic and interpret the results for a hypothesis test concerning the mean difference of two normally distributed populations;
- identify the appropriate test statistic and interpret the results for a hypothesis test concerning 1) the variance of a normally distributed population, and 2) the equality of the variances of two normally distributed populations based on two independent random samples;
- formulate a test of the hypothesis that the population correlation coefficient equals zero and determine whether the hypothesis is rejected at a given level of significance;
- distinguish between parametric and nonparametric tests and describe situations in which the use of nonparametric tests may be appropriate.

6. SUMMARY

In this chapter, we have presented the concepts and methods of statistical inference and hypothesis testing.

- A hypothesis is a statement about one or more populations.
- The steps in testing a hypothesis are as follows:
  1. Stating the hypotheses.
  2. Identifying the appropriate test statistic and its probability distribution.
  3. Specifying the significance level.
  4. Stating the decision rule.
  5. Collecting the data and calculating the test statistic.
  6. Making the statistical decision.
  7. Making the economic or investment decision.
- We state two hypotheses: The null hypothesis is the hypothesis to be tested; the alternative hypothesis is the hypothesis accepted when the null hypothesis is rejected.
- There are three ways to formulate hypotheses:
  1. $H_0: \theta = \theta_0$ versus $H_a: \theta \neq \theta_0$
  2. $H_0: \theta \leq \theta_0$ versus $H_a: \theta > \theta_0$
  3. $H_0: \theta \geq \theta_0$ versus $H_a: \theta < \theta_0$

  where θ_0 is a hypothesized value of the population parameter and θ is the true value of the population parameter. In the above, Formulation 1 is a two-sided test and Formulations 2 and 3 are one-sided tests.
- When we have a "suspected" or "hoped for" condition for which we want to find supportive evidence, we frequently set up that condition as the alternative hypothesis and use a one-sided test. To emphasize a neutral attitude, however, the researcher may select a "not equal to" alternative hypothesis and conduct a two-sided test.
- A test statistic is a quantity, calculated on the basis of a sample, whose value is the basis for deciding whether to reject or not reject the null hypothesis. To decide whether to reject, or not to reject, the null hypothesis, we compare the computed value of the test statistic to a critical value (rejection point) for the same test statistic.
- In reaching a statistical decision, we can make two possible errors: We may reject a true null hypothesis (a Type I error), or we may fail to reject a false null hypothesis (a Type II error).
- The level of significance of a test is the probability of a Type I error that we accept in conducting a hypothesis test. The probability of a Type I error is denoted by the Greek letter alpha, α. The standard approach to hypothesis testing involves specifying a level of significance (probability of Type I error) only.
- The power of a test is the probability of correctly rejecting the null (rejecting the null when it is false).
- A decision rule consists of determining the rejection points (critical values) with which to compare the test statistic to decide whether to reject or not to reject the null hypothesis. When we reject the null hypothesis, the result is said to be statistically significant.
- The $(1 - \alpha)$ confidence interval represents the range of values of the test statistic for which the null hypothesis will not be rejected at an α significance level.
- The statistical decision consists of rejecting or not rejecting the null hypothesis. The economic decision takes into consideration all economic issues pertinent to the decision.

- The *p*-value is the smallest level of significance at which the null hypothesis can be rejected. The smaller the *p*-value, the stronger the evidence against the null hypothesis and in favor of the alternative hypothesis. The *p*-value approach to hypothesis testing does not involve setting a significance level; rather it involves computing a *p*-value for the test statistic and allowing the consumer of the research to interpret its significance.
- For hypothesis tests concerning the population mean of a normally distributed population with unknown (known) variance, the theoretically correct test statistic is the *t*-statistic (*z*-statistic). In the unknown variance case, given large samples (generally, samples of 30 or more observations), the *z*-statistic may be used in place of the *t*-statistic because of the force of the central limit theorem.
- The *t*-distribution is a symmetrical distribution defined by a single parameter: degrees of freedom. Compared to the standard normal distribution, the *t*-distribution has fatter tails.
- When we want to test whether the observed difference between two means is statistically significant, we must first decide whether the samples are independent or dependent (related). If the samples are independent, we conduct tests concerning differences between means. If the samples are dependent, we conduct tests of mean differences (paired comparisons tests).
- When we conduct a test of the difference between two population means from normally distributed populations with unknown variances, if we can assume the variances are equal, we use a *t*-test based on pooling the observations of the two samples to estimate the common (but unknown) variance. This test is based on an assumption of independent samples.
- When we conduct a test of the difference between two population means from normally distributed populations with unknown variances, if we cannot assume that the variances are equal, we use an approximate *t*-test using modified degrees of freedom given by a formula. This test is based on an assumption of independent samples.
- In tests concerning two means based on two samples that are not independent, we often can arrange the data in paired observations and conduct a test of mean differences (a paired comparisons test). When the samples are from normally distributed populations with unknown variances, the appropriate test statistic is a *t*-statistic. The denominator of the *t*-statistic, the standard error of the mean differences, takes account of correlation between the samples.
- In tests concerning the variance of a single, normally distributed population, the test statistic is chi-square (χ^2) with $n - 1$ degrees of freedom, where n is sample size.
- For tests concerning differences between the variances of two normally distributed populations based on two random, independent samples, the appropriate test statistic is based on an *F*-test (the ratio of the sample variances).
- The *F*-statistic is defined by the numerator and denominator degrees of freedom. The numerator degrees of freedom (number of observations in the sample minus 1) is the divisor used in calculating the sample variance in the numerator. The denominator degrees of freedom (number of observations in the sample minus 1) is the divisor used in calculating the sample variance in the denominator. In forming an *F*-test, a convention is to use the larger of the two ratios, s_1^2/s_2^2 or s_2^2/s_1^2, as the actual test statistic.
- In tests concerning correlation, we use a *t*-statistic to test whether a population correlation coefficient is significantly different from 0. If we have n observations for two variables, this test statistic has a *t*-distribution with $n - 2$ degrees of freedom.

- A parametric test is a hypothesis test concerning a parameter or a hypothesis test based on specific distributional assumptions. In contrast, a nonparametric test either is not concerned with a parameter or makes minimal assumptions about the population from which the sample comes.
- A nonparametric test is primarily used in three situations: when data do not meet distributional assumptions, when data are given in ranks, or when the hypothesis we are addressing does not concern a parameter.
- The Spearman rank correlation coefficient is calculated on the ranks of two variables within their respective samples.

PRACTICE PROBLEMS

1. Which of the following statements about hypothesis testing is correct?
   A. The null hypothesis is the condition a researcher hopes to support.
   B. The alternative hypothesis is the proposition considered true without conclusive evidence to the contrary.
   C. The alternative hypothesis exhausts all potential parameter values not accounted for by the null hypothesis.

2. Identify the appropriate test statistic or statistics for conducting the following hypothesis tests. (Clearly identify the test statistic and, if applicable, the number of degrees of freedom. For example, "We conduct the test using an x-statistic with y degrees of freedom.")
   A. H_0: $\mu = 0$ versus H_a: $\mu \neq 0$, where μ is the mean of a normally distributed population with unknown variance. The test is based on a sample of 15 observations.
   B. H_0: $\mu = 0$ versus H_a: $\mu \neq 0$, where μ is the mean of a normally distributed population with unknown variance. The test is based on a sample of 40 observations.
   C. H_0: $\mu \leq 0$ versus H_a: $\mu > 0$, where μ is the mean of a normally distributed population with known variance σ^2. The sample size is 45.
   D. H_0: $\sigma^2 = 200$ versus H_a: $\sigma^2 \neq 200$, where σ^2 is the variance of a normally distributed population. The sample size is 50.
   E. $H_0 : \sigma_1^2 = \sigma_2^2$ versus $H_a : \sigma_1^2 \neq \sigma_2^2$, where σ_1^2 is the variance of one normally distributed population and σ_2^2 is the variance of a second normally distributed population. The test is based on two independent random samples.
   F. H_0: (Population mean 1) – (Population mean 2) = 0 versus H_a: (Population mean 1) – (Population mean 2) $\neq$ 0, where the samples are drawn from normally distributed populations with unknown variances. The observations in the two samples are correlated.
   G. H_0: (Population mean 1) – (Population mean 2) = 0 versus H_a: (Population mean 1) – (Population mean 2) $\neq$ 0, where the samples are drawn from normally distributed populations with unknown but assumed equal variances. The observations in the two samples (of size 25 and 30, respectively) are independent.

3. For each of the following hypothesis tests concerning the population mean, μ, state the rejection point condition or conditions for the test statistic (e.g., $t > 1.25$); n denotes sample size.
   A. H_0: $\mu = 10$ versus H_a: $\mu \neq 10$, using a t-test with $n = 26$ and $\alpha = 0.05$
   B. H_0: $\mu = 10$ versus H_a: $\mu \neq 10$, using a t-test with $n = 40$ and $\alpha = 0.01$
   C. H_0: $\mu \leq 10$ versus H_a: $\mu > 10$, using a t-test with $n = 40$ and $\alpha = 0.01$
   D. H_0: $\mu \leq 10$ versus H_a: $\mu > 10$, using a t-test with $n = 21$ and $\alpha = 0.05$
   E. H_0: $\mu \geq 10$ versus H_a: $\mu < 10$, using a t-test with $n = 19$ and $\alpha = 0.10$
   F. H_0: $\mu \geq 10$ versus H_a: $\mu < 10$, using a t-test with $n = 50$ and $\alpha = 0.05$

4. For each of the following hypothesis tests concerning the population mean, μ, state the rejection point condition or conditions for the test statistic (e.g., $z > 1.25$); n denotes sample size.
   A. H_0: $\mu = 10$ versus H_a: $\mu \neq 10$, using a z-test with $n = 50$ and $\alpha = 0.01$
   B. H_0: $\mu = 10$ versus H_a: $\mu \neq 10$, using a z-test with $n = 50$ and $\alpha = 0.05$
   C. H_0: $\mu = 10$ versus H_a: $\mu \neq 10$, using a z-test with $n = 50$ and $\alpha = 0.10$
   D. H_0: $\mu \leq 10$ versus H_a: $\mu > 10$, using a z-test with $n = 50$ and $\alpha = 0.05$

5. Willco is a manufacturer in a mature cyclical industry. During the most recent industry cycle, its net income averaged \$30 million per year with a standard deviation of \$10 million ($n = 6$ observations). Management claims that Willco's performance during the most recent cycle results from new approaches and that we can dismiss profitability expectations based on its average or normalized earnings of \$24 million per year in prior cycles.
   A. With μ as the population value of mean annual net income, formulate null and alternative hypotheses consistent with testing Willco management's claim.
   B. Assuming that Willco's net income is at least approximately normally distributed, identify the appropriate test statistic.
   C. Identify the rejection point or points at the 0.05 level of significance for the hypothesis tested in Part A.
   D. Determine whether or not to reject the null hypothesis at the 0.05 significance level.

The following information relates to Questions 6–7

Performance in Forecasting Quarterly Earnings per Share

	Number of Forecasts	Mean Forecast Error (Predicted – Actual)	Standard Deviations of Forecast Errors
Analyst A	101	0.05	0.10
Analyst B	121	0.02	0.09

6. Investment analysts often use earnings per share (EPS) forecasts. One test of forecasting quality is the zero-mean test, which states that optimal forecasts should have a mean forecasting error of 0. (Forecasting error = Predicted value of variable – Actual value of variable.)

You have collected data (shown in the table above) for two analysts who cover two different industries: Analyst A covers the telecom industry; Analyst B covers automotive parts and suppliers.

A. With μ as the population mean forecasting error, formulate null and alternative hypotheses for a zero-mean test of forecasting quality.

B. For Analyst A, using both a t-test and a z-test, determine whether to reject the null at the 0.05 and 0.01 levels of significance.

C. For Analyst B, using both a t-test and a z-test, determine whether to reject the null at the 0.05 and 0.01 levels of significance.

7. Reviewing the EPS forecasting performance data for Analysts A and B, you want to investigate whether the larger average forecast errors of Analyst A are due to chance or to a higher underlying mean value for Analyst A. Assume that the forecast errors of both analysts are normally distributed and that the samples are independent.

A. Formulate null and alternative hypotheses consistent with determining whether the population mean value of Analyst A's forecast errors (μ_1) are larger than Analyst B's (μ_2).

B. Identify the test statistic for conducting a test of the null hypothesis formulated in Part A.

C. Identify the rejection point or points for the hypothesis tested in Part A, at the 0.05 level of significance.

D. Determine whether or not to reject the null hypothesis at the 0.05 level of significance.

8. The table below gives data on the monthly returns on the S&P 500 and small-cap stocks for a forty-year period and provides statistics relating to their mean differences. Furthermore, the entire sample period is split into two subperiods of 20 years each and the returns data for these subperiods is also given in the table.

Measure	S&P 500 Return (%)	Small-Cap Stock Return (%)	Differences (S&P 500– Small-Cap Stock)
Entire sample period, 480 months			
Mean	1.0542	1.3117	–0.258
Standard deviation	4.2185	5.9570	3.752
First subperiod, 240 months			
Mean	0.6345	1.2741	–0.640
Standard deviation	4.0807	6.5829	4.096
Second subperiod, 240 months			
Mean	1.4739	1.3492	0.125
Standard deviation	4.3197	5.2709	3.339

Let μ_d stand for the population mean value of difference between S&P 500 returns and small-cap stock returns. Use a significance level of 0.05 and suppose that mean differences are approximately normally distributed.

A. Formulate null and alternative hypotheses consistent with testing whether any difference exists between the mean returns on the S&P 500 and small-cap stocks.
B. Determine whether or not to reject the null hypothesis at the 0.05 significance level for the entire sample period.
C. Determine whether or not to reject the null hypothesis at the 0.05 significance level for the first subperiod.
D. Determine whether or not to reject the null hypothesis at the 0.05 significance level for the second subperiod.

9. During a 10-year period, the standard deviation of annual returns on a portfolio you are analyzing was 15 percent a year. You want to see whether this record is sufficient evidence to support the conclusion that the portfolio's underlying variance of return was less than 400, the return variance of the portfolio's benchmark.
A. Formulate null and alternative hypotheses consistent with the verbal description of your objective.
B. Identify the test statistic for conducting a test of the hypotheses in Part A.
C. Identify the rejection point or points at the 0.05 significance level for the hypothesis tested in Part A.
D. Determine whether the null hypothesis is rejected or not rejected at the 0.05 level of significance.

10. You are investigating whether the population variance of returns on the S&P 500/ BARRA Growth Index changed subsequent to the October 1987 market crash. You gather the following data for 120 months of returns before October 1987 and for 120 months of returns after October 1987. You have specified a 0.05 level of significance.

Time Period	n	Mean Monthly Return (%)	Variance of Returns
Before October 1987	120	1.416	22.367
After October 1987	120	1.436	15.795

A. Formulate null and alternative hypotheses consistent with the verbal description of the research goal.
B. Identify the test statistic for conducting a test of the hypotheses in Part A.
C. Determine whether or not to reject the null hypothesis at the 0.05 level of significance. (Use the F-tables in the back of this volume.)

11. The following table shows the sample correlations between the monthly returns for four different mutual funds and the S&P 500. The correlations are based on 36 monthly observations. The funds are as follows:

Fund 1   Large-cap fund
Fund 2   Mid-cap fund
Fund 3   Large-cap value fund
Fund 4   Emerging markets fund
S&P 500   US domestic stock index

	Fund 1	Fund 2	Fund 3	Fund 4	S&P 500
Fund 1	1				
Fund 2	0.9231	1			
Fund 3	0.4771	0.4156	1		
Fund 4	0.7111	0.7238	0.3102	1	
S&P 500	0.8277	0.8223	0.5791	0.7515	1

Test the null hypothesis that each of these correlations, individually, is equal to zero against the alternative hypothesis that it is not equal to zero. Use a 5 percent significance level.

12. In the step "stating a decision rule" in testing a hypothesis, which of the following elements must be specified?
    A. Critical value
    B. Power of a test
    C. Value of a test statistic

13. Which of the following statements is correct with respect to the null hypothesis?
    A. It is considered to be true unless the sample provides evidence showing it is false.
    B. It can be stated as "not equal to" provided the alternative hypothesis is stated as "equal to."
    C. In a two-tailed test, it is rejected when evidence supports equality between the hypothesized value and population parameter.

14. An analyst is examining a large sample with an unknown population variance. To test the hypothesis that the historical average return on an index is less than or equal to 6%, which of the following is the *most* appropriate test?
    A. One-tailed z-test
    B. Two-tailed z-test
    C. One-tailed F-test

15. A hypothesis test for a normally-distributed population at a 0.05 significance level implies a:
    A. 95% probability of rejecting a true null hypothesis.
    B. 95% probability of a Type I error for a two-tailed test.
    C. 5% critical value rejection region in a tail of the distribution for a one-tailed test.

16. Which of the following statements regarding a one-tailed hypothesis test is correct?
    A. The rejection region increases in size as the level of significance becomes smaller.
    B. A one-tailed test more strongly reflects the beliefs of the researcher than a two-tailed test.
    C. The absolute value of the rejection point is larger than that of a two-tailed test at the same level of significance.

17. The value of a test statistic is *best* described as the basis for deciding whether to:
    A. reject the null hypothesis.
    B. accept the null hypothesis.
    C. reject the alternative hypothesis.

18. Which of the following is a Type I error?
    A. Rejecting a true null hypothesis
    B. Rejecting a false null hypothesis
    C. Failing to reject a false null hypothesis

19. A Type II error is *best* described as:
    A. rejecting a true null hypothesis.
    B. failing to reject a false null hypothesis.
    C. failing to reject a false alternative hypothesis.

20. The level of significance of a hypothesis test is *best* used to:
    A. calculate the test statistic.
    B. define the test's rejection points.
    C. specify the probability of a Type II error.

21. You are interested in whether excess risk-adjusted return (alpha) is correlated with mutual fund expense ratios for US large-cap growth funds. The following table presents the sample.

Mutual Fund	1	2	3	4	5	6	7	8	9
Alpha (X)	−0.52	−0.13	−0.60	−1.01	−0.26	−0.89	−0.42	−0.23	−0.60
Expense Ratio (Y)	1.34	0.92	1.02	1.45	1.35	0.50	1.00	1.50	1.45

    A. Formulate null and alternative hypotheses consistent with the verbal description of the research goal.
    B. Identify the test statistic for conducting a test of the hypotheses in Part A.
    C. Justify your selection in Part B.
    D   Determine whether or not to reject the null hypothesis at the 0.05 level of significance.

22. All else equal, is specifying a smaller significance level in a hypothesis test likely to increase the probability of a:

	Type I error?	Type II error?
A.	No	No
B.	No	Yes
C.	Yes	No

23. The probability of correctly rejecting the null hypothesis is the:
    A. *p*-value.
    B. power of a test.
    C. level of significance.

24. The power of a hypothesis test is:
    A. equivalent to the level of significance.
    B. the probability of not making a Type II error.
    C. unchanged by increasing a small sample size.

25. When making a decision in investments involving a statistically significant result, the:
    A. economic result should be presumed meaningful.
    B. statistical result should take priority over economic considerations.
    C. economic logic for the future relevance of the result should be further explored.

26. An analyst tests the profitability of a trading strategy with the null hypothesis being that the average abnormal return before trading costs equals zero. The calculated t-statistic is 2.802, with critical values of $\pm$ 2.756 at significance level $\alpha = 0.01$. After considering trading costs, the strategy's return is near zero. The results are *most likely*:
    A. statistically but not economically significant.
    B. economically but not statistically significant.
    C. neither statistically nor economically significant.

27. Which of the following statements is correct with respect to the p-value?
    A. It is a less precise measure of test evidence than rejection points.
    B. It is the largest level of significance at which the null hypothesis is rejected.
    C. It can be compared directly with the level of significance in reaching test conclusions.

28. Which of the following represents a correct statement about the p-value?
    A. The p-value offers less precise information than does the rejection points approach.
    B. A larger p-value provides stronger evidence in support of the alternative hypothesis.
    C. A p-value less than the specified level of significance leads to rejection of the null hypothesis.

29. Which of the following statements on p-value is correct?
    A. The p-value is the smallest level of significance at which H_0 can be rejected.
    B. The p-value indicates the probability of making a Type II error.
    C. The lower the p-value, the weaker the evidence for rejecting the H_0.

30. The following table shows the significance level (α) and the p-value for three hypothesis tests.

	α	p-value
Test 1	0.05	0.10
Test 2	0.10	0.08
Test 3	0.10	0.05

The evidence for rejecting H_0 is strongest for:
    A. Test 1.
    B. Test 2.
    C. Test 3.

31. Which of the following tests of a hypothesis concerning the population mean is *most* appropriate?
    A. A z-test if the population variance is unknown and the sample is small
    B. A z-test if the population is normally distributed with a known variance
    C. A t-test if the population is non-normally distributed with unknown variance and a small sample

32. For a small sample with unknown variance, which of the following tests of a hypothesis concerning the population mean is most appropriate?
    A. A *t*-test if the population is normally distributed
    B. A *t*-test if the population is non-normally distributed
    C. A *z*-test regardless of the normality of the population distribution

33. For a small sample from a normally distributed population with unknown variance, the *most* appropriate test statistic for the mean is the:
    A. *z*-statistic.
    B. *t*-statistic.
    C. χ^2 statistic.

34. An investment consultant conducts two independent random samples of 5-year performance data for US and European absolute return hedge funds. Noting a 50-basis point-return advantage for US managers, the consultant decides to test whether the two means are statistically different from one another at a 0.05 level of significance. The two populations are assumed to be normally distributed with unknown but equal variances. Results of the hypothesis test are contained in the tables below.

	Sample Size	Mean Return %	Standard Deviation
US Managers	50	4.7	5.4
European Managers	50	4.2	4.8

Null and Alternative Hypotheses	$H_0: \mu_{US} - \mu_E = 0; H_a: \mu_{US} - \mu_E \neq 0$
Test Statistic	0.4893
Critical Value Rejection Points	± 1.984

μ_{US} is the mean return for US funds and μ_E is the mean return for European funds. The results of the hypothesis test indicate that the:
    A. null hypothesis is not rejected.
    B. alternative hypothesis is statistically confirmed.
    C. difference in mean returns is statistically different from zero.

35. A pooled estimator is used when testing a hypothesis concerning the:
    A. equality of the variances of two normally distributed populations.
    B. difference between the means of two at least approximately normally distributed populations with unknown but assumed equal variances.
    C. difference between the means of two at least approximately normally distributed populations with unknown and assumed unequal variances.

36. When evaluating mean differences between two dependent samples, the *most* appropriate test is a:
    A. chi-square test.
    B. paired comparisons test.
    C. *z*-test.

37. A fund manager reported a 2% mean quarterly return over the past ten years for its entire base of 250 client accounts that all follow the same investment strategy. A consultant employing the manager for 45 client accounts notes that their mean quarterly returns were 0.25% less over the same period. The consultant tests the hypothesis that the return disparity between the returns of his clients and the reported returns of the fund manager's 250 client accounts are significantly different from zero. Assuming normally distributed populations with unknown population variances, the *most* appropriate test statistic is:
    A. a paired comparisons *t*-test.
    B. a *t*-test of the difference between the two population means.
    C. an approximate *t*-test of mean differences between the two populations.

38. A chi-square test is *most* appropriate for tests concerning:
    A. a single variance.
    B. differences between two population means with variances assumed to be equal.
    C. differences between two population means with variances assumed to not be equal.

39. Which of the following should be used to test the difference between the variances of two normally distributed populations?
    A. *t*-test
    B. *F*-test
    C. Paired comparisons test

40. Jill Batten is analyzing how the returns on the stock of Stellar Energy Corp. are related with the previous month's percent change in the US Consumer Price Index for Energy (CPIENG). Based on 248 observations, she has computed the sample correlation between the Stellar and CPIENG variables to be –0.1452. She also wants to determine whether the sample correlation is statistically significant. The critical value for the test statistic at the 0.05 level of significance is approximately 1.96. Batten should conclude that the statistical relationship between Stellar and CPIENG is:
    A. significant, because the calculated test statistic has a lower absolute value than the critical value for the test statistic.
    B. significant, because the calculated test statistic has a higher absolute value than the critical value for the test statistic.
    C. not significant, because the calculated test statistic has a higher absolute value than the critical value for the test statistic.

41. In which of the following situations would a non-parametric test of a hypothesis *most likely* be used?
    A. The sample data are ranked according to magnitude.
    B. The sample data come from a normally distributed population.
    C. The test validity depends on many assumptions about the nature of the population.

42. An analyst is examining the monthly returns for two funds over one year. Both funds' returns are non-normally distributed. To test whether the mean return of one fund is greater than the mean return of the other fund, the analyst can use:
    A. a parametric test only.
    B. a nonparametric test only.
    C. both parametric and nonparametric tests.

CHAPTER 7

INTRODUCTION TO LINEAR REGRESSION

LEARNING OUTCOMES

The candidate should be able to:

- distinguish between the dependent and independent variables in a linear regression;
- explain the assumptions underlying linear regression and interpret regression coefficients;
- calculate and interpret the standard error of estimate, the coefficient of determination, and a confidence interval for a regression coefficient;
- formulate a null and alternative hypothesis about a population value of a regression coefficient and determine the appropriate test statistic and whether the null hypothesis is rejected at a given level of significance;
- calculate the predicted value for the dependent variable, given an estimated regression model and a value for the independent variable;
- calculate and interpret a confidence interval for the predicted value of the dependent variable; and
- describe the use of analysis of variance (ANOVA) in regression analysis, interpret ANOVA results, and calculate and interpret the *F*-statistic.

SUMMARY

- The dependent variable in a linear regression is the variable that the regression model tries to explain. The independent variables are the variables that a regression model uses to explain the dependent variable.
- If there is one independent variable in a linear regression and there are n observations of the dependent and independent variables, the regression model is $Y_i = b_0 + b_1 X_i + \varepsilon_i$, $i = 1, \ldots, n$, where Y_i is the dependent variable, X_i is the independent variable, and ε_i is the error term. In this model, the coefficient b_0 is the intercept. The intercept is the predicted value of the dependent variable when the independent variable has a value of zero. In this model, the coefficient b_1 is the slope of the regression line. If the value of the independent variable increases by one unit, then the model predicts that the value of the dependent variable will increase by b_1 units.

- The assumptions of the classic normal linear regression model are the following:
  - A linear relation exists between the dependent variable and the independent variable.
  - The independent variable is not random.
  - The expected value of the error term is 0.
  - The variance of the error term is the same for all observations (homoskedasticity).
  - The error term is uncorrelated across observations.
  - The error term is normally distributed.

- The estimated parameters in a linear regression model minimize the sum of the squared regression residuals.
- The standard error of estimate measures how well the regression model fits the data. If the SEE is small, the model fits well.
- The coefficient of determination measures the fraction of the total variation in the dependent variable that is explained by the independent variable. In a linear regression with one independent variable, the simplest way to compute the coefficient of determination is to square the correlation of the dependent and independent variables.
- To calculate a confidence interval for an estimated regression coefficient, we must know the standard error of the estimated coefficient and the critical value for the t-distribution at the chosen level of significance, t_c.
- To test whether the population value of a regression coefficient, b_1, is equal to a particular hypothesized value, B_1, we must know the estimated coefficient, $\hat{b}_1$, the standard error of the estimated coefficient, $s_{\hat{b}_1}$, and the critical value for the t-distribution at the chosen level of significance, t_c. The test statistic for this hypothesis is $(\hat{b}_1 - B_1)/s_{\hat{b}_1}$. If the absolute value of this statistic is greater than t_c, then we reject the null hypothesis that $b_1 = B_1$.
- In the regression model $Y_i = b_0 + b_1 X_i + \varepsilon_i$, if we know the estimated parameters, $\hat{b}_0$ and $\hat{b}_1$, for any value of the independent variable, X, then the predicted value of the dependent variable Y is $\hat{Y} = \hat{b}_0 + \hat{b}_1 X$.
- The prediction interval for a regression equation for a particular predicted value of the dependent variable is $\hat{Y} \pm t_c s_f$, where s_f is the square root of the estimated variance of the prediction error and t_c is the critical level for the t-statistic at the chosen significance level. This computation specifies a $(1 - \alpha)$ percent confidence interval. For example, if $\alpha = 0.05$, then this computation yields a 95% confidence interval.

PRACTICE PROBLEMS

1. Julie Moon is an energy analyst examining electricity, oil, and natural gas consumption in different regions over different seasons. She ran a regression explaining the variation in energy consumption as a function of temperature. The total variation of the dependent variable was 140.58, the explained variation was 60.16, and the unexplained variation was 80.42. She had 60 monthly observations.
   A. Compute the coefficient of determination.
   B. What was the sample correlation between energy consumption and temperature?
   C. Compute the standard error of the estimate of Moon's regression model.
   D. Compute the sample standard deviation of monthly energy consumption.

2. You are examining the results of a regression estimation that attempts to explain the unit sales growth of a business you are researching. The analysis of variance output for the regression is given in the table below. The regression was based on five observations ($n = 5$).

ANOVA	df	SS	MSS	F	Significance F
Regression	1	88.0	88.0	36.667	0.00904
Residual	3	7.2	2.4		
Total	4	95.2			

A. How many independent variables are in the regression to which the ANOVA refers?
B. Define Total SS.
C. Calculate the sample variance of the dependent variable using information in the above table.
D. Define regression SS and explain how its value of 88 is obtained in terms of other quantities reported in the above table.
E. What hypothesis does the F-statistic test?
F. Explain how the value of the F-statistic of 36.667 is obtained in terms of other quantities reported in the above table.
G. Is the F-test significant at the 5 percent significance level?

3. An economist collected the monthly returns for KDL's portfolio and a diversified stock index. The data collected are shown below:

Month	Portfolio Return (%)	Index Return (%)
1	1.11	−0.59
2	72.10	64.90
3	5.12	4.81
4	1.01	1.68
5	−1.72	−4.97
6	4.06	−2.06

The economist calculated the correlation between the two returns and found it to be 0.996. The regression results with the KDL return as the dependent variable and the index return as the independent variable are given as follows:

Regression Statistics

Multiple R	0.996
R^2	0.992
Standard error	2.861
Observations	6

ANOVA	DF	SS	MSS	F	Significance F
Regression	1	4,101.62	4,101.62	500.79	0
Residual	4	32.76	8.19		
Total	5	4,134.38			

	Coefficients	Standard Error		t-Statistic	p-Value
Intercept	2.252	1.274		1.768	0.1518
Slope	1.069	0.0477		22.379	0

When reviewing the results, Andrea Fusilier suspected that they were unreliable. She found that the returns for Month 2 should have been 7.21 percent and 6.49 percent, instead of the large values shown in the first table. Correcting these values resulted in a revised correlation of 0.824 and the revised regression results shown as follows:

Regression Statistics

Multiple R	0.824
R^2	0.678
Standard error	2.062
Observations	6

ANOVA	DF	SS	MSS	F	Significance F
Regression	1	35.89	35.89	35.89	0.044
Residual	4	17.01	4.25		
Total	5	52.91			

	Coefficients	Standard Error		t-Statistic	p-Value
Intercept	2.242	0.863		2.597	0.060
Slope	0.623	0.214		2.905	0.044

Explain how the bad data affected the results.

The following information relates to Questions 4–9

Kenneth McCoin, CFA, is a fairly tough interviewer. Last year, he handed each job applicant a sheet of paper with the information in the following table, and he then asked several questions about regression analysis. Some of McCoin's questions, along with a sample of the answers he received to each, are given below. McCoin told the applicants that the independent variable is the ratio of net income to sales for restaurants with a market cap of more than $100 million and the dependent variable is the ratio of cash flow from operations to sales for those restaurants. Which of the choices provided is the best answer to each of McCoin's questions?

Regression Statistics					
Multiple R	0.8623				
R^2	0.7436				
Standard error	0.0213				
Observations	24				
ANOVA	df	SS	MSS	F	Significance F
Regression	1	0.029	0.029000	63.81	0
Residual	22	0.010	0.000455		
Total	23	0.040			
	Coefficients	**Standard Error**		**t-Statistic**	**p-Value**
Intercept	0.077	0.007		11.328	0
Slope	0.826	0.103		7.988	0

4. What is the value of the coefficient of determination?
    A. 0.8261
    B. 0.7436
    C. 0.8623

	Standard Error of the Estimate	R^2
A	Decrease	Decrease
B	Decrease	Increase
C	Increase	Decrease

5. Suppose that you deleted several of the observations that had small residual values. If you re-estimated the regression equation using this reduced sample, what would likely happen to the standard error of the estimate and the R^2?

6. What is the correlation between X and Y?
    A. −0.7436
    B. 0.7436
    C. 0.8623

7. Where did the F-value in the ANOVA table come from?
   A. You look up the F-value in a table. The F depends on the numerator and denominator degrees of freedom.
   B. Divide the "mean square" for the regression by the "mean square" of the residuals.
   C. The F-value is equal to the reciprocal of the t-value for the slope coefficient.

8. If the ratio of net income to sales for a restaurant is 5 percent, what is the predicted ratio of cash flow from operations to sales?
   A. $0.007 + 0.103(5.0) = 0.524$.
   B. $0.077 - 0.826(5.0) = -4.054$.
   C. $0.077 + 0.826(5.0) = 4.207$.

9. Is the relationship between the ratio of cash flow to operations and the ratio of net income to sales significant at the 5 percent level?
   A. No, because the R^2 is greater than 0.05.
   B. No, because the p-values of the intercept and slope are less than 0.05.
   C. Yes, because the p-values for F and t for the slope coefficient are less than 0.05.

The following information relates to Questions 10–14

Howard Golub, CFA, is preparing to write a research report on Stellar Energy Corp. common stock. One of the world's largest companies, Stellar is in the business of refining and marketing oil. As part of his analysis, Golub wants to evaluate the sensitivity of the stock's returns to various economic factors. For example, a client recently asked Golub whether the price of Stellar Energy Corp. stock has tended to rise following increases in retail energy prices. Golub believes the association between the two variables is negative, but he does not know the strength of the association.

Golub directs his assistant, Jill Batten, to study the relationships between Stellar monthly common stock returns versus the previous month's percentage change in the US Consumer Price Index for Energy (CPIENG) and Stellar monthly common stock returns versus the previous month's percentage change in the US Producer Price Index for Crude Energy Materials (PPICEM). Golub wants Batten to run both a correlation and a linear regression analysis. In response, Batten compiles the summary statistics shown in Exhibit 1

EXHIBIT 1   Descriptive Statistics

	Monthly Return Stellar Common Stock	Lagged Monthly Change	
		CPIENG	PPICEM
Mean	0.0123	0.0023	0.0042
Standard deviation	0.0717	0.0160	0.0534
Covariance, Stellar vs. CPIENG	−0.00017		
Covariance, Stellar vs. PPICEM	−0.00048		
Covariance, CPIENG vs. PPICEM	0.00044		
Correlation, Stellar vs. CPIENG	−0.1452		

for the 248 months between January 1980 and August 2000. All of the data are in decimal form, where 0.01 indicates a 1% return. Batten also runs a regression analysis using Stellar monthly returns as the dependent variable and the monthly change in CPIENG as the independent variable. Exhibit 2 displays the results of this regression model.

EXHIBIT 2   Regression Analysis with CPIENG

Regression Statistics

Multiple R	0.1452
R^2	0.0211
Standard error of the estimate	0.0710
Observations	248

	Coefficients	Standard Error	*t*-Statistic
Intercept	0.0138	0.0046	3.0275
Slope coefficient	−0.6486	0.2818	−2.3014

	Data Type	Expected Value of Error Term
A	Time series	0
B	Time series	ε_i
C	Cross sectional	0

10. Did Batten's regression analyze cross-sectional or time-series data, and what was the expected value of the error term from that regression?

11. Based on the regression, which used data in decimal form, if the CPIENG *decreases* by 1.0 percent, what is the expected return on Stellar common stock during the next period?
    A. 0.0073 (0.73%)
    B. 0.0138 (1.38%)
    C. 0.0203 (2.03%)

12. Based on Batten's regression model, the coefficient of determination indicates that:
    A. Stellar's returns explain 2.11% of the variability in CPIENG.
    B. Stellar's returns explain 14.52% of the variability in CPIENG.
    C. changes in CPIENG explain 2.11% of the variability in Stellar's returns.

13. For Batten's regression model, the standard error of the estimate shows that the standard deviation of:
    A. the residuals from the regression is 0.0710.
    B. values estimated from the regression is 0.0710.
    C. Stellar's observed common stock returns is 0.0710.

14. For the analysis run by Batten, which of the following is an *incorrect* conclusion from the regression output?
    A. The estimated intercept coefficient from Batten's regression is statistically significant at the 0.05 level.
    B. In the month after the CPIENG declines, Stellar's common stock is expected to exhibit a positive return.
    C. Viewed in combination, the slope and intercept coefficients from Batten's regression are not statistically significant at the 0.05 level.

The following information relates to Questions 15–24

Anh Liu is an analyst researching whether a company's debt burden affects investors' decision to short the company's stock. She calculates the short interest ratio (the ratio of short interest to average daily share volume, expressed in days) for 50 companies as of the end of 2016 and compares this ratio with the companies' debt ratio (the ratio of total liabilities to total assets, expressed in decimal form).

Liu provides a number of statistics in Exhibit 1. She also estimates a simple regression to investigate the effect of the debt ratio on a company's short interest ratio. The results of this simple regression, including the analysis of variance (ANOVA), are shown in Exhibit 2.

EXHIBIT 1   Summary Statistics

Statistic	Debt Ratio X_i	Short Interest Ratio Y_i
Sum	19.8550	192.3000
Average	0.3971	3.8460
Sum of squared deviations from the mean	$\sum_{i=1}^{n} (X_i - \bar{X})^2 = 2.2225.$	$\sum_{i=1}^{n} (Y_i - \bar{Y})^2 = 412.2042.$
Sum of cross-products of deviations from the mean	$\sum_{i=1}^{n}(X_i - \bar{X})(Y_i - \bar{Y}) = -9.2430.$	

EXHIBIT 2   Regression of the Short Interest Ratio on the Debt Ratio

ANOVA	Degrees of Freedom (df)	Sum of Squares (SS)	Mean Square (MS)
Regression	1	38.4404	38.4404
Residual	48	373.7638	7.7867
Total	49	412.2042	

Regression Statistics			
Multiple R	0.3054		
R^2	0.0933		
Standard error of estimate	2.7905		
Observations	50		
	Coefficients	Standard Error	t-Statistic
Intercept	5.4975	0.8416	6.5322
Debt ratio	−4.1589	1.8718	−2.2219

In addition to estimating a regression equation, Liu graphs the 50 observations using a scatter plot, with the short interest ratio on the vertical axis and the debt ratio on the horizontal axis.

Liu is considering three interpretations of these results for her report on the relationship between debt ratios and short interest ratios:

Interpretation 1:   Companies' higher debt ratios cause lower short interest ratios.
Interpretation 2:   Companies' higher short interest ratios cause higher debt ratios.
Interpretation 3:   Companies with higher debt ratios tend to have lower short interest ratios.

She is especially interested in using her estimation results to predict the short interest ratio for MQD Corporation, which has a debt ratio of 0.40.

15. Based on Exhibits 1 and 2, if Liu were to graph the 50 observations, the scatter plot summarizing this relation would be *best* described as:
  A. horizontal.
  B. upward sloping.
  C. downward sloping.

16. Based on Exhibit 1, the sample covariance is *closest to*:
  A. −9.2430.
  B. −0.1886.
  C.   8.4123.

17. Based on Exhibits 1 and 2, the correlation between the debt ratio and the short interest ratio is *closest to*:
  A. −0.3054.
  B.   0.0933.
  C.   0.3054.

18. Which of the interpretations *best* describes Liu's findings for her report?
  A. Interpretation 1
  B. Interpretation 2
  C. Interpretation 3

19. The dependent variable in Liu's regression analysis is the:
  A. intercept.
  B. debt ratio.
  C. short interest ratio.

20. Based on Exhibit 2, the degrees of freedom for the *t*-test of the slope coefficient in this regression are:
  A. 48.
  B. 49.
  C. 50.

21. The upper bound for the 95 percent confidence interval for the coefficient on the debt ratio in the regression is *closest* to:
  A. −1.0199.
  B. −0.3947.
  C.   1.4528.

22. Which of the following should Liu conclude from these results shown in Exhibit 2?
    A. The average short interest ratio is 5.4975.
    B. The estimated slope coefficient is statistically significant at the 0.05 level.
    C. The debt ratio explains 30.54 percent of the variation in the short interest ratio.

23. Based on Exhibit 2, the short interest ratio expected for MQD Corporation is *closest* to:
    A. 3.8339.
    B. 5.4975.
    C. 6.2462.

24 Based on Liu's regression results in Exhibit 2, the *F*-statistic for testing whether the slope coefficient is equal to zero is *closest* to:
    A −2.2219.
    B 3.5036.
    C 4.9367.

The following information relates to Questions 25–30

Elena Vasileva recently joined EnergyInvest as a junior portfolio analyst. Vasileva's supervisor asks her to evaluate a potential investment opportunity in Amtex, a multinational oil and gas corporation based in the United States. Vasileva's supervisor suggests using regression analysis to examine the relation between Amtex shares and returns on crude oil.

Vasileva notes the following assumptions of regression analysis:

Assumption 1   The error term is uncorrelated across observations.
Assumption 2   The variance of the error term is the same for all observations.
Assumption 3   The expected value of the error term is equal to the mean value of the dependent variable.

Vasileva runs a regression of Amtex share returns on crude oil returns using the monthly data she collected. Selected data used in the regression are presented in Exhibit 1, and selected regression output is presented in Exhibit 2.

Vasileva expects the crude oil return next month, Month 37, to be −0.01. She computes the variance of the prediction error to be 0.0022.

EXHIBIT 1   Selected Data for Crude Oil Returns and Amtex Share Returns

	Oil Return (X_i)	Amtex Return (Y_i)	Cross-Product $(X_i - \bar{X})(Y_i - \bar{Y})$	Predicted Amtex Return $(\hat{Y})$	Regression Residual $(Y_i - \hat{Y})$	Squared Residual $(Y_i - \hat{Y})^2$
Month 1	−0.032000	0.033145	−0.000388	0.002011	−0.031134	0.000969
⋮	⋮	⋮	⋮	⋮	⋮	⋮
Month 36	0.028636	0.062334	0.002663	0.016282	−0.046053	0.002121
Sum			0.085598			0.071475
Average	−0.018056	0.005293				

EXHIBIT 2   Selected Regression Output, Dependent Variable: Amtex Share Return

	Coefficient	Standard Error
Intercept	0.0095	0.0078
Oil return	0.2354	0.0760

Note: The critical *t*-value for a two-sided *t*-test at the 1% significance level (df = 34) is 2.728.

25. Which of Vasileva's assumptions regarding regression analysis is *incorrect?*
    A. Assumption 1
    B. Assumption 2
    C. Assumption 3

26. Based on Exhibit 1, the standard error of the estimate is *closest* to:
    A. 0.044558.
    B. 0.045850.
    C. 0.050176.

27. Based on Exhibit 2, Vasileva should reject the null hypothesis that:
    A. the slope is less than or equal to 0.15.
    B. the intercept is less than or equal to 0.
    C. crude oil returns do not explain Amtex share returns.

28. Based on Exhibit 2, Vasileva should compute the:
    A. 99% confidence interval for the slope coefficient to be 0.1594 to 0.3114.
    B. 95% confidence interval for the intercept to be −0.0037 to 0.0227.
    C. 95% confidence interval for the slope coefficient to be 0.0810 to 0.3898.

29. Based on Exhibit 2 and Vasileva's prediction of the crude oil return for Month 37, the estimate of Amtex share return for Month 37 is *closest* to:
    A. −0.0024.
    B.   0.0071.
    C.   0.0119.

30. Using information from Exhibit 2, Vasileva should compute the 95% prediction interval for Amtex share return for Month 37 to be:
    A. −0.0882 to 0.1025.
    B. −0.0835 to 0.1072.
    C.   0.0027 to 0.0116.

The following information relates to Question 31–33

Doug Abitbol is a portfolio manager for Polyi Investments, a hedge fund that trades in the United States. Abitbol manages the hedge fund with the help of Robert Olabudo, a junior portfolio manager.

Abitbol looks at economists' inflation forecasts and would like to examine the relationship between the US Consumer Price Index (US CPI) consensus forecast and actual US CPI using regression analysis. Olabudo estimates regression coefficients to test whether the consensus forecast is unbiased. Regression results are presented in Exhibit 1. Additionally,

EXHIBIT 1   Regression Output: Estimating US CPI

Regression Statistics			
Multiple R	0.9929		
R^2	0.9859		
Standard error of estimate	0.0009		
Observations	60		
	Coefficients	**Standard Error**	**t-Statistic**
Intercept	0.0001	0.0002	0.5351
US CPI consensus forecast	0.9830	0.0155	63.6239

Notes:
1. The absolute value of the critical value for the t-statistic is 2.0 at the 5% level of significance.
2. The standard deviation of the US CPI consensus forecast is $s_x = 0.7539$.
3. The mean of the US CPI consensus forecast is $\bar{X} = 1.3350$.

Olabudo calculates the 95 percent prediction interval of the actual CPI using a US CPI consensus forecast of 2.8.

To conclude their meeting, Abitbol and Olabudo discuss the limitations of regression analysis. Olabudo notes the following limitations of regression analysis:

Limitation 1: Public knowledge of regression relationships may negate their future usefulness.
Limitation 2: Hypothesis tests and predictions based on linear regression will not be valid if regression assumptions are violated.

31. Based on Exhibit 1, Olabudo should:
    A. conclude that the inflation predictions are unbiased.
    B. reject the null hypothesis that the slope coefficient equals 1.
    C. reject the null hypothesis that the intercept coefficient equals 0.

32. Based on Exhibit 1, Olabudo should calculate a prediction interval for the actual US CPI *closest* to:
    A. 2.7506 to 2.7544.
    B. 2.7521 to 2.7529.
    C. 2.7981 to 2.8019.

33. Which of Olabudo's noted limitations of regression analysis is correct?
    A. Only Limitation 1
    B. Only Limitation 2
    C. Both Limitation 1 and Limitation 2

CHAPTER **8**

MULTIPLE REGRESSION

LEARNING OUTCOMES

The candidate should be able to:

- formulate a multiple regression equation to describe the relation between a dependent variable and several independent variables, and determine the statistical significance of each independent variable;
- interpret estimated regression coefficients and their *p*-values;
- formulate a null and an alternative hypothesis about the population value of a regression coefficient, calculate the value of the test statistic, and determine whether to reject the null hypothesis at a given level of significance;
- interpret the results of hypothesis tests of regression coefficients;
- calculate and interpret a predicted value for the dependent variable, given an estimated regression model and assumed values for the independent variables;
- explain the assumptions of a multiple regression model;
- calculate and interpret the *F*-statistic, and describe how it is used in regression analysis;
- distinguish between and interpret the R^2 and adjusted R^2 in multiple regression;
- evaluate how well a regression model explains the dependent variable by analyzing the output of the regression equation and an ANOVA table;
- formulate and interpret a multiple regression, including qualitative independent variables;
- explain the types of heteroskedasticity and how heteroskedasticity and serial correlation affect statistical inference;
- describe multicollinearity, and explain its causes and effects in regression analysis;
- describe how model misspecification affects the results of a regression analysis, and describe how to avoid common forms of misspecification;
- interpret an estimated logistic regression;
- evaluate and interpret a multiple regression model and its results.

SUMMARY

We have presented the multiple linear regression model and discussed violations of regression assumptions, model specification and misspecification, and models with qualitative variables.

- The general form of a multiple linear regression model is $Y_i = b_0 + b_1 X_{1i} + b_2 X_{2i} + \ldots + b_k X_{ki} + \varepsilon_i$.
- We conduct hypothesis tests concerning the population values of regression coefficients using t-tests of the form

$$t = \frac{\hat{b}_j - b_j}{s_{\hat{b}_j}}.$$

- The lower the p-value reported for a test, the more significant the result.
- The assumptions of classical normal multiple linear regression model are as follows:
  1. A linear relation exists between the dependent variable and the independent variables.
  2. The independent variables are not random. Also, no exact linear relation exists between two or more of the independent variables.
  3. The expected value of the error term, conditioned on the independent variables, is 0.
  4. The variance of the error term is the same for all observations.
  5. The error term is uncorrelated across observations.
  6. The error term is normally distributed.

- To make a prediction using a multiple linear regression model, we take the following three steps:
  1. Obtain estimates of the regression coefficients.
  2. Determine the assumed values of the independent variables.
  3. Compute the predicted value of the dependent variable.

- When predicting the dependent variable using a linear regression model, we encounter two types of uncertainty: uncertainty in the regression model itself, as reflected in the standard error of estimate, and uncertainty about the estimates of the regression coefficients.
- The F-test is reported in an ANOVA table. The F-statistic is used to test whether at least one of the slope coefficients on the independent variables is significantly different from 0.

$$F = \frac{RSS/k}{SSE/[n - (k + 1)]} = \frac{\text{Mean regression sum of squares}}{\text{Mean squared error}}.$$

Under the null hypothesis that all the slope coefficients are jointly equal to 0, this test statistic has a distribution of $F_{k, n - (k+1)}$, where the regression has n observations and k independent variables. The F-test measures the overall significance of the regression.

- R^2 is nondecreasing in the number of independent variables, so it is less reliable as a measure of goodness of fit in a regression with more than one independent variable than in a one-independent-variable regression.

  Analysts often choose to use adjusted R^2 because it does not necessarily increase when one adds an independent variable.

- Dummy variables in a regression model can help analysts determine whether a particular qualitative independent variable explains the model's dependent variable. A dummy variable takes on the value of 0 or 1. If we need to distinguish among n categories, the regression should include $n - 1$ dummy variables.
- When using intercept dummies, the intercept of the regression measures the average value of the dependent variable of the omitted category, and the coefficient on each dummy variable measures the average incremental effect of that dummy variable on the dependent variable.
- When using slope dummies, the coefficient on each dummy measures the average incremental effect on the slope coefficient of the independent variable.
- If a regression shows significant conditional heteroskedasticity, the standard errors and test statistics computed by regression programs will be incorrect unless they are adjusted for heteroskedasticity.
- One simple test for conditional heteroskedasticity is the Breusch–Pagan test. Breusch and Pagan showed that, under the null hypothesis of no conditional heteroskedasticity, nR^2 (from the regression of the squared residuals on the independent variables from the original regression) will be a χ^2 random variable with the number of degrees of freedom equal to the number of independent variables in the regression.
- The principal effect of serial correlation in a linear regression is that the standard errors and test statistics computed by regression programs will be incorrect unless adjusted for serial correlation. Positive serial correlation typically inflates the t-statistics of estimated regression coefficients as well as the F-statistic for the overall significance of the regression.
- The most commonly used test for serial correlation is based on the Durbin–Watson statistic. If the Durbin–Watson statistic differs sufficiently from 2, then the regression errors have significant serial correlation.
- Multicollinearity occurs when two or more independent variables (or combinations of independent variables) are highly (but not perfectly) correlated with each other. With multicollinearity, the regression coefficients may not be individually statistically significant even when the overall regression is significant, as judged by the F-statistic.
- Model specification refers to the set of variables included in the regression and the regression equation's functional form. The following principles can guide model specification:
  - The model should be grounded in cogent economic reasoning.
  - The functional form chosen for the variables in the regression should be appropriate given the nature of the variables.
  - The model should be parsimonious.
  - The model should be examined for violations of regression assumptions before being accepted.
  - The model should be tested and found useful out of sample before being accepted.
- If a regression is misspecified, then statistical inference using OLS is invalid and the estimated regression coefficients may be inconsistent.
- Assuming that a model has the correct functional form when in fact it does not is one example of misspecification. This assumption may be violated in several ways:
  - One or more important variables could be omitted from the regression.
  - One or more of the regression variables may need to be transformed before estimating the regression.
  - The regression model pools data from different samples that should not be pooled.

- Another type of misspecification occurs when independent variables are correlated with the error term. This is a violation of Regression Assumption 3, that the error term has a mean of 0, and causes the estimated regression coefficients to be biased and inconsistent. Three common problems that create this type of time-series misspecification are:
  - including lagged dependent variables as independent variables in regressions with serially correlated errors;
  - including a function of the dependent variable as an independent variable, sometimes as a result of the incorrect dating of variables; and
  - independent variables that are measured with error.

- Logit models estimate the probability of a discrete outcome (the value of a qualitative dependent variable, such as whether a company enters bankruptcy) given the values of the independent variables used to explain that outcome. The logit model, which is based on the logistic distribution, estimates the probability that $Y = 1$ (a condition is fulfilled) given the values of the independent variables.

PRACTICE PROBLEMS

1. With many US companies operating globally, the effect of the US dollar's strength on a US company's returns has become an important investment issue. You would like to determine whether changes in the US dollar's value and overall US equity market returns affect an asset's returns. You decide to use the S&P 500 Index to represent the US equity market.

   A. Write a multiple regression equation to test whether changes in the value of the dollar and equity market returns affect an asset's returns. Use the notations below.

   R_{it} = return on the asset in period t

   R_{Mt} = return on the S&P 500 in period t

   ΔX_t = change in period t in the log of a trade-weighted index of the foreign exchange value of US dollar against the currencies of a broad group of major US trading partners.

   B. You estimate the regression for Archer Daniels Midland Company (NYSE: ADM). You regress its monthly returns for the period January 1990 to December 2002 on S&P 500 Index returns and changes in the log of the trade-weighted exchange value of the US dollar. The table below shows the coefficient estimates and their standard errors.

Coefficient Estimates from Regressing ADM's Returns: Monthly Data, January 1990–December 2002

	Coefficient	Standard Error
Intercept	0.0045	0.0062
R_{Mt}	0.5373	0.1332
ΔX_t	−0.5768	0.5121
$n = 156$		

Determine whether S&P 500 returns affect ADM's returns. Then determine whether changes in the value of the US dollar affect ADM's returns. Use a 0.05 significance level to make your decisions.

C. Based on the estimated coefficient on R_{Mt}, is it correct to say that "for a 1 percentage point increase in the return on the S&P 500 in period t, we expect a 0.5373 percentage point increase in the return on ADM"?

2. One of the most important questions in financial economics is what factors determine the cross-sectional variation in an asset's returns. Some have argued that book-to-market ratio and size (market value of equity) play an important role.

A. Write a multiple regression equation to test whether book-to-market ratio and size explain the cross-section of asset returns. Use the notations below.

$$(B/M)_i = \text{book-to-market ratio for asset } i$$
$$R_i = \text{return on asset } i \text{ in a particular month}$$
$$\text{Size}_i = \text{natural log of the market value of equity for asset } i$$

B. The table below shows the results of the linear regression for a cross-section of 66 companies. The size and book-to-market data for each company are for December 2001. The return data for each company are for January 2002.

Results from Regressing Returns on the Book-to-Market Ratio and Size

	Coefficient	Standard Error
Intercept	0.0825	0.1644
$(B/M)_i$	−0.0541	0.0588
Size_i	−0.0164	0.0350
$n = 66$		

Source: FactSet.

Determine whether the book-to-market ratio and size are each useful for explaining the cross-section of asset returns. Use a 0.05 significance level to make your decision.

3. There is substantial cross-sectional variation in the number of financial analysts who follow a company. Suppose you hypothesize that a company's size (market cap) and financial risk (debt-to-equity ratios) influence the number of financial analysts who follow a company. You formulate the following regression model:

$$(\text{Analyst following})_i = b_0 + b_1 \text{Size}_i + b_2(D/E)_i + \varepsilon_i$$

where

$(\text{Analyst following})_i = $ the natural log of $(1 + n)$, where n_i is the number of analysts following company i

$\text{Size}_i = $ the natural log of the market capitalization of company i in millions of dollars

$(D/E)_i = $ the debt-to-equity ratio for company i

In the definition of Analyst following, 1 is added to the number of analysts following a company because some companies are not followed by any analysts, and the natural log of 0 is indeterminate. The following table gives the coefficient estimates of the above regression model for a randomly selected sample of 500 companies. The data are for the year 2002.

Coefficient Estimates from Regressing Analyst Following on Size and Debt-to-Equity Ratio

	Coefficient	Standard Error	t-Statistic
Intercept	−0.2845	0.1080	−2.6343
$Size_i$	0.3199	0.0152	21.0461
$(D/E)_i$	−0.1895	0.0620	−3.0565
$n = 500$			

Source: First Call/Thomson Financial, Compustat.

A. Consider two companies, both of which have a debt-to-equity ratio of 0.75. The first company has a market capitalization of $100 million, and the second company has a market capitalization of $1 billion. Based on the above estimates, how many more analysts will follow the second company than the first company?

B. Suppose the p-value reported for the estimated coefficient on $(D/E)_i$ is 0.00236. State the interpretation of 0.00236.

4. In early 2001, US equity marketplaces started trading all listed shares in minimal increments (ticks) of $0.01 (decimalization). After decimalization, bid–ask spreads of stocks traded on the NASDAQ tended to decline. In response, spreads of NASDAQ stocks cross-listed on the Toronto Stock Exchange (TSE) tended to decline as well. Researchers Oppenheimer and Sabherwal (2003) hypothesized that the percentage decline in TSE spreads of cross-listed stocks was related to company size, the predecimalization ratio of spreads on NASDAQ to those on the TSE, and the percentage decline in NASDAQ spreads. The following table gives the regression coefficient estimates from estimating that relationship for a sample of 74 companies. Company size is measured by the natural logarithm of the book value of company's assets in thousands of Canadian dollars.

Coefficient Estimates from Regressing Percentage Decline in TSE Spreads on Company Size, Predecimalization Ratio of NASDAQ to TSE Spreads, and Percentage Decline in NASDAQ Spreads

	Coefficient	t-Statistic
Intercept	−0.45	−1.86
$Size_i$	0.05	2.56
$(Ratio\ of\ spreads)_i$	−0.06	−3.77
$(Decline\ in\ NASDAQ\ spreads)_i$	0.29	2.42
$n = 74$		

Source: Oppenheimer and Sabherwal (2003).

The average company in the sample has a book value of assets of C$900 million and a predecimalization ratio of spreads equal to 1.3. Based on the above model, what is the predicted decline in spread on the TSE for a company with these average characteristics, given a 1 percentage point decline in NASDAQ spreads?

5. The neglected-company effect claims that companies that are followed by fewer analysts will earn higher returns on average than companies that are followed by many analysts. To test the neglected-company effect, you have collected data on 66 companies and the number of analysts providing earnings estimates for each company. You decide to also include size as an independent variable, measuring size as the log of the market value of the company's equity, to try to distinguish any small-company effect from a neglected-company effect. The small-company effect asserts that small-company stocks may earn average higher risk-adjusted returns than large-company stocks.

The table below shows the results from estimating the model $R_i = b_0 + b_1 \text{Size}_i + b_2(\text{Number of analysts})_i + \varepsilon_i$ for a cross-section of 66 companies. The size and number of analysts for each company are for December 2001. The return data are for January 2002.

Results from Regressing Returns on Size and Number of Analysts

	Coefficient	Standard Error	t-Statistic
Intercept	0.0388	0.1556	0.2495
Size_i	−0.0153	0.0348	−0.4388
$(\text{Number of analysts})_i$	0.0014	0.0015	0.8995

ANOVA	DF	SS	MSS
Regression	2	0.0094	0.0047
Residual	63	0.6739	0.0107
Total	65	0.6833	

Residual standard error	0.1034
R-squared	0.0138
Observations	66

Source: First Call/Thomson Financial, FactSet.

A. What test would you conduct to see whether the two independent variables are *jointly* statistically related to returns ($H_0: b_1 = b_2 = 0$)?
B. What information do you need to conduct the appropriate test?
C. Determine whether the two variables jointly are statistically related to returns at the 0.05 significance level.
D. Explain the meaning of adjusted R^2 and state whether adjusted R^2 for the regression would be smaller than, equal to, or larger than 0.0138.

6. Some developing nations are hesitant to open their equity markets to foreign investment because they fear that rapid inflows and outflows of foreign funds will increase volatility. In July 1993, India implemented substantial equity market reforms, one of which allowed foreign institutional investors into the Indian equity markets. You want to test

whether the volatility of returns of stocks traded on the Bombay Stock Exchange (BSE) increased after July 1993, when foreign institutional investors were first allowed to invest in India. You have collected monthly return data for the BSE from February 1990 to December 1997. Your dependent variable is a measure of return volatility of stocks traded on the BSE; your independent variable is a dummy variable that is coded 1 if foreign investment was allowed during the month and 0 otherwise.

You believe that market return volatility actually *decreases* with the opening up of equity markets. The table below shows the results from your regression.

Results from Dummy Regression for Foreign Investment in India with a Volatility Measure as the Dependent Variable

	Coefficient	Standard Error	t-Statistic
Intercept	0.0133	0.0020	6.5351
Dummy	−0.0075	0.0027	−2.7604
$n = 95$			

Source: FactSet.

A. State null and alternative hypotheses for the slope coefficient of the dummy variable that are consistent with testing your stated belief about the effect of opening the equity markets on stock return volatility.
B. Determine whether you can reject the null hypothesis at the 0.05 significance level (in a one-sided test of significance).
C. According to the estimated regression equation, what is the level of return volatility before and after the market-opening event?

7.

Both researchers and the popular press have discussed the question as to which of the two leading US political parties, Republicans or Democrats, is better for the stock market.

A. Write a regression equation to test whether overall market returns, as measured by the annual returns on the S&P 500 Index, tend to be higher when the Republicans or the Democrats control the White House. Use the notations below.

$$R_{Mt} = \text{return on the S\&P 500 in period } t$$

$$\text{Party}_t = \text{the political party controlling the White House (1 for a Republican president; 0 for a Democratic president) in period } t$$

B. The table below shows the results of the linear regression from Part A using annual data for the S&P 500 and a dummy variable for the party that controlled the White House. The data are from 1926 to 2002.

Results from Regressing S&P 500 Returns on a Dummy Variable for the Party That Controlled the White House, 1926–2002

	Coefficient	Standard Error	*t*-Statistic
Intercept	0.1494	0.0323	4.6270
Party$_t$	−0.0570	0.0466	−1.2242

ANOVA	DF	SS	MSS	F	Significance F
Regression	1	0.0625	0.0625	1.4987	0.2247
Residual	75	3.1287	0.0417		
Total	76	3.1912			

Residual standard error	0.2042
R-squared	0.0196
Observations	77

Source: FactSet.

Based on the coefficient and standard error estimates, verify to two decimal places the *t*-statistic for the coefficient on the dummy variable reported in the table.

C. Determine at the 0.05 significance level whether overall US equity market returns tend to differ depending on the political party controlling the White House.

8. Problem 3 addressed the cross-sectional variation in the number of financial analysts who follow a company. In that problem, company size and debt-to-equity ratios were the independent variables. You receive a suggestion that membership in the S&P 500 Index should be added to the model as a third independent variable; the hypothesis is that there is greater demand for analyst coverage for stocks included in the S&P 500 because of the widespread use of the S&P 500 as a benchmark.

A. Write a multiple regression equation to test whether analyst following is systematically higher for companies included in the S&P 500 Index. Also include company size and debt-to-equity ratio in this equation. Use the notations below.

(Analyst following)$_i$ = natural log of (1 + Number of analysts following company i)

Size$_i$ = natural log of the market capitalization of company i in millions of dollars

(D/E)$_i$ = debt-to-equity ratio for company i

S&P$_i$ = inclusion of company i in the S&P 500 Index (1 if included, 0 if not included)

In the above specification for analyst following, 1 is added to the number of analysts following a company because some companies are not followed by any analyst, and the natural log of 0 is indeterminate.

B. State the appropriate null hypothesis and alternative hypothesis in a two-sided test of significance of the dummy variable.

C. The following table gives estimates of the coefficients of the above regression model for a randomly selected sample of 500 companies. The data are for the year 2002. Determine whether you can reject the null hypothesis at the 0.05 significance level (in a two-sided test of significance).

Coefficient Estimates from Regressing Analyst Following on Size, Debt-to-Equity Ratio, and S&P 500 Membership, 2002

	Coefficient	Standard Error	t-Statistic
Intercept	−0.0075	0.1218	−0.0616
$Size_i$	0.2648	0.0191	13.8639
$(D/E)_i$	−0.1829	0.0608	−3.0082
$S\&P_i$	0.4218	0.0919	4.5898
$n = 500$			

Source: First Call/Thomson Financial, Compustat.

D. Consider a company with a debt-to-equity ratio of 2/3 and a market capitalization of $10 billion. According to the estimated regression equation, how many analysts would follow this company if it were not included in the S&P 500 Index, and how many would follow if it were included in the index?

E. In Problem 3, using the sample, we estimated the coefficient on the size variable as 0.3199, versus 0.2648 in the above regression. Discuss whether there is an inconsistency in these results.

9. You believe there is a relationship between book-to-market ratios and subsequent returns. The output from a cross-sectional regression and a graph of the actual and predicted relationship between the book-to-market ratio and return are shown below.

Results from Regressing Returns on the Book-to-Market Ratio

	Coefficient	Standard Error	t-Statistic
Intercept	12.0130	3.5464	3.3874
$\left(\frac{Book\ value}{Market\ value}\right)_i$	−9.2209	8.4454	−1.0918

ANOVA	DF	SS	MSS	F	Significance F
Regression	1	154.9866	154.9866	1.1921	0.2831
Residual	32	4162.1895	130.0684		
Total	33	4317.1761			

Residual standard error	11.4048
R-squared	0.0359
Observations	34

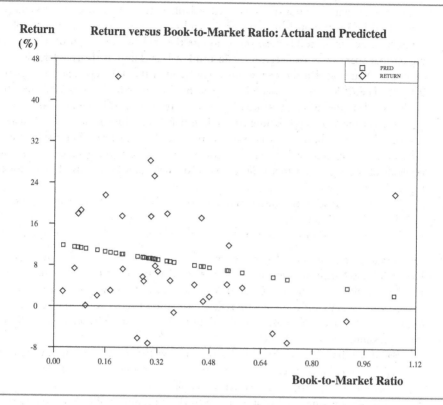

Return versus Book-to-Market Ratio: Actual and Predicted

A. You are concerned with model specification problems and regression assumption violations. Focusing on assumption violations, discuss symptoms of conditional heteroskedasticity based on the graph of the actual and predicted relationship.
B. Describe in detail how you could formally test for conditional heteroskedasticity in this regression.
C. Describe a recommended method for correcting for conditional heteroskedasticity.

10. You are examining the effects of the January 2001 NYSE implementation of the trading of shares in minimal increments (ticks) of $0.01 (decimalization). In particular, you are analyzing a sample of 52 Canadian companies cross-listed on both the NYSE and the Toronto Stock Exchange (TSE). You find that the bid–ask spreads of these shares decline on both exchanges after the NYSE decimalization. You run a linear regression analyzing the decline in spreads on the TSE, and find that the decline on the TSE is related to company size, predecimalization ratio of NYSE to TSE spreads, and decline in the NYSE spreads. The relationships are statistically significant. You want to be sure, however, that the results are not influenced by conditional heteroskedasticity. Therefore, you regress the squared residuals of the regression model on the three independent variables. The R^2 for this regression is 14.1 percent. Perform a statistical test to determine if conditional heteroskedasticity is present.

11. You are analyzing if institutional investors such as mutual funds and pension funds prefer to hold shares of companies with less volatile returns. You have the percentage of shares held by institutional investors at the end of 1998 for a random sample of 750 companies. For these companies, you compute the standard deviation of daily returns during that year. Then you regress the institutional holdings on the standard deviation of returns. You find that the regression is significant at the 0.01 level and the F-statistic is 12.98. The R^2 for this regression is 1.7 percent. As expected, the regression coefficient of the standard deviation of returns is negative. Its t-statistic is -3.60, which is also significant at the 0.01 level. Before concluding that institutions prefer to hold shares of less volatile stocks, however, you want to be sure that the regression results are not influenced by conditional heteroskedasticity. Therefore, you regress the squared residuals of the regression model on the standard deviation of returns. The R^2 for this regression is 0.6 percent.

   A. Perform a statistical test to determine if conditional heteroskedasticity is present at the 0.05 significance level.

   B. In view of your answer to Part A, what remedial action, if any, is appropriate?

12. In estimating a regression based on monthly observations from January 1987 to December 2002 inclusive, you find that the coefficient on the independent variable is positive and significant at the 0.05 level. You are concerned, however, that the t-statistic on the independent variable may be inflated because of serial correlation between the error terms. Therefore, you examine the Durbin–Watson statistic, which is 1.8953 for this regression.

   A. Based on the value of the Durbin–Watson statistic, what can you say about the serial correlation between the regression residuals? Are they positively correlated, negatively correlated, or not correlated at all?

   B. Compute the sample correlation between the regression residuals from one period and those from the previous period.

   C. Perform a statistical test to determine if serial correlation is present. Assume that the critical values for 192 observations when there is a single independent variable are about 0.09 above the critical values for 100 observations.

13. The book-to-market ratio and the size of a company's equity are two factors that have been asserted to be useful in explaining the cross-sectional variation in subsequent returns. Based on this assertion, you want to estimate the following regression model:

$$R_i = b_0 + b_1 \left(\frac{\text{Book}}{\text{Market}} \right)_i + b_2 \text{Size}_i + \varepsilon_i$$

where
R_i = Return of company i's shares (in the following period)
$\left(\frac{\text{Book}}{\text{Market}} \right)_i$ = company i's book-to-market ratio
Size_i = Market value of company i's equity
A colleague suggests that this regression specification may be erroneous, because he believes that the book-to-market ratio may be strongly related to (correlated with) company size.

   A. To what problem is your colleague referring, and what are its consequences for regression analysis?

Regression of Return on Book-to-Market and Size

	Coefficient	Standard Error	t-Statistic
Intercept	14.1062	4.220	3.3427
$\left(\frac{\text{Book}}{\text{Market}}\right)_i$	−12.1413	9.0406	−1.3430
$Size_i$	−0.00005502	0.00005977	−0.92047
R-squared	0.06156		
Observations	34		

Correlation Matrix

	Book-to-Market Ratio	Size
Book-to-Market Ratio	1.0000	
Size	−0.3509	1.0000

B. With respect to multicollinearity, critique the choice of variables in the regression model above.

C. State the classic symptom of multicollinearity and comment on that basis whether multicollinearity appears to be present, given the additional fact that the F-test for the above regression is not significant.

14. You are analyzing the variables that explain the returns on the stock of the Boeing Company. Because overall market returns are likely to explain a part of the returns on Boeing, you decide to include the returns on a value-weighted index of all the companies listed on the NYSE, AMEX, and NASDAQ as an independent variable. Further, because Boeing is a large company, you also decide to include the returns on the S&P 500 Index, which is a value-weighted index of the larger market-capitalization companies. Finally, you decide to include the changes in the US dollar's value. To conduct your test, you have collected the following data for the period 1990–2002.

R_t = monthly return on the stock of Boeing in month t

R_{ALLt} = monthly return on a value-weighted index of all the companies listed on the NYSE, AMEX, and NASDAQ in month t

R_{SPt} = monthly return on the S&P 500 Index in month t

ΔX_t = change in month t in the log of a trade-weighted index of the foreign exchange value of the US dollar against the currencies of a broad group of major US trading partners

The following table shows the output from regressing the monthly return on Boeing stock on the three independent variables.

Regression of Boeing Returns on Three Explanatory Variables: Monthly Data, January 1990–December 2002

	Coefficient	Standard Error	t-Statistic
Intercept	0.0026	0.0066	0.3939
R_{ALLt}	−0.1337	0.6219	−0.2150
R_{SPt}	0.8875	0.6357	1.3961
ΔX_t	0.2005	0.5399	0.3714

ANOVA	DF	SS	MSS
Regression	3	0.1720	0.0573
Residual	152	0.8947	0.0059
Total	155	1.0667	

Residual standard error	0.0767
R-squared	0.1610
Observations	156

Source: FactSet, Federal Reserve Bank of Philadelphia.

From the *t*-statistics, we see that none of the explanatory variables is statistically significant at the 5 percent level or better. You wish to test, however, if the three variables *jointly* are statistically related to the returns on Boeing.

A. Your null hypothesis is that all three population slope coefficients equal 0—that the three variables *jointly* are statistically not related to the returns on Boeing. Conduct the appropriate test of that hypothesis.

B. Examining the regression results, state the regression assumption that may be violated in this example. Explain your answer.

C. State a possible way to remedy the violation of the regression assumption identified in Part B.

15. You are analyzing the cross-sectional variation in the number of financial analysts that follow a company (also the subject of Problems 3 and 8). You believe that there is less analyst following for companies with a greater debt-to-equity ratio and greater analyst following for companies included in the S&P 500 Index. Consistent with these beliefs, you estimate the following regression model.

$$(\text{Analysts following})_i = b_0 + b_1(D/E)_i + b_2(S\&P)_i + \varepsilon_i$$

where

$(\text{Analysts following})_i$ = natural log of (1 + Number of analysts following company *i*)
$(D/E)_i$ = debt-to-equity ratio for company *i*
$S\&P_i$ = inclusion of company *i* in the S&P 500 Index (1 if included; 0 if not included)

In the preceding specification, 1 is added to the number of analysts following a company because some companies are not followed by any analysts, and the natural log of 0 is indeterminate. The following table gives the coefficient estimates of the above regression model for a randomly selected sample of 500 companies. The data are for the year 2002.

Coefficient Estimates from Regressing Analyst Following on Debt-to-Equity Ratio and S&P 500 Membership, 2002

	Coefficient	Standard Error	t-Statistic
Intercept	1.5367	0.0582	26.4038
$(D/E)_i$	−0.1043	0.0712	−1.4649
$S\&P_i$	1.2222	0.0841	14.5327
$n = 500$			

Source: First Call/Thomson Financial, Compustat.

You discuss your results with a colleague. She suggests that this regression specification may be erroneous, because analyst following is likely to be also related to the size of the company.

A. What is this problem called, and what are its consequences for regression analysis?

B. To investigate the issue raised by your colleague, you decide to collect data on company size also. You then estimate the model after including an additional variable, Size i, which is the natural log of the market capitalization of company i in millions of dollars. The following table gives the new coefficient estimates.

Coefficient Estimates from Regressing Analyst Following on Size, Debt-to-Equity Ratio, and S&P 500 Membership, 2002

	Coefficient	Standard Error	t-Statistic
Intercept	−0.0075	0.1218	−0.0616
$Size_i$	0.2648	0.0191	13.8639
$(D/E)_i$	−0.1829	0.0608	−3.0082
$S\&P_i$	0.4218	0.0919	4.5898
$n = 500$			

Source: First Call/Thomson Financial, Compustat.

What do you conclude about the existence of the problem mentioned by your colleague in the original regression model you had estimated?

16. You have noticed that hundreds of non-US companies are listed not only on a stock exchange in their home market but also on one of the exchanges in the United States. You have also noticed that hundreds of non-US companies are listed only in their home market and not in the United States. You are trying to predict whether or not a non-US company will choose to list on a US exchange. One of the factors that you think will affect whether or not a company lists in the United States is its size relative to the size of other companies in its home market.

A. What kind of a dependent variable do you need to use in the model?

B. What kind of a model should be used?

The following information relates to Questions 17–22

Gary Hansen is a securities analyst for a mutual fund specializing in small-capitalization growth stocks. The fund regularly invests in initial public offerings (IPOs). If the fund subscribes to an offer, it is allocated shares at the offer price. Hansen notes that IPOs frequently are underpriced, and the price rises when open market trading begins. The initial return for an IPO is calculated as the change in price on the first day of trading divided by the offer price. Hansen is developing a regression model to predict the initial return for IPOs. Based on past research, he selects the following independent variables to predict IPO initial returns:

Underwriter rank	=	1–10, where 10 is highest rank
Pre-offer price adjustment[a]	=	(Offer price − Initial filing price)/Initial filing price
Offer size ($ millions)	=	Shares sold × Offer price
Fraction retained[a]	=	Fraction of total company shares retained by insiders

[a]Expressed as a decimal

Hansen collects a sample of 1,725 recent IPOs for his regression model. Regression results appear in Exhibit 1, and ANOVA results appear in Exhibit 2.

Hansen wants to use the regression results to predict the initial return for an upcoming IPO. The upcoming IPO has the following characteristics:

- Underwriter rank = 6
- Pre-offer price adjustment = 0.04
- Offer size = $40 million
- Fraction retained = 0.70

EXHIBIT 1   Hansen's Regression Results Dependent Variable: IPO Initial Return (Expressed in Decimal Form, i.e., 1% = 0.01)

Variable	Coefficient (b_j)	Standard Error	t-Statistic
Intercept	0.0477	0.0019	25.11
Underwriter rank	0.0150	0.0049	3.06
Pre-offer price adjustment	0.4350	0.0202	21.53
Offer size	−0.0009	0.0011	−0.82
Fraction retained	0.0500	0.0260	1.92

EXHIBIT 2   Selected ANOVA Results for Hansen's Regression

	Degrees of Freedom (DF)	Sum of Squares (SS)
Regression	4	51.433
Residual	1,720	91.436
Total	1,724	142.869
	Multiple R-squared = 0.36	

Because he notes that the pre-offer price adjustment appears to have an important effect on initial return, Hansen wants to construct a 95 percent confidence interval for the coefficient on this variable. He also believes that for each 1 percent increase in pre-offer price adjustment, the initial return will increase by less than 0.5 percent, holding other variables constant. Hansen wishes to test this hypothesis at the 0.05 level of significance.

Before applying his model, Hansen asks a colleague, Phil Chang, to review its specification and results. After examining the model, Chang concludes that the model suffers from two problems: 1) conditional heteroskedasticity, and 2) omitted variable bias. Chang makes the following statements:

Statement 1.   "Conditional heteroskedasticity will result in consistent coefficient estimates, but both the *t*-statistics and *F*-statistic will be biased, resulting in false inferences."

Statement 2.   "If an omitted variable is correlated with variables already included in the model, coefficient estimates will be biased and inconsistent and standard errors will also be inconsistent."

Selected values for the *t*-distribution and *F*-distribution appear in Exhibits 3 and 4, respectively.

EXHIBIT 3   Selected Values for the *t*-Distribution (DF = ∞)

Area in Right Tail	*t*-Value
0.050	1.645
0.025	1.960
0.010	2.326
0.005	2.576

EXHIBIT 4   Selected Values for the *F*-Distribution ($\alpha = 0.01$) (DF1/DF2: Numerator/Denominator Degrees of Freedom)

		DF1	
		4	∞
DF2	4	16.00	13.50
	∞	3.32	1.00

17. Based on Hansen's regression, the predicted initial return for the upcoming IPO is *closest* to:
    A.   0.0943.
    B.   0.1064.
    C.   0.1541.

18. The 95 percent confidence interval for the regression coefficient for the pre-offer price adjustment is *closest* to:
    A.   0.156 to 0.714.
    B.   0.395 to 0.475.
    C.   0.402 to 0.468.

	Null Hypothesis	Conclusion about b_j (0.05 Level of Significance)
A	H_0: $b_j = 0.5$	Reject H_0
B	H_0: $b_j \geq 0.5$	Fail to reject H_0
C	H_0: $b_j \geq 0.5$	Reject H_0

19. The *most* appropriate null hypothesis and the *most* appropriate conclusion regarding Hansen's belief about the magnitude of the initial return relative to that of the pre-offer price adjustment (reflected by the coefficient b_j) are:

20. The *most* appropriate interpretation of the multiple R-squared for Hansen's model is that:
    A. unexplained variation in the dependent variable is 36 percent of total variation.
    B. correlation between predicted and actual values of the dependent variable is 0.36.
    C. correlation between predicted and actual values of the dependent variable is 0.60.

21. Is Chang's Statement 1 correct?
    A. Yes.
    B. No, because the model's F-statistic will not be biased.
    C. No, because the model's t-statistics will not be biased.

22. Is Chang's Statement 2 correct?
    A. Yes.
    B. No, because the model's coefficient estimates will be unbiased.
    C. No, because the model's coefficient estimates will be consistent.

The following information relates to Questions 23–28

Adele Chiesa is a money manager for the Bianco Fund. She is interested in recent findings showing that certain business condition variables predict excess US stock market returns (one-month market return minus one-month T-bill return). She is also familiar with evidence showing how US stock market returns differ by the political party affiliation of the US president. Chiesa estimates a multiple regression model to predict monthly excess stock market returns accounting for business conditions and the political party affiliation of the US president:

$$\text{Excess stock market return}_t = a_0 + a_1 \text{Default spread}_{t-1} + a_2 \text{Term spread}_{t-1} + a_3 \text{Pres party dummy}_{t-1} + e_t$$

Default spread is equal to the yield on Baa bonds minus the yield on Aaa bonds. Term spread is equal to the yield on a 10-year constant-maturity US Treasury index minus the yield on a 1-year constant-maturity US Treasury index. Pres party dummy is equal to 1 if the US president is a member of the Democratic Party and 0 if a member of the Republican Party.

Chiesa collects 432 months of data (all data are in percent form, i.e., $0.01 = 1$ percent). The regression is estimated with 431 observations because the independent variables are lagged one month. The regression output is in Exhibit 1. Exhibits 2 through 5 contain critical values for selected test statistics.

EXHIBIT 1   Multiple Regression Output (the Dependent Variable Is the One-Month Market Return in Excess of the One-Month T-Bill Return)

	Coefficient	t-Statistic	p-Value
Intercept	−4.60	−4.36	<0.01
Default spread$_{t-1}$	3.04	4.52	<0.01
Term spread$_{t-1}$	0.84	3.41	<0.01
Pres party dummy$_{t-1}$	3.17	4.97	<0.01
Number of observations		431	
Test statistic from Breusch–Pagan (BP) test		7.35	
R^2		0.053	
Adjusted R^2		0.046	
Durbin–Watson (DW)		1.65	
Sum of squared errors (SSE)		19,048	
Regression sum of squares (SSR)		1,071	

An intern working for Chiesa has a number of questions about the results in Exhibit 1:

Question 1.   How do you test to determine whether the overall regression model is significant?

Question 2.   Does the estimated model conform to standard regression assumptions? For instance, is the error term serially correlated, or is there conditional heteroskedasticity?

Question 3.   How do you interpret the coefficient for the Pres party dummy variable?

Question 4.   Default spread appears to be quite important. Is there some way to assess the precision of its estimated coefficient? What is the economic interpretation of this variable?

After responding to her intern's questions, Chiesa concludes with the following statement: "Predictions from Exhibit 1 are subject to parameter estimate uncertainty, but not regression model uncertainty."

EXHIBIT 2   Critical Values for the Durbin–Watson Statistic ($\alpha = 0.05$)

N	K = 3	
	d_l	d_u
420	1.825	1.854
430	1.827	1.855
440	1.829	1.857

EXHIBIT 3   Table of the Student's t-Distribution (One-Tailed Probabilities for DF = ∞)

P	t
0.10	1.282
0.05	1.645
0.025	1.960
0.01	2.326

EXHIBIT 4   Values of χ^2

	Probability in Right Tail			
DF	0.975	0.95	0.05	0.025
1	0.0001	0.0039	3.841	5.024
2	0.0506	0.1026	5.991	7.378
3	0.2158	0.3518	7.815	9.348
4	0.4840	0.7110	9.488	11.14

EXHIBIT 5   Table of the F-Distribution (Critical Values for Right-Hand Tail Area Equal to 0.05) Numerator: DF1 and Denominator: DF2

	DF1				
DF2	1	2	3	4	427
1	161	200	216	225	254
2	18.51	19.00	19.16	19.25	19.49
3	10.13	9.55	9.28	9.12	8.53
4	7.71	6.94	6.59	6.39	5.64
427	3.86	3.02	2.63	2.39	1.17

23. Regarding the intern's Question 1, is the regression model as a whole significant at the 0.05 level?
    A. No, because the calculated F-statistic is less than the critical value for F.
    B. Yes, because the calculated F-statistic is greater than the critical value for F.
    C. Yes, because the calculated χ^2 statistic is greater than the critical value for χ^2.

24. Which of the following is Chiesa's *best* response to Question 2 regarding serial correlation in the error term? At a 0.05 level of significance, the test for serial correlation indicates that there is:
    A. no serial correlation in the error term.
    B. positive serial correlation in the error term.
    C. negative serial correlation in the error term.

25. Regarding Question 3, the Pres party dummy variable in the model indicates that the mean monthly value for the excess stock market return is:
    A.   1.43 percent larger during Democratic presidencies than Republican presidencies.
    B.   3.17 percent larger during Democratic presidencies than Republican presidencies.
    C.   3.17 percent larger during Republican presidencies than Democratic presidencies.

26. In response to Question 4, the 95 percent confidence interval for the regression coefficient for the default spread is *closest* to:
    A.   0.13 to 5.95.
    B.   1.72 to 4.36.
    C.   1.93 to 4.15.

27. With respect to the default spread, the estimated model indicates that when business conditions are:
    A.   strong, expected excess returns will be higher.
    B.   weak, expected excess returns will be lower.
    C.   weak, expected excess returns will be higher.

28. Is Chiesa's concluding statement correct regarding parameter estimate uncertainty and regression model uncertainty?
    A.   Yes.
    B.   No, predictions are not subject to parameter estimate uncertainty.
    C.   No, predictions are subject to regression model uncertainty and parameter estimate uncertainty.

The following information relates to Questions 29–36

Doris Honoré is a securities analyst with a large wealth management firm. She and her colleague Bill Smith are addressing three research topics: how investment fund characteristics affect fund total returns, whether a fund rating system helps predict fund returns, and whether stock and bond market returns explain the returns of a portfolio of utility shares run by the firm.

   To explore the first topic, Honoré decides to study US mutual funds using a sample of 555 large-cap US equity funds. The sample includes funds in style classes of value, growth, and blend (i.e., combining value and growth characteristics). The dependent variable is the average annualized rate of return (in percent) over the past five years. The independent variables are fund expense ratio, portfolio turnover, the natural logarithm of fund size, fund age, and three dummy variables. The multiple manager dummy variable has a value of 1 if the fund has multiple managers (and a value of 0 if it has a single manager). The fund style is indicated by a growth dummy (value of 1 for growth funds and 0 otherwise) and a blend dummy (value of 1 for blend funds and 0 otherwise). If the growth and blend dummies are both zero, the fund is a value fund. The regression output is given in Exhibit 1.

EXHIBIT 1   Multiple Regression Output for Large-Cap Mutual Fund Sample

	Coefficient	Standard Error	t-Statistic
Intercept	10.9375	1.3578	8.0551
Expense ratio (%)	−1.4839	0.2282	−6.5039
Portfolio turnover (%)	0.0017	0.0016	1.0777
ln (fund size in $)	0.1467	0.0612	2.3976
Manager tenure (years)	−0.0098	0.0102	−0.9580
Multiple manager dummy	0.0628	0.1533	0.4100
Fund age (years)	−0.0123	0.0047	−2.6279
Growth dummy	2.4368	0.1886	12.9185
Blend dummy	0.5757	0.1881	3.0611

ANOVA	DF	SS	MSS
Regression	8	714.169	89.2712
Residual	546	1583.113	2.8995
Total	554	2297.282	

Multiple R	0.5576
R^2	0.3109
Adjusted R^2	0.3008
Standard error (%)	1.7028
Observations	555

Based on the results shown in Exhibit 1, Honoré wants to test the hypothesis that all of the regression coefficients are equal to zero. For the 555 fund sample, she also wants to compare the performance of growth funds with the value funds.

Honoré is concerned about the possible presence of multicollinearity in the regression. She states that adding a new independent variable that is highly correlated with one or more independent variables already in the regression model, has three potential consequences:

1. The R^2 is expected to decline.
2. The regression coefficient estimates can become imprecise and unreliable.
3. The standard errors for some or all of the regression coefficients will become inflated.

Another concern for the regression model (in Exhibit 1) is conditional heteroskedasticity. Honoré is concerned that the presence of heteroskedasticity can cause both the F-test for the overall significance of the regression and the t-tests for significance of individual regression coefficients to be unreliable. She runs a regression of the squared residuals from the model in Exhibit 1 on the eight independent variables, and finds the R^2 is 0.0669.

As a second research project, Honoré wants to test whether including Morningstar's rating system, which assigns a one- through five-star rating to a fund, as an independent variable will improve the predictive power of the regression model. To do this, she needs to examine whether values of the independent variables in a given period predict fund return in the next period. Smith suggests three different methods of adding the Morningstar ratings to the model:

- Method 1: Add an independent variable that has a value equal to the number of stars in the rating of each fund.
- Method 2: Add five dummy variables, one for each rating.
- Method 3: Add dummy variables for four of the five ratings.

As a third research project, Honoré wants to establish whether bond market returns (proxied by returns of long-term US Treasuries) and stock market returns (proxied by returns of the S&P 500 Index) explain the returns of a portfolio of utility stocks being recommended to clients. Exhibit 2 presents the results of a regression of 10 years of monthly percentage total returns for the utility portfolio on monthly total returns for US Treasuries and the S&P 500.

EXHIBIT 2   Regression Analysis of Utility Portfolio Returns

	Coefficient	Standard Error	t-Statistic	p-Value
Intercept	−0.0851	0.2829	−0.3008	0.7641
US Treasury	0.4194	0.0848	4.9474	<0.0001
S&P 500	0.6198	0.0666	9.3126	<0.0001

ANOVA	DF	SS	MSS	F	Significance F
Regression	2	827.48	413.74	46.28	<0.0001
Residual	117	1045.93	8.94		
Total	119	1873.41			

Multiple R	0.6646
R^2	0.4417
Adjusted R^2	0.4322
Standard error (%)	2.99
Observations	120

For the time-series model in Exhibit 2, Honoré says that positive serial correlation would not require that the estimated coefficients be adjusted, but that the standard errors of the regression coefficients would be underestimated. This issue would cause the t-statistics of the regression coefficients to be inflated. Honoré tests the null hypothesis that the there is no serial correlation in the regression residuals and finds that the Durbin–Watson statistic is equal to 1.81. The critical values at the 0.05 significance level for the Durbin–Watson statistic are $d_l = 1.63$ and $d_u = 1.72$.

Smith asks whether Honoré should have estimated the models in Exhibit 1 and Exhibit 2 using a probit or logit model instead of using a traditional regression analysis.

29. Considering Exhibit 1, the F-statistic is closest to:
    A. 3.22.
    B. 8.06.
    C. 30.79.

30. Based on Exhibit 1, the difference between the predicted annualized returns of a growth fund and an otherwise similar value fund is *closest* to:
    A. 1.86%.
    B. 2.44%.
    C. 3.01%.

31. Honoré describes three potential consequences of multicollinearity. Are all three consequences correct?
    A. Yes
    B. No, 1 is incorrect
    C. No, 2 is incorrect

32. Which of the three methods suggested by Smith would *best* capture the ability of the Morningstar rating system to predict mutual fund performance?
    A. Method 1
    B. Method 2
    C. Method 3

33. Honoré is concerned about the consequences of heteroskedasticity. Is she correct regarding the effect of heteroskedasticity on the reliability of the F-test and t-tests?
    A. Yes
    B. No, she is incorrect with regard to the F-test
    C. No, she is incorrect with regard to the t-tests

34. Is Honoré's description of the effects of positive serial correlation (in Exhibit 2) correct regarding the estimated coefficients and the standard errors?
    A. Yes
    B. No, she is incorrect about only the estimated coefficients
    C. No, she is incorrect about only the standard errors of the regression coefficients

35. Based on her estimated Durbin–Watson statistic, Honoré should:
    A. fail to reject the null hypothesis.
    B. reject the null hypothesis because there is significant positive serial correlation.
    C. reject the null hypothesis because there is significant negative serial correlation.

36. Should Honoré have estimated the models in Exhibit 1 and Exhibit 2 using probit or logit models instead of traditional regression analysis?
    A. Both should be estimated with probit or logit models.
    B. Neither should be estimated with probit or logit models.
    C. Only the analysis in Exhibit 1 should be done with probit or logit models.

The following information relates to Questions 37–45

Brad Varden, a junior analyst at an actively managed mutual fund, is responsible for research on a subset of the 500 large-cap equities the fund follows. Recently, the fund has been paying close attention to management turnover and to publicly available environmental, social, and governance (ESG) ratings. Varden is given the task of investigating whether any significant relationship exists between a company's profitability and either of these two characteristics. Colleen Quinni, a senior analyst at the fund, suggests that as an initial step in his investigation, Varden should perform a multiple regression analysis on the variables and report back to her.

Varden knows that Quinni is an expert at quantitative research, and she once told Varden that after you get an idea, you should formulate a hypothesis, test the hypothesis, and analyze the results. Varden expects to find that ESG rating is negatively related to ROE and CEO tenure is positively related to ROE. He considers a relationship meaningful when it is statistically significant at the 0.05 level. To begin, Varden collects values for ROE, CEO tenure, and ESG rating for a sample of 40 companies from the large-cap security universe. He performs a multiple regression with ROE (in percent) as the dependent variable and ESG rating and CEO tenure (in years) as the independent variables: $Y_i = b_0 + b_1X_{1i} + b_2X_{2i} + \varepsilon_i$.

Exhibit 1 shows the regression results.

EXHIBIT 1   Regression Statistics

$\widehat{Y}_i = 9.442 + 0.069X_{1i} + 0.681X_{2i}$

	Coefficient	Standard Error	t-Statistic	p-Value
Intercept	9.442	3.343	2.824	0.008
b_1 (ESG variable)	0.069	0.058	1.201	0.238
b_2 (Tenure variable)	0.681	0.295	2.308	0.027

ANOVA	DF	SS	MSS	F	Significance F
Regression	2	240.410	120.205	4.161	0.023
Residual	37	1069.000	28.892		
Total	39	1309.410			

Multiple R	0.428
R^2	0.183
Adjusted R^2	0.139
Standard error (%)	5.375
Observations	40

DF Associates is one of the companies Varden follows. He wants to predict its ROE using his regression model. DF Associates' corporate ESG rating is 55, and the company's CEO has been in that position for 10.5 years.

Varden also wants to check on the relationship between these variables and the dividend growth rate (divgr), so he completes the correlation matrix shown in Exhibit 2.

EXHIBIT 2   Correlation Matrix

	ROE	ESG	Tenure	Divgr
ROE	1.0			
ESG	0.446	1.0		
Tenure	0.369	0.091	1.0	
Divgr	0.117	0.046	0.028	1.0

Investigating further, Varden determines that dividend growth is not a linear combination of CEO tenure and ESG rating. He is unclear about how additional independent variables would affect the significance of the regression, so he asks Quinni, "Given this correlation matrix, will both R^2 and adjusted R^2 automatically increase if I add dividend growth as a third independent variable?"

The discussion continues, and Quinni asks two questions.

1. What does your F-statistic of 4.161 tell you about the regression?
2. In interpreting the overall significance of your regression model, which statistic do you believe is most relevant: R^2, adjusted R^2, or the F-statistic?

Varden answers both questions correctly and says he wants to check two more ideas. He believes the following:

1. ROE is less correlated with the dividend growth rate in firms whose CEO has been in office more than 15 years, and
2. CEO tenure is a normally distributed random variable.

Later, Varden includes the dividend growth rate as a third independent variable and runs the regression on the fund's entire group of 500 large-cap equities. He finds that the adjusted R^2 is much higher than the results in Exhibit 1. He reports this to Quinni and says, "Adding the dividend growth rate gives a model with a higher adjusted R^2. The three-variable model is clearly better." Quinni cautions, "I don't think you can conclude that yet."

37. Based on Exhibit 1 and given Varden's expectations, which is the *best* null hypothesis and conclusion regarding CEO tenure?
    A. $b_2 \leq 0$; reject the null hypothesis
    B. $b_2 = 0$; cannot reject the null hypothesis
    C. $b_2 \geq 0$; reject the null hypothesis

38. At a significance level of 1%, which of the following is the *best* interpretation of the regression coefficients with regard to explaining ROE?
    A. ESG is significant, but tenure is not.
    B. Tenure is significant, but ESG is not.
    C. Neither ESG nor tenure is significant.

39. Based on Exhibit 1, which independent variables in Varden's model are significant at the 0.05 level?
    A. ESG only
    B. Tenure only
    C. Neither ESG nor tenure

40. Based on Exhibit 1, the predicted ROE for DF Associates is *closest* to:
    A. 10.957%.
    B. 16.593%.
    C. 20.388%.

41. Based on Exhibit 2, Quinni's *best* answer to Varden's question about the effect of adding a third independent variable is:
    A. no for R^2 and no for adjusted R^2.
    B. yes for R^2 and no for adjusted R^2.
    C. yes for R^2 and yes for adjusted R^2.

42. Based on Exhibit 1, Varden's *best* answer to Quinni's question about the *F*-statistic is:
    A. both independent variables are significant at the 0.05 level.
    B. neither independent variable is significant at the 0.05 level.
    C. at least one independent variable is significant at the 0.05 level.

43. Varden's *best* answer to Quinni's question about overall significance is:
    A. R^2.
    B. adjusted R^2.
    C. the *F*-statistic.

44. If Varden's beliefs about ROE and CEO tenure are true, which of the following would violate the assumptions of multiple regression analysis?
    A. The assumption about CEO tenure distribution only
    B. The assumption about the ROE/dividend growth correlation only
    C. The assumptions about both the ROE/dividend growth correlation and CEO tenure distribution

45. The *best* rationale for Quinni's caution about the three-variable model is that the:
    A. dependent variable is defined differently.
    B. sample sizes are different in the two models.
    C. dividend growth rate is positively correlated with the other independent variables.

CHAPTER 9

TIME-SERIES ANALYSIS

LEARNING OUTCOMES

The candidate should be able to:

- calculate and evaluate the predicted trend value for a time series, modeled as either a linear trend or a log-linear trend, given the estimated trend coefficients;
- describe factors that determine whether a linear or a log-linear trend should be used with a particular time series and evaluate limitations of trend models;
- explain the requirement for a time series to be covariance stationary and describe the significance of a series that is not stationary;
- describe the structure of an autoregressive (AR) model of order p and calculate one- and two-period-ahead forecasts given the estimated coefficients;
- explain how autocorrelations of the residuals can be used to test whether the autoregressive model fits the time series;
- explain mean reversion and calculate a mean-reverting level;
- contrast in-sample and out-of-sample forecasts and compare the forecasting accuracy of different time-series models based on the root mean squared error criterion;
- explain the instability of coefficients of time-series models;
- describe characteristics of random walk processes and contrast them to covariance stationary processes;
- describe implications of unit roots for time-series analysis, explain when unit roots are likely to occur and how to test for them, and demonstrate how a time series with a unit root can be transformed so it can be analyzed with an AR model;
- describe the steps of the unit root test for nonstationarity and explain the relation of the test to autoregressive time-series models;
- explain how to test and correct for seasonality in a time-series model and calculate and interpret a forecasted value using an AR model with a seasonal lag;
- explain autoregressive conditional heteroskedasticity (ARCH) and describe how ARCH models can be applied to predict the variance of a time series;
- explain how time-series variables should be analyzed for nonstationarity and/or cointegration before use in a linear regression; and

- determine an appropriate time-series model to analyze a given investment problem and justify that choice.

SUMMARY

- The predicted trend value of a time series in period t is $\widehat{b}_0 + \widehat{b}_1 t$ in a linear trend model; the predicted trend value of a time series in a log-linear trend model is $e^{\widehat{b}_0 + \widehat{b}_1 t}$.
- Time series that tend to grow by a constant amount from period to period should be modeled by linear trend models, whereas time series that tend to grow at a constant rate should be modeled by log-linear trend models.
- Trend models often do not completely capture the behavior of a time series, as indicated by serial correlation of the error term. If the Durbin–Watson statistic from a trend model differs significantly from 2, indicating serial correlation, we need to build a different kind of model.
- An autoregressive model of order p, denoted AR(p), uses p lags of a time series to predict its current value: $x_t = b_0 + b_1 x_{t-1} + b_2 x_{t-2} + \ldots + b_p x_{t-p} + \varepsilon_t$.
- A time series is covariance stationary if the following three conditions are satisfied: First, the expected value of the time series must be constant and finite in all periods. Second, the variance of the time series must be constant and finite in all periods. Third, the covariance of the time series with itself for a fixed number of periods in the past or future must be constant and finite in all periods. Inspection of a nonstationary time-series plot may reveal an upward or downward trend (nonconstant mean) and/or nonconstant variance. The use of linear regression to estimate an autoregressive time-series model is not valid unless the time series is covariance stationary.
- For a specific autoregressive model to be a good fit to the data, the autocorrelations of the error term should be 0 at all lags.
- A time series is mean reverting if it tends to fall when its level is above its long-run mean and rise when its level is below its long-run mean. If a time series is covariance stationary, then it will be mean reverting.
- The one-period-ahead forecast of a variable x_t from an AR(1) model made in period t for period $t + 1$ is $\widehat{x}_{t+1} = \widehat{b}_0 + \widehat{b}_1 x_t$. This forecast can be used to create the two-period-ahead forecast from the model made in period t, $\widehat{x}_{t+2} = \widehat{b}_0 + \widehat{b}_1 x_{t+1}$. Similar results hold for AR (p) models.
- In-sample forecasts are the in-sample predicted values from the estimated time-series model. Out-of-sample forecasts are the forecasts made from the estimated time-series model for a time period different from the one for which the model was estimated. Out-of-sample forecasts are usually more valuable in evaluating the forecasting performance of a time-series model than are in-sample forecasts. The root mean squared error (RMSE), defined as the square root of the average squared forecast error, is a criterion for comparing the forecast accuracy of different time-series models; a smaller RMSE implies greater forecast accuracy.
- Just as in regression models, the coefficients in time-series models are often unstable across different sample periods. In selecting a sample period for estimating a time-series model, we should seek to assure ourselves that the time series was stationary in the sample period.
- A random walk is a time series in which the value of the series in one period is the value of the series in the previous period plus an unpredictable random error. If the time series is a

random walk, it is not covariance stationary. A random walk with drift is a random walk with a nonzero intercept term. All random walks have unit roots. If a time series has a unit root, then it will not be covariance stationary.

- If a time series has a unit root, we can sometimes transform the time series into one that is covariance stationary by first-differencing the time series; we may then be able to estimate an autoregressive model for the first-differenced series.
- An n-period moving average of the current and past $(n - 1)$ values of a time series, x_t, is calculated as $[x_t + x_{t-1} + \ldots + x_{t-(n-1)}]/n$.
- A moving-average model of order q, denoted MA(q), uses q lags of a random error term to predict its current value.
- The order q of a moving-average model can be determined using the fact that if a time series is a moving-average time series of order q, its first q autocorrelations are nonzero while autocorrelations beyond the first q are zero.
- The autocorrelations of most autoregressive time series start large and decline gradually, whereas the autocorrelations of an MA(q) time series suddenly drop to 0 after the first q autocorrelations. This helps in distinguishing between autoregressive and moving-average time series.
- If the error term of a time-series model shows significant serial correlation at seasonal lags, the time series has significant seasonality. This seasonality can often be modeled by including a seasonal lag in the model, such as adding a term lagged four quarters to an AR(1) model on quarterly observations.
- The forecast made in time t for time $t + 1$ using a quarterly AR(1) model with a seasonal lag would be $x_{t+1} = \widehat{b}_0 + \widehat{b}_1 x_t + \widehat{b}_2 x_{t-3}$.
- ARMA models have several limitations: The parameters in ARMA models can be very unstable; determining the AR and MA order of the model can be difficult; and even with their additional complexity, ARMA models may not forecast well.
- The variance of the error in a time-series model sometimes depends on the variance of previous errors, representing autoregressive conditional heteroskedasticity (ARCH). Analysts can test for first-order ARCH in a time-series model by regressing the squared residual on the squared residual from the previous period. If the coefficient on the squared residual is statistically significant, the time-series model has ARCH(1) errors.
- If a time-series model has ARCH(1) errors, then the variance of the errors in period $t + 1$ can be predicted in period t using the formula $\widehat{\sigma}^2_{t+1} = \widehat{a}_0 + \widehat{a}_1 \widehat{\varepsilon}^2_t$.
- If linear regression is used to model the relationship between two time series, a test should be performed to determine whether either time series has a unit root:
  . If neither of the time series has a unit root, then we can safely use linear regression.
  . If one of the two time series has a unit root, then we should not use linear regression.
  . If both time series have a unit root and the time series are cointegrated, we may safely use linear regression; however, if they are not cointegrated, we should not use linear regression. The (Engle–Granger) Dickey–Fuller test can be used to determine whether time series are cointegrated.

PRACTICE PROBLEMS

Note: In the problems and solutions for this chapter, we use the hat (⌢) to indicate an estimate if we are trying to differentiate between an estimated and an actual value. However, we suppress the hat when we are clearly showing regression output.

EXHIBIT 1   Estimating a Linear Trend in the Civilian Unemployment Rate: Monthly Observations, January 2013–August 2019

Regression Statistics			
R^2	0.9316		
Standard error	0.3227		
Observations	80		
Durbin–Watson	0.1878		
	Coefficient	**Standard Error**	**t-Statistic**
Intercept	7.2237	0.0728	99.1704
Trend	–0.0510	0.0016	–32.6136

1. The civilian unemployment rate (UER) is an important component of many economic models. Exhibit 1 gives regression statistics from estimating a linear trend model of the unemployment rate: $UER_t = b_0 + b_1 t + \varepsilon_t$.
   A. Using the regression output in the previous table, what is the model's prediction of the unemployment rate for July 2013?
   B. How should we interpret the Durbin–Watson (DW) statistic for this regression? What does the value of the DW statistic say about the validity of a t-test on the coefficient estimates?

2. Exhibit 2 compares the predicted civilian unemployment rate (PRED) with the actual civilian unemployment rate (UER) from January 2013 to August 2019. The predicted results come from estimating the linear time trend model $UER_t = b_0 + b_1 t + \varepsilon_t$. What can we conclude about the appropriateness of this model?

EXHIBIT 2   Predicted and Actual Civilian Unemployment Rates

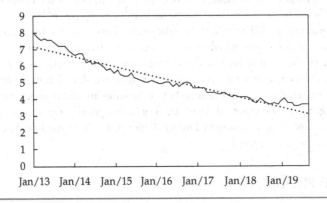

3. You have been assigned to analyze automobile manufacturers, and as a first step in your analysis, you decide to model monthly sales of lightweight vehicles to determine sales growth in that part of the industry. Exhibit 3 gives lightweight vehicle monthly sales (annualized) from January 1992 to December 2000.

EXHIBIT 3   Lightweight Vehicle Sales

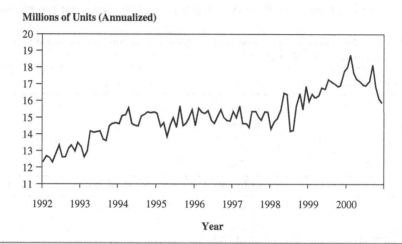

Monthly sales in the lightweight vehicle sector, $Sales_t$, have been increasing over time, but you suspect that the growth rate of monthly sales is relatively constant. Write the simplest time-series model for $Sales_t$ that is consistent with your perception.

4. Exhibit 4 shows a plot of the first differences in the civilian unemployment rate (UER) between January 2013 and August 2019, $\Delta UER_t = UER_t - UER_{t-1}$.

EXHIBIT 4   Change in Civilian Unemployment Rate

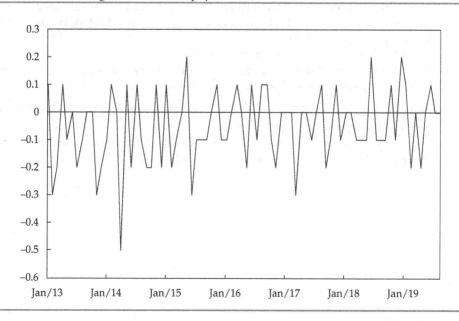

    A. Has differencing the data made the new series, ΔUER_t, covariance stationary? Explain your answer.

    B. Given the graph of the change in the unemployment rate shown in the figure, describe the steps we should take to determine the appropriate autoregressive time-series model specification for the series ΔUER_t.

5. Exhibit 5 gives the regression output of an AR(1) model on first differences in the unemployment rate. Describe how to interpret the DW statistic for this regression.

EXHIBIT 5   Estimating an AR(1) Model of Changes in the Civilian Unemployment Rate: Monthly Observations, February 2013–August 2019

Regression Statistics			
R^2	0.0546		
Standard error	0.1309		
Observations	79		
Durbin–Watson	2.0756		
	Coefficient	Standard Error	t-Statistic
Intercept	−0.0668	0.0158	−4.2278
ΔUER_{t-1}	−0.2320	0.1100	−2.191

6. Assume that changes in the civilian unemployment rate are covariance stationary and that an AR(1) model is a good description for the time series of changes in the unemployment rate. Specifically, we have $\Delta UER_t = -0.0668 - 0.2320\Delta UER_{t-1}$ (using the coefficient estimates given in the previous problem). Given this equation, what is the mean-reverting level to which changes in the unemployment rate converge?

7. Suppose the following model describes changes in the civilian unemployment rate: $\Delta UER_t = -0.0668 - 0.2320\Delta UER_{t-1}$. The current change (first difference) in the unemployment rate is 0.0300. Assume that the mean-reverting level for changes in the unemployment rate is −0.0542.

    A. What is the best prediction of the next change?

    B. What is the prediction of the change following the next change?

    C. Explain your answer to Part B in terms of equilibrium.

8. Exhibit 6 gives the actual sales, log of sales, and changes in the log of sales of Cisco Systems for the period 1Q 2019 to 4Q 2019.

    Forecast the first- and second-quarter sales of Cisco Systems for 2020 using the regression $\Delta \ln(Sales_t) = 0.0068 + 0.2633\Delta \ln(Sales_{t-1})$.

EXHIBIT 6

Date	Actual Sales ($ Millions)	Log of Sales	Changes in Log of Sales $\Delta\ln(\text{Sales}_t)$
1Q 2019	13,072	9.4782	0.0176
2Q 2019	12,446	9.4292	-0.0491
3Q 2019	12,958	9.4695	0.403
4Q 2019	13,428	9.5051	0.0356
1Q 2020			
2Q 2020			

9. Exhibit 7 gives the actual change in the log of sales of Cisco Systems from 1Q 2019 to 4Q 2019, along with the forecasts from the regression model $\Delta\ln(\text{Sales}_t) = 0.0068 + 0.2633\Delta\ln(\text{Sales}_{t-1})$ estimated using data from 1Q 2001 to 4Q 2018. (Note that the observations after the fourth quarter of 2018 are out of sample.)

EXHIBIT 7

Date	Actual Value of Changes in the Log of Sales $\Delta\ln(\text{Sales}_t)$	Forecast Value of Changes in the Log of Sales $\Delta\ln(\text{Sales}_t)$
1Q 2019	0.0176	0.0147
2Q 2019	-0.0491	0.0107
3Q 2019	0.4030	0.0096
4Q 2019	0.0356	0.0093

    A. Calculate the RMSE for the out-of-sample forecast errors.

    B. Compare the forecasting performance of the model given with that of another model having an out-of-sample RMSE of 2 percent.

10. A. The AR(1) model for the civilian unemployment rate, $\Delta\text{UER}_t = -0.0405 - 0.4674\Delta\text{UER}_{t-1}$, was developed with five years of data. What would be the drawback to using the AR(1) model to predict changes in the civilian unemployment rate 12 months or more ahead, as compared with 1 month ahead?

    B. For purposes of estimating a predictive equation, what would be the drawback to using 30 years of civilian unemployment data rather than only 5 years?

11. Exhibit 8 shows monthly observations on the natural log of lightweight vehicle sales, ln (Sales_t), for January 1992 to December 2000.

EXHIBIT 8   Lightweight Vehicle Sales

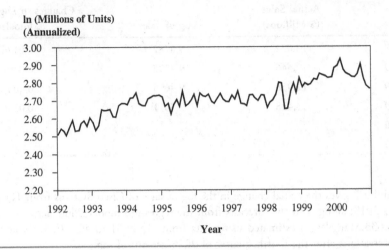

A. Using the figure, comment on whether the specification $\ln(Sales_t) = b_0 + b_1[\ln(Sales_{t-1})] + \varepsilon_t$ is appropriate.

B. State an appropriate transformation of the time series.

12. Exhibit 9 shows a plot of first differences in the log of monthly lightweight vehicle sales over the same period as in Problem 11. Has differencing the data made the resulting series, $\Delta\ln(Sales_t) = \ln(Sales_t) - \ln(Sales_{t-1})$, covariance stationary?

EXHIBIT 9   Change in Natural Log of Lightweight Vehicle Sales

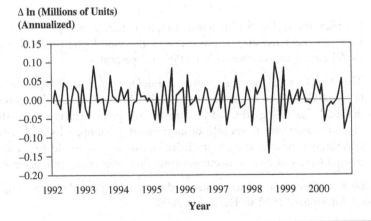

13. Using monthly data from January 1992 to December 2000, we estimate the following equation for lightweight vehicle sales: $\Delta\ln(Sales_t) = 2.7108 + 0.3987\Delta\ln(Sales_{t-1}) + \varepsilon_t$. Exhibit 10 gives sample autocorrelations of the errors from this model.

A. Use the information in the table to assess the appropriateness of the specification given by the equation.

B. If the residuals from the AR(1) model above violate a regression assumption, how would you modify the AR(1) specification?

EXHIBIT 10   Different Order Autocorrelations of Differences in the Logs of Vehicle Sales

Lag	Autocorrelation	Standard Error	*t*-Statistic
1	0.9358	0.0962	9.7247
2	0.8565	0.0962	8.9005
3	0.8083	0.0962	8.4001
4	0.7723	0.0962	8.0257
5	0.7476	0.0962	7.7696
6	0.7326	0.0962	7.6137
7	0.6941	0.0962	7.2138
8	0.6353	0.0962	6.6025
9	0.5867	0.0962	6.0968
10	0.5378	0.0962	5.5892
11	0.4745	0.0962	4.9315
12	0.4217	0.0962	4.3827

14. Exhibit 11 shows the quarterly sales of Cisco Systems from 3Q 2001 to 2Q 2019.

EXHIBIT 11   Quarterly Sales at Cisco

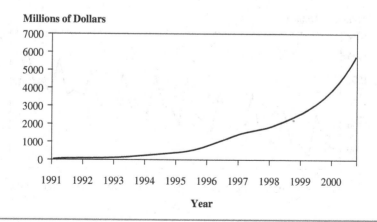

Exhibit 12 gives the regression statistics from estimating the model $\Delta \ln(Sales_t) = b_0 + b_1 \Delta \ln(Sales_{t-1}) + \varepsilon_t$.

EXHIBIT 12   Change in the Natural Log of Sales for Cisco Quarterly Observations, 3Q 1991–4Q 2000

Regression Statistics

R^2	0.2899		
Standard error	0.0408		
Observations	38		
Durbin–Watson	1.5707		
	Coefficient	**Standard Error**	**t-Statistic**
Intercept	0.0661	0.0175	3.7840
$\Delta \ln(Sales_{t-1})$	0.4698	0.1225	3.8339

A. Describe the salient features of the quarterly sales series.
B. Describe the procedures we should use to determine whether the AR(1) specification is correct.
C. Assuming the model is correctly specified, what is the long-run change in the log of sales toward which the series will tend to converge?

15. Exhibit 13 shows the quarterly sales of Avon Products from 1Q 1992 to 2Q 2002. Describe the salient features of the data shown.

EXHIBIT 13   Quarterly Sales at Avon

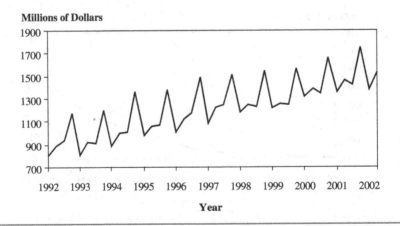

16. Exhibit 14 shows the autocorrelations of the residuals from an AR(1) model fit to the changes in the gross profit margin (GPM) of the Home Depot, Inc.

EXHIBIT 14   Autocorrelations of the Residuals from Estimating the Regression $\Delta GPM_t = 0.0006 - 0.3330\Delta GPM_{t-1} + \varepsilon_t$, 1Q 1992–4Q 2001 (40 Observations)

Lag	Autocorrelation
1	-0.1106
2	-0.5981
3	-0.1525
4	0.8496
5	-0.1099

Exhibit 15 shows the output from a regression on changes in the GPM for Home Depot, where we have changed the specification of the AR regression.

EXHIBIT 15   Change in Gross Profit Margin for Home Depot, 1Q 1992–4Q 2001

Regression Statistics			
R^2	0.9155		
Standard error	0.0057		
Observations	40		
Durbin–Watson	2.6464		
	Coefficient	Standard Error	t-Statistic
Intercept	-0.0001	0.0009	-0.0610
ΔGPM_{t-1}	-0.0608	0.0687	-0.8850
ΔGPM_{t-4}	0.8720	0.0678	12.8683

A. Identify the change that was made to the regression model.
B. Discuss the rationale for changing the regression specification.

17. Suppose we decide to use an autoregressive model with a seasonal lag because of the seasonal autocorrelation in the previous problem. We are modeling quarterly data, so we estimate Equation 15: $(\ln Sales_t - \ln Sales_{t-1}) = b_0 + b_1(\ln Sales_{t-1} - \ln Sales_{t-2}) + b_2(\ln Sales_{t-4} - \ln Sales_{t-5}) + \varepsilon_t$. Exhibit 16 shows the regression statistics from this equation.

EXHIBIT 16   Log Differenced Sales: AR(1) Model with Seasonal Lag Johnson & Johnson Quarterly
Observations, January 1985–December 2001

Regression Statistics

R^2	0.4220		
Standard error	0.0318		
Observations	68		
Durbin–Watson	1.8784		
	Coefficient	**Standard Error**	**t-Statistic**
Intercept	0.0121	0.0053	2.3055
Lag 1	−0.0839	0.0958	−0.8757
Lag 4	0.6292	0.0958	6.5693

Autocorrelations of the Residual

Lag	Autocorrelation	Standard Error	t-Statistic
1	0.0572	0.1213	0.4720
2	−0.0700	0.1213	−0.5771
3	0.0065	0.1213	−0.0532
4	−0.0368	0.1213	−0.3033

A. Using the information in Exhibit 16, determine whether the model is correctly specified.

B. If sales grew by 1 percent last quarter and by 2 percent four quarters ago, use the model to predict the sales growth for this quarter.

18. Describe how to test for autoregressive conditional heteroskedasticity (ARCH) in the residuals from the AR(1) regression on first differences in the civilian unemployment rate, $\Delta UER_t = b_0 + b_1 \Delta UER_{t-1} + \varepsilon_t$.

19. Suppose we want to predict the annualized return of the five-year T-bill using the annualized return of the three-month T-bill with monthly observations from January 1993 to December 2002. Our analysis produces the data shown in Exhibit 17.
Can we rely on the regression model in Exhibit 17 to produce me
aningful predictions? Specify what problem might be a concern with this regression.

EXHIBIT 17   Regression with Three-Month T-Bill as the Independent Variable and the Five-Year
T-Bill as the Dependent Variable: Monthly Observations, January 1993–December 2002

Regression Statistics

R^2	0.5829		
Standard error	0.6598		
Observations	120		
Durbin–Watson	0.1130		
	Coefficient	**Standard Error**	**t-Statistic**
Intercept	3.0530	0.2060	14.8181
Three-month	0.5722	0.0446	12.8408

The following information relates to Questions 20–26

Angela Martinez, an energy sector analyst at an investment bank, is concerned about the future level of oil prices and how it might affect portfolio values. She is considering whether to recommend a hedge for the bank portfolio's exposure to changes in oil prices. Martinez examines West Texas Intermediate (WTI) monthly crude oil price data, expressed in US dollars per barrel, for the 181-month period from August 2000 through August 2015. The end-of-month WTI oil price was $51.16 in July 2015 and $42.86 in August 2015 (Month 181).

After reviewing the time-series data, Martinez determines that the mean and variance of the time series of oil prices are not constant over time. She then runs the following four regressions using the WTI time-series data.

- Linear trend model: Oil price$_t$ = b_0 + $b_1 t$ + e_t.
- Log-linear trend model: ln Oil price$_t$ = b_0 + $b_1 t$ + e_t.
- AR(1) model: Oil price$_t$ = b_0 + b_1Oil price$_{t-1}$ + e_t.
- AR(2) model: Oil price$_t$ = b_0 + b_1Oil price$_{t-1}$ + b_2Oil price$_{t-2}$ + e_t.

Exhibit 1 presents selected data from all four regressions, and Exhibit 2 presents selected autocorrelation data from the AR(1) models.

EXHIBIT 1   Crude Oil Price per Barrel, August 2000–August 2015

	Regression Statistics (t-statistics for coefficients are reported in parentheses)			
	Linear	Log-Linear	AR(1)	AR(2)
R^2	0.5703	0.6255	0.9583	0.9656
Standard error	18.6327	0.3034	5.7977	5.2799
Observations	181	181	180	179
Durbin–Watson	0.10	0.08	1.16	2.08
RMSE			2.0787	2.0530
Coefficients:				
Intercept	28.3278	3.3929	1.5948	2.0017
	(10.1846)	(74.9091)	(1.4610)	(1.9957)
t (Trend)	0.4086	0.0075		
	(15.4148)	(17.2898)		
Oil price$_{t-1}$			0.9767	1.3946
			(63.9535)	(20.2999)
Oil price$_{t-2}$				-0.4249
				(-6.2064)

EXHIBIT 2   Autocorrelations of the Residual from AR(1) Model

Lag	Autocorrelation	t-Statistic
1	0.4157	5.5768
2	0.2388	3.2045
3	0.0336	0.4512
4	−0.0426	−0.5712

Note: At the 5 percent significance level, the critical value for a t-statistic is 1.97.

In Exhibit 1, at the 5 percent significance level, the lower critical value for the Durbin–Watson test statistic is 1.75 for both the linear and log-linear regressions.

After reviewing the data and regression results, Martinez draws the following conclusions.

Conclusion 1.   The time series for WTI oil prices is covariance stationary.

Conclusion 2.   Out-of-sample forecasting using the AR(1) model appears to be more accurate than that of the AR(2) model.

20.   Based on Exhibit 1, the predicted WTI oil price for October 2015 using the linear trend model is *closest* to:
A. $29.15.
B. $74.77.
C. $103.10.

21.   Based on Exhibit 1, the predicted WTI oil price for September 2015 using the log-linear trend model is *closest* to:
A. $29.75.
B. $29.98.
C. $116.50.

22.   Based on the regression output in Exhibit 1, there is evidence of positive serial correlation in the errors in:
A.   the linear trend model but not the log-linear trend model.
B.   both the linear trend model and the log-linear trend model.
C.   neither the linear trend model nor the log-linear trend model.

23.   Martinez's Conclusion 1 is:
A.   correct.
B.   incorrect because the mean and variance of WTI oil prices are not constant over time.
C.   incorrect because the Durbin–Watson statistic of the AR(2) model is greater than 1.75.

24.   Based on Exhibit 1, the forecasted oil price in September 2015 based on the AR(2) model is *closest* to:
A. $38.03.
B. $40.04.
C. $61.77.

25. Based on the data for the AR(1) model in Exhibits 1 and 2, Martinez can conclude that the:
    A. residuals are not serially correlated.
    B. autocorrelations do not differ significantly from zero.
    C. standard error for each of the autocorrelations is 0.0745.

26. Based on the mean-reverting level implied by the AR(1) model regression output in Exhibit 1, the forecasted oil price for September 2015 is *most likely* to be:
    A. less than $42.86.
    B. equal to $42.86.
    C. greater than $42.86.

The following information relates to Question 27–35

Max Busse is an analyst in the research department of a large hedge fund. He was recently asked to develop a model to predict the future exchange rate between two currencies. Busse gathers monthly exchange rate data from the most recent 10-year period and runs a regression based on the following AR(1) model specification:

Regression 1: $x_t = b_0 + b_1 x_{t-1} + \varepsilon_t$, where x_t is the exchange rate at time t.

Based on his analysis of the time series and the regression results, Busse reaches the following conclusions:

Conclusion 1.   The variance of x_t increases over time.
Conclusion 2.   The mean-reverting level is undefined.
Conclusion 3. b_0 does not appear to be significantly different from 0.

Busse decides to do additional analysis by first-differencing the data and running a new regression.

Regression 2: $y_t = b_0 + b_1 y_{t-1} + \varepsilon_t$, where $y_t = x_t - x_{t-1}$.

Exhibit 1 shows the regression results.

EXHIBIT 1   First-Differenced Exchange Rate AR(1) Model: Month-End Observations, Last 10 Years

Regression Statistics

R^2	0.0017
Standard error	7.3336
Observations	118
Durbin–Watson	1.9937

	Coefficient	Standard Error	t-Statistic
Intercept	−0.8803	0.6792	−1.2960
$x_{t-1} - x_{t-2}$	0.0412	0.0915	0.4504

Autocorrelations of the Residual

Lag	Autocorrelation	Standard Error	t-Statistic
1	0.0028	0.0921	0.0300
2	0.0205	0.0921	0.2223
3	0.0707	0.0921	0.7684
4	0.0485	0.0921	0.5271

Note: The critical *t*-statistic at the 5 percent significance level is 1.98.

Busse decides that he will need to test the data for nonstationarity using a Dickey–Fuller test. To do so, he knows he must model a transformed version of Regression 1.

Busse's next assignment is to develop a model to predict future quarterly sales for PoweredUP, Inc., a major electronics retailer. He begins by running the following regression:

Regression 3: $\ln Sales_t - \ln Sales_{t-1} = b_0 + b_1(\ln Sales_{t-1} - \ln Sales_{t-2}) + \varepsilon_t$.

Exhibit 2 presents the results of this regression.

EXHIBIT 2   Log Differenced Sales AR(1) Model: PoweredUP, Inc., Last 10 Years of Quarterly Sales

Regression Statistics

R^2	0.2011
Standard error	0.0651
Observations	38
Durbin–Watson	1.9677

	Coefficient	Standard Error	t-Statistic
Intercept	0.0408	0.0112	3.6406
ln Sales$_{t-1}$ – ln Sales$_{t-2}$	–0.4311	0.1432	–3.0099

Autocorrelations of the Residual

Lag	Autocorrelation	Standard Error	t-Statistic
1	0.0146	0.1622	0.0903
2	–0.1317	0.1622	–0.8119
3	–0.1123	0.1622	–0.6922
4	0.6994	0.1622	4.3111

Note: The critical *t*-statistic at the 5 percent significance level is 2.02.

Because the regression output from Exhibit 2 raises some concerns, Busse runs a different regression. These regression results, along with quarterly sales data for the past five quarters, are presented in Exhibits 3 and 4, respectively.

EXHIBIT 3   Log Differenced Sales AR(1) Model with Seasonal Lag: PoweredUP, Inc., Last 10 Years of Quarterly Sales

Regression Statistics

R^2	0.6788
Standard error	0.0424
Observations	35
Durbin–Watson	1.8799

	Coefficient	Standard Error	t-Statistic
Intercept	0.0092	0.0087	1.0582
ln Sales$_{t-1}$ – ln Sales$_{t-2}$	−0.1279	0.1137	−1.1252
ln Sales$_{t-4}$ – ln Sales$_{t-5}$	0.7239	0.1093	6.6209

Autocorrelations of the Residual

Lag	Autocorrelation	Standard Error	t-Statistic
1	0.0574	0.1690	0.3396
2	0.0440	0.1690	0.2604
3	0.1923	0.1690	1.1379
4	−0.1054	0.1690	−0.6237

Note: The critical *t*-statistic at the 5 percent significance level is 2.03.

EXHIBIT 4   Most Recent Quarterly Sales Data (in billions)

Dec 2015 (Sales$_{t-1}$)	$3.868
Sep 2015 (Sales$_{t-2}$)	$3.780
June 2015 (Sales$_{t-3}$)	$3.692
Mar 2015 (Sales$_{t-4}$)	$3.836
Dec 2014 (Sales$_{t-5}$)	$3.418

After completing his work on PoweredUP, Busse is asked to analyze the relationship of oil prices and the stock prices of three transportation companies. His firm wants to know whether the stock prices can be predicted by the price of oil. Exhibit 5 shows selected information from the results of his analysis.

EXHIBIT 5   Analysis Summary of Stock Prices for Three Transportation Stocks and the Price of Oil

	Unit Root?	Linear or Exponential Trend?	Serial Correlation of Residuals in Trend Model?	ARCH(1)?	Comments
Company 1	Yes	Exponential	Yes	Yes	Not cointegrated with oil price
Company 2	Yes	Linear	Yes	No	Cointegrated with oil price
Company 3	No	Exponential	Yes	No	Not cointegrated with oil price
Oil Price	Yes				

To assess the relationship between oil prices and stock prices, Busse runs three regressions using the time series of each company's stock prices as the dependent variable and the time series of oil prices as the independent variable.

27. Which of Busse's conclusions regarding the exchange rate time series is consistent with both the properties of a covariance-stationary time series and the properties of a random walk?
    A. Conclusion 1
    B. Conclusion 2
    C. Conclusion 3

28. Based on the regression output in Exhibit 1, the first-differenced series used to run Regression 2 is consistent with:
    A. a random walk.
    B. covariance stationarity.
    C. a random walk with drift.

29. Based on the regression results in Exhibit 1, the *original* time series of exchange rates:
    A. has a unit root.
    B. exhibits stationarity.
    C. can be modeled using linear regression.

30. In order to perform the nonstationarity test, Busse should transform the Regression 1 equation by:
    A. adding the second lag to the equation.
    B. changing the regression's independent variable.
    C. subtracting the independent variable from both sides of the equation.

31. Based on the regression output in Exhibit 2, what should lead Busse to conclude that the Regression 3 equation is not correctly specified?
    A. The Durbin–Watson statistic
    B. The *t*-statistic for the slope coefficient
    C. The *t*-statistics for the autocorrelations of the residual

32. Based on the regression output in Exhibit 3 and sales data in Exhibit 4, the forecasted value of quarterly sales for March 2016 for PoweredUP is *closest* to:
    A. $4.193 billion.
    B. $4.205 billion.
    C. $4.231 billion.

33. Based on Exhibit 5, Busse should conclude that the variance of the error terms for Company 1:
    A. is constant.
    B. can be predicted.
    C. is homoskedastic.

34. Based on Exhibit 5, for which company would the regression of stock prices on oil prices be expected to yield valid coefficients that could be used to estimate the long-term relationship between stock price and oil price?
    A. Company 1
    B. Company 2
    C. Company 3

35. Based on Exhibit 5, which single time-series model would *most likely* be appropriate for Busse to use in predicting the future stock price of Company 3?
    A. Log-linear trend model
    B. First-differenced AR(2) model
    C. First-differenced log AR(1) model

CHAPTER 10

MACHINE LEARNING

LEARNING OUTCOMES

The candidate should be able to:

- distinguish between supervised machine learning, unsupervised machine learning, and deep learning;
- describe overfitting and identify methods of addressing it;
- describe supervised machine learning algorithms—including penalized regression, support vector machine, k-nearest neighbor, classification and regression tree, ensemble learning, and random forest—and determine the problems for which they are best suited;
- describe unsupervised machine learning algorithms—including principal components analysis, k-means clustering, and hierarchical clustering—and determine the problems for which they are best suited;
- describe neural networks, deep learning nets, and reinforcement learning.

SUMMARY

Machine learning methods are gaining usage at many stages in the investment management value chain. Among the major points made are the following:

- Machine learning aims at extracting knowledge from large amounts of data by learning from known examples to determine an underlying structure in the data. The emphasis is on generating structure or predictions without human intervention. An elementary way to think of ML algorithms is to "find the pattern, apply the pattern."
- Supervised learning depends on having labeled training data as well as matched sets of observed inputs (Xs, or features) and the associated output (Y, or target). Supervised learning can be divided into two categories: regression and classification. If the target variable to be predicted is continuous, then the task is one of regression. If the target variable is categorical or ordinal (e.g., determining a firm's rating), then it is a classification problem.

- With unsupervised learning, algorithms are trained with no labeled data, so they must infer relations between features, summarize them, or present underlying structure in their distributions that has not been explicitly provided. Two important types of problems well suited to unsupervised ML are dimension reduction and clustering.
- In deep learning, sophisticated algorithms address complex tasks (e.g., image classification, natural language processing). Deep learning is based on neural networks, highly flexible ML algorithms for solving a variety of supervised and unsupervised tasks characterized by large datasets, non-linearities, and interactions among features. In reinforcement learning, a computer learns from interacting with itself or data generated by the same algorithm.
- Generalization describes the degree to which an ML model retains its explanatory power when predicting out-of-sample. Overfitting, a primary reason for lack of generalization, is the tendency of ML algorithms to tailor models to the training data at the expense of generalization to new data points.
- Bias error is the degree to which a model fits the training data. Variance error describes how much a model's results change in response to new data from validation and test samples. Base error is due to randomness in the data. Out-of-sample error equals bias error plus variance error plus base error.
- K-fold cross-validation is a technique for mitigating the holdout sample problem (excessive reduction of the training set size). The data (excluding test sample and fresh data) are shuffled randomly and then divided into k equal sub-samples, with $k - 1$ samples used as training samples and one sample, the kth, used as a validation sample.
- Regularization describes methods that reduce statistical variability in high-dimensional data estimation or prediction problems via reducing model complexity.
- LASSO (least absolute shrinkage and selection operator) is a popular type of penalized regression where the penalty term involves summing the absolute values of the regression coefficients. The greater the number of included features, the larger the penalty. So, a feature must make a sufficient contribution to model fit to offset the penalty from including it.
- Support vector machine (SVM) is a classifier that aims to seek the optimal hyperplane— the one that separates the two sets of data points by the maximum margin (and thus is typically used for classification).
- K-nearest neighbor (KNN) is a supervised learning technique most often used for classification. The idea is to classify a new observation by finding similarities ("nearness") between it and its k-nearest neighbors in the existing dataset.
- Classification and regression tree (CART) can be applied to predict either a categorical target variable, producing a classification tree, or a continuous target variable, producing a regression tree.
- A binary CART is a combination of an initial root node, decision nodes, and terminal nodes. The root node and each decision node represent a single feature (f) and a cutoff value (c) for that feature. The CART algorithm iteratively partitions the data into subgroups until terminal nodes are formed that contain the predicted label.
- Ensemble learning is a technique of combining the predictions from a collection of models. It typically produces more accurate and more stable predictions than any single model.
- A random forest classifier is a collection of many different decision trees generated by a bagging method or by randomly reducing the number of features available during training.

- Principal components analysis (PCA) is an unsupervised ML algorithm that reduces highly correlated features into fewer uncorrelated composite variables by transforming the feature covariance matrix. PCA produces eigenvectors that define the principal components (i.e., the new uncorrelated composite variables) and eigenvalues, which give the proportion of total variance in the initial data that is explained by each eigenvector and its associated principal component.
- *K*-means is an unsupervised ML algorithm that partitions observations into a fixed number (*k*) of non-overlapping clusters. Each cluster is characterized by its centroid, and each observation belongs to the cluster with the centroid to which that observation is closest.
- Hierarchical clustering is an unsupervised iterative algorithm that is used to build a hierarchy of clusters. Two main strategies are used to define the intermediary clusters (i.e., those clusters between the initial dataset and the final set of clustered data).
- Agglomerative (bottom-up) hierarchical clustering begins with each observation being its own cluster. Then, the algorithm finds the two closest clusters, defined by some measure of distance, and combines them into a new, larger cluster. This process is repeated until all observations are clumped into a single cluster.
- Divisive (top-down) hierarchical clustering starts with all observations belonging to a single cluster. The observations are then divided into two clusters based on some measure of distance. The algorithm then progressively partitions the intermediate clusters into smaller clusters until each cluster contains only one observation.
- Neural networks consist of nodes connected by links. They have three types of layers: an input layer, hidden layers, and an output layer. Learning takes place in the hidden layer nodes, each of which consists of a summation operator and an activation function. Neural networks have been successfully applied to a variety of investment tasks characterized by non-linearities and complex interactions among variables.
- Neural networks with many hidden layers (at least 2 but often more than 20) are known as deep neural networks (DNNs) and are the backbone of the artificial intelligence revolution.
- Reinforcement learning (RL) involves an agent that should perform actions that will maximize its rewards over time, taking into consideration the constraints of its environment.

PRACTICE PROBLEMS

The following information relates to Questions 1–10

Alef Associates manages a long-only fund specializing in global small-cap equities. Since its founding a decade ago, Alef maintains a portfolio of 100 stocks (out of an eligible universe of about 10,000 stocks). Some of these holdings are the result of screening the universe for attractive stocks based on several ratios that use readily available market and accounting data; others are the result of investment ideas generated by Alef's professional staff of five securities analysts and two portfolio managers.

Although Alef's investment performance has been good, its chief investment officer, Paul Moresanu, is contemplating a change in the investment process aimed at achieving even better returns. After attending multiple workshops and being approached by data vendors, Moresanu feels that data science should play a role in the way Alef selects its investments.

He has also noticed that much of Alef's past outperformance is due to stocks that became takeover targets. After some research and reflection, Moresanu writes the following email to the Alef's CEO.

Subject: Investment Process Reorganization

I have been thinking about modernizing the way we select stock investments. Given that our past success has put Alef Associates in an excellent financial position, now seems to be a good time to invest in our future. What I propose is that we continue managing a portfolio of 100 global small-cap stocks but restructure our process to benefit from machine learning (ML). Importantly, the new process will still allow a role for human insight, for example, in providing domain knowledge. In addition, I think we should make a special effort to identify companies that are likely to be acquired. Specifically, I suggest following the four steps which would be repeated every quarter.

Step 1. We apply ML techniques to a model including fundamental and technical variables (features) to predict next quarter's return for each of the 100 stocks currently in our portfolio. Then, the 20 stocks with the lowest estimated return are identified for replacement.

Step 2. We utilize ML techniques to divide our investable universe of about 10,000 stocks into 20 different groups, based on a wide variety of the most relevant financial and non-financial characteristics. The idea is to prevent unintended portfolio concentration by selecting stocks from each of these distinct groups.

Step 3. For each of the 20 different groups, we use labeled data to train a model that will predict the five stocks (in any given group) that are most likely to become acquisition targets in the next one year.

Step 4. Our five experienced securities analysts are each assigned four of the groups, and then each analyst selects their one best stock pick from each of their assigned groups. These 20 "high-conviction" stocks will be added to our portfolio (in replacement of the 20 relatively underperforming stocks to be sold in Step 1).

A couple of additional comments related to the above:

Comment 1. The ML algorithms will require large amounts of data. We would first need to explore using free or inexpensive historical datasets and then evaluate their usefulness for the ML-based stock selection processes before deciding on using data that requires subscription.

Comment 2. As time passes, we expect to find additional ways to apply ML techniques to refine Alef's investment processes.

What do you think?
Paul Moresanu

1. The machine learning techniques appropriate for executing Step 1 are *most* likely to be based on:
   A. regression
   B. classification
   C. clustering

2. Assuming regularization is utilized in the machine learning technique used for executing Step 1, which of the following ML models would be *least* appropriate:
   A. Regression tree with pruning.
   B. LASSO with lambda (λ) equal to 0.
   C. LASSO with lambda (λ) between 0.5 and 1.

3. Which of the following machine learning techniques is *most* appropriate for executing Step 2:
   A. K-Means Clustering
   B. Principal Components Analysis (PCA)
   C. Classification and Regression Trees (CART)

4. The hyperparameter in the ML model to be used for accomplishing Step 2 is?
   A. 100, the number of small-cap stocks in Alef's portfolio.
   B. 10,000, the eligible universe of small-cap stocks in which Alef can potentially invest.
   C. 20, the number of different groups (i.e. clusters) into which the eligible universe of small-cap stocks will be divided.

5. The target variable for the labelled training data to be used in Step 3 is *most* likely which one of the following?
   A. A continuous target variable.
   B. A categorical target variable.
   C. An ordinal target variable.

6. Comparing two ML models that could be used to accomplish Step 3, which statement(s) *best* describe(s) the advantages of using Classification and Regression Trees (CART) instead of K-Nearest Neighbor (KNN)?
   Statement I. For CART there is no requirement to specify an initial hyperparameter (like K).
   Statement II. For CART there is no requirement to specify a similarity (or distance) measure.
   Statement III. For CART the output provides a visual explanation for the prediction.
   A. Statement I only.
   B. Statement III only.
   C. Statements I, II and III.

7. Assuming a Classification and Regression Tree (CART) model is used to accomplish Step 3, which of the following is *most* likely to result in model overfitting?
   A. Using the k–fold cross-validation method
   B. Including an overfitting penalty (i.e., regularization term).
   C. Using a fitting curve to select a model with low bias error and high variance error.

8. Assuming a Classification and Regression Tree (CART) model is initially used to accomplish Step 3, as a further step which of the following techniques is most likely to result in more accurate predictions?

   A. Discarding CART and using the predictions of a Support Vector Machine (SVM) model instead.

   B. Discarding CART and using the predictions of a K-Nearest Neighbor (KNN) model instead.

   C. Combining the predictions of the CART model with the predictions of other models – such as logistic regression, SVM, and KNN – via ensemble learning.

9. Regarding Comment #2, Moresanu has been thinking about the applications of neural networks (NNs) and deep learning (DL) to investment management. Which statement(s) *best* describe(s) the tasks for which NNs and DL are well-suited?

   Statement I.   NNs and DL are well-suited for image and speech recognition, and natural language processing.

   Statement II.   NNs and DL are well-suited for developing single variable ordinary least squares regression models.

   Statement III. NNs and DL are well-suited for modelling non-linearities and complex interactions among many features.

   A. Statement II only.

   B. Statements I and III.

   C. Statements I, II and III.

10. Regarding neural networks (NNs) that Alef might potentially implement, which of the following statements is *least* accurate?

   A. NNs must have at least 10 hidden layers to be considered deep learning nets.

   B. The activation function in a node operates like a light dimmer switch since it decreases or increases the strength of the total net input.

   C. The summation operator receives input values, multiplies each by a weight, sums up the weighted values into the total net input, and passes it to the activation function.

CHAPTER 11

BIG DATA PROJECTS

LEARNING OUTCOMES

The candidate should be able to:

- state and explain steps in a data analysis project;
- describe objectives, steps, and examples of preparing and wrangling data;
- describe objectives, methods, and examples of data exploration;
- describe objectives, steps, and techniques in model training;
- describe preparing, wrangling, and exploring text-based data for financial forecasting;
- describe methods for extracting, selecting and engineering features from textual data;
- evaluate the fit of a machine learning algorithm.

SUMMARY

In this chapter, we have discussed the major steps in big data projects involving the development of machine learning (ML) models—namely, those combining textual big data with structured inputs.

- Big data—defined as data with volume, velocity, variety, and potentially lower veracity—has tremendous potential for various fintech applications, including several related to investment management.
- The main steps for traditional ML model building are conceptualization of the problem, data collection, data preparation and wrangling, data exploration, and model training.
- For textual ML model building, the first four steps differ somewhat from those used in the traditional model: Text problem formulation, text curation, text preparation and wrangling, and text exploration are typically necessary.
- For structured data, data preparation and wrangling entail data cleansing and data preprocessing. Data cleansing typically involves resolving incompleteness errors, invalidity errors, inaccuracy errors, inconsistency errors, non-uniformity errors, and duplication errors.

- Preprocessing for structured data typically involves performing the following transformations: extraction, aggregation, filtration, selection, and conversion.
- Preparation and wrangling text (unstructured) data involves a set of text-specific cleansing and preprocessing tasks. Text cleansing typically involves removing the following: html tags, punctuation, most numbers, and white spaces.
- Text preprocessing requires performing normalization that involves the following: lowercasing, removing stop words, stemming, lemmatization, creating bag of words (BOW) and n-grams, and organizing the BOW and n-grams into a document term matrix (DTM).
- Data exploration encompasses exploratory data analysis, feature selection, and feature engineering. Whereas histograms, box plots, and scatterplots are common techniques for exploring structured data, word clouds are an effective way to gain a high-level picture of the composition of textual content. These visualization tools help share knowledge among the team (business subject matter experts, quants, technologists, etc.) to help derive optimal solutions.
- Feature selection methods used for text data include term frequency, document frequency, chi-square test, and a mutual information measure. Feature engineering for text data includes converting numbers into tokens, creating n-grams, and using name entity recognition and parts of speech to engineer new feature variables.
- The model training steps (method selection, performance evaluation, and model tuning) often do not differ much for structured versus unstructured data projects.
- Model selection is governed by the following factors: whether the data project involves labeled data (supervised learning) or unlabeled data (unsupervised learning); the type of data (numerical, continuous, or categorical; text data; image data; speech data; etc.); and the size of the dataset.
- Model performance evaluation involves error analysis using confusion matrixes, determining receiver operating characteristics, and calculating root mean square error.
- To carry out an error analysis for each model, a confusion matrix is created; true positives (TPs), true negatives (TNs), false positives (FPs), and false negatives (FNs) are determined. Then, the following performance metrics are calculated: accuracy, F1 score, precision, and recall. The higher the accuracy and F1 score, the better the model performance.
- To carry out receiver operating characteristic (ROC) analysis, ROC curves and area under the curve (AUC) of various models are calculated and compared. The more convex the ROC curve and the higher the AUC, the better the model performance.
- Model tuning involves managing the trade-off between model bias error, associated with underfitting, and model variance error, associated with overfitting. A fitting curve of in-sample (training sample) error and out-of-sample (cross-validation sample) error on the y-axis versus model complexity on the x-axis is useful for managing the bias vs. variance error trade-off.
- In a real-world big data project involving text data analysis for classifying and predicting sentiment of financial text for particular stocks, the text data are transformed into structured data for populating the DTM, which is then used as the input for the ML algorithm.
- To derive term frequency (TF) at the sentence level and TF–IDF, both of which can be inputs to the DTM, the following frequency measures should be used to create a term frequency measures table: TotalWordsInSentence; TotalWordCount; TermFrequency (Collection Level); WordCountInSentence; SentenceCountWithWord; Document Frequency; and Inverse Document Frequency.

PRACTICE PROBLEMS

The following information relates to Questions 1–15

Aaliyah Schultz is a fixed-income portfolio manager at Aries Investments. Schultz supervises Ameris Steele, a junior analyst.

A few years ago, Schultz developed a proprietary machine learning (ML) model that aims to predict downgrades of publicly-traded firms by bond rating agencies. The model currently relies only on structured financial data collected from different sources. Schultz thinks the model's predictive power may be improved by incorporating sentiment data derived from textual analysis of news articles and Twitter content relating to the subject companies.

Schultz and Steele meet to discuss plans for incorporating the sentiment data into the model. They discuss the differences in the steps between building ML models that use traditional structured data and building ML models that use textual big data. Steele tells Schultz:

Statement 1:   The second step in building text-based ML models is text preparation and wrangling, whereas the second step in building ML models using structured data is data collection.

Statement 2:   The fourth step in building both types of models encompasses data/text exploration.

Steele expresses concern about using Twitter content in the model, noting that research suggests that as much as 10–15 percent of social media content is from fake accounts. Schultz tells Steele that she understands her concern but thinks the potential for model improvement outweighs the concern.

Steele begins building a model that combines the structured financial data and the sentiment data. She starts with cleansing and wrangling the raw structured financial data. Exhibit 1 presents a small sample of the raw dataset before cleansing: Each row represents data for a particular firm.

EXHIBIT 1   Sample of Raw Structured Data Before Cleansing

ID	Ticker	IPO Date	Industry (NAICS)	EBIT	Interest Expense	Total Debt
1	ABC	4/6/17	44	9.4	0.6	10.1
2	BCD	November 15, 2004	52	5.5	0.4	6.2
3	HIJ	26-Jun-74	54	8.9	1.2	15.8
4	KLM	14-Mar-15	72	5.7	1.5	0.0

After cleansing the data, Steele then preprocesses the dataset. She creates two new variables: an "Age" variable based on the firm's IPO date and an "Interest Coverage Ratio" variable equal to EBIT divided by interest expense. She also deletes the "IPO Date" variable from the dataset. After applying these transformations, Steele scales the financial data using normalization. She notes that over the full sample dataset, the "Interest Expense" variable ranges from a minimum of 0.2 and a maximum of 12.2, with a mean of 1.1 and a standard deviation of 0.4.

Steele and Schultz then discuss how to preprocess the raw text data. Steele tells Schultz that the process can be completed in the following three steps:

Step 1:   Cleanse the raw text data.
Step 2:   Split the cleansed data into a collection of words for them to be normalized.
Step 3:   Normalize the collection of words from Step 2 and create a distinct set of tokens from the normalized words.

With respect to Step 1, Steele tells Schultz:

"I believe I should remove all html tags, punctuation, numbers, and extra white spaces from the data before normalizing them."

After properly cleansing the raw text data, Steele completes Steps 2 and 3. She then performs exploratory data analysis. To assist in feature selection, she wants to create a visualization that shows the most informative words in the dataset based on their term frequency (TF) values. After creating and analyzing the visualization, Steele is concerned that some tokens are likely to be noise features for ML model training; therefore, she wants to remove them.

Steele and Schultz discuss the importance of feature selection and feature engineering in ML model training. Steele tells Schultz:

"Appropriate feature selection is a key factor in minimizing model overfitting, whereas feature engineering tends to prevent model underfitting."

Once satisfied with the final set of features, Steele selects and runs a model on the training set that classifies the text as having positive sentiment (Class "1" or negative sentiment (Class "0"). She then evaluates its performance using error analysis. The resulting confusion matrix is presented in Exhibit 2.

EXHIBIT 2   Confusion Matrix

		Actual Training Results	
		Class "1"	Class "0"
Predicted Results	Class "1"	TP = 182	FP = 52
	Class "0"	FN = 31	TN = 96

1. Which of Steele's statements relating to the steps in building structured data-based and text-based ML models is correct?
   A. Only Statement 1 is correct.
   B. Only Statement 2 is correct.
   C. Statement 1 and Statement 2 are correct.

2. Steele's concern about using Twitter data in the model *best* relates to:
   A. volume.
   B. velocity.
   C. veracity.

3. What type of error appears to be present in the IPO Date column of Exhibit 1?
   A. invalidity error.
   B. inconsistency error.
   C. non-uniformity error.

4. What type of error is most likely present in the last row of data (ID #4) in Exhibit 1?
   A. Inconsistency error
   B. Incompleteness error
   C. Non-uniformity error

5. During the preprocessing of the data in Exhibit 1, what type of data transformation did Steele perform during the data preprocessing step?
   A. Extraction
   B. Conversion
   C. Aggregation

6. Based on Exhibit 1, for the firm with ID #3, Steele should compute the scaled value for the "Interest Expense" variable as:
   A. 0.008.
   B. 0.083.
   C. 0.250.

7. Is Steele's statement regarding Step 1 of the preprocessing of raw text data correct?
   A. Yes.
   B. No, because her suggested treatment of punctuation is incorrect.
   C. No, because her suggested treatment of extra white spaces is incorrect.

8. Steele's Step 2 can be *best* described as:
   A. tokenization.
   B. lemmatization.
   C. standardization.

9. The output created in Steele's Step 3 can be *best* described as a:
   A. bag of words.
   B. set of n-grams.
   C. document term matrix.

10. Given her objective, the visualization that Steele should create in the exploratory data analysis step is a:
    A. scatter plot.
    B. word cloud.
    C. document term matrix.

11. To address her concern in her exploratory data analysis, Steele should focus on those tokens that have:
    A. low chi-square statistics.
    B. low mutual information (ML) values.
    C. very low and very high term frequency (TF) values.

12. Is Steele's statement regarding the relationship between feature selection/feature engineering and model fit correct?
    A. Yes.
    B. No, because she is incorrect with respect to feature selection.
    C. No, because she is incorrect with respect to feature engineering.

13. Based on Exhibit 2, the model's precision metric is *closest* to:
    A. 78 percent.
    B. 81 percent.
    C. 85 percent.

14. Based on Exhibit 2, the model's F1 score is *closest* to:
    A. 77 percent.
    B. 81 percent.
    C. 85 percent.

15. Based on Exhibit 2, the model's accuracy metric is *closest* to:
    A. 77 percent.
    B. 81 percent.
    C. 85 percent.

The following information relates to Questions 16–22

Iesha Azarov is a senior analyst at Ganymede Moon Partners (Ganymede), where he works with junior analyst Pàola Bector. Azarov would like to incorporate machine learning (ML) models into the company's analytical process. Azarov asks Bector to develop ML models for two unstructured stock sentiment datasets, Dataset ABC and Dataset XYZ. Both datasets have been cleaned and preprocessed in preparation for text exploration and model training.

Following an exploratory data analysis that revealed Dataset ABC's most frequent tokens, Bector conducts a collection frequency analysis. Bector then computes TF–IDF (term frequency–inverse document frequency) for several words in the collection and tells Azarov the following:

Statement 1: IDF is equal to the inverse of the document frequency measure.
Statement 2: TF at the collection level is multiplied by IDF to calculate TF–IDF.
Statement 3: TF–IDF values vary by the number of documents in the dataset, and there-fore, model performance can vary when applied to a dataset with just a few documents.

Bector notes that Dataset ABC is characterized by the absence of ground truth.

Bector turns his attention to Dataset XYZ, containing 84,000 tokens and 10,000 sen-tences. Bector chooses an appropriate feature selection method to identify and remove unnecessary tokens from the dataset and then focuses on model training. For performance evaluation purposes, Dataset XYZ is split into a training set, cross-validation (CV) set, and test set. Each of the sentences has already been labeled as either a positive sentiment (Class "1") or a negative sentiment (Class "0") sentence. There is an unequal class distribution between the positive sentiment and negative sentiment sentences in Dataset XYZ. Simple random sampling is applied within levels of the sentiment class labels to balance the class distributions within the splits. Bector's view is that the false positive and false negative eval-uation metrics should be given equal weight. Select performance data from the cross-valida-tion set confusion matrices is presented in Exhibit 1:

EXHIBIT 1   Performance Metrics for Dataset XYZ

Confusion Matrix	CV Data (threshold *p*-value)	Performance Metrics			
		Precision	Recall	F1 Score	Accuracy
A	0.50	0.95	0.87	0.91	0.91
B	0.35	0.93	0.90	0.91	0.92
C	0.65	0.86	0.97	0.92	0.91

Azarov and Bector evaluate the Dataset XYZ performance metrics for Confusion Matrices A, B, and C in Exhibit 1. Azarov says, "For Ganymede's purposes, we should be most concerned with the cost of Type I errors."

Azarov requests that Bector apply the ML model to the test dataset for Dataset XYZ, assuming a threshold *p*-value of 0.65. Exhibit 2 contains a sample of results from the test dataset corpus.

EXHIBIT 2   10 Sample Results of Test Data for Dataset XYZ

Sentence #	Actual Sentiment	Target *p*-Value
1	1	0.75
2	0	0.45
3	1	0.64
4	1	0.81
5	0	0.43
6	1	0.78
7	0	0.59
8	1	0.60
9	0	0.67
10	0	0.54

Bector makes the following remarks regarding model training:

Remark 1: Method selection is governed by such factors as the type of data and the size of data.
Remark 2: In the performance evaluation stage, model fitting errors, such as bias error and variance error, are used to measure goodness of fit.

16. Based on the text exploration method used for Dataset ABC, tokens that potentially carry important information useful for differentiating the sentiment embedded in the text are *most likely* to have values that are:
    A. low.
    B. intermediate.
    C. high.

Quantitative Investment Analysis

17. Which of Bector's statements regarding TF, IDF, and TF–IDF is correct?
    A. Statement 1
    B. Statement 2
    C. Statement 3

18. What percentage of Dataset ABC should be allocated to a training subset?
    A. 0 percent
    B. 20 percent
    C. 60 percent

19. Based only on Dataset XYZ's composition and Bector's view regarding false positive and false negative evaluation metrics, which performance measure is *most appropriate*?
    A. Recall
    B. F1 score
    C. Precision

20. Based on Exhibit 1, which confusion matrix demonstrates the *most* favorable value of the performance metric that *best* addresses Azarov's concern?
    A. Confusion Matrix A
    B. Confusion Matrix B
    C. Confusion Matrix C

21. Based on Exhibit 2, the accuracy metric for Dataset XYZ's test set sample is *closest to*:
    A. 0.67.
    B. 0.70.
    C. 0.75.

22. Which of Bector's remarks related to model training is correct?
    A. Only Remark 1
    B. Only Remark 2
    C. Both Remark 1 and Remark 2

The following information relates to Questions 23–31

Bernadette Rivera is a portfolio manager at Voxkor, a private equity company that provides financing to early-stage start-up businesses. Rivera is working with a data analyst, Tim Achler, on a text-based machine-learning (ML) model to enhance Voxkor's predictive ability to identify successful start-ups.

Voxkor currently uses ML models based only on traditional, structured financial data but would like to develop a new ML model that analyzes textual big data gathered from the internet. The model will classify text information into positive or negative sentiment classes for each respective start-up. Rivera wants to confirm her understanding of any differences in the ML model building steps between data analysis projects that use traditional structured data and projects that involve unstructured, text-based data. Rivera makes the following statements:

Statement 1: Some of the methods used in the exploration step are different for structured and unstructured data, but for both types of data, the step involves feature selection and feature engineering.

Statement 2:   A major difference when developing a text-based ML model is the curation step, which involves cleansing, preprocessing, and converting the data into a structured format usable for model training.

Achler uses a web spidering program to obtain the data for the text-based model. The program extracts raw content from social media webpages, which contains English language sentences and special characters. After curating the text, Achler removes unnecessary elements from the raw text using regular expression software and completes additional text cleansing and preprocessing tasks.

Next, Achler and Rivera discuss remaining text wrangling tasks—specifically, which tokens to include in the document term matrix (DTM). Achler divides unique tokens into three groups; a sample of each group is shown in Exhibit 1.

EXHIBIT 1   Summary of Sample Tokens

Token Group 1	Token Group 2	Token Group 3
"not_increas_market"	"not_increased_market"	"not," "increased," "market"
"currencysign"	"currencysign"	"EUR"
"sale_decreas"	"sale_decreased"	"Sales," "decreased"

The dataset is now ready for the text exploration step. At this point in the process, Rivera wants to better comprehend the collection of unique words. Achler recommends an exploratory data analysis technique that visualizes words by varying their font size proportionately to the number of occurrences of each word in the corpus.

As an additional part of the text exploration step, Achler conducts a term frequency analysis to identify outliers. Achler summarizes the analysis in Exhibit 2.

EXHIBIT 2   Words with Highest and Lowest Frequency Value

Group 1		Group 2	
Word	Frequency	Word	Frequency
the	0.04935	naval	1.0123e-05
and	0.04661	stereotype	1.5185e-05
to	0.04179	till	1.5185e-05
that	0.03577	ribbon	2.0247e-05
in	0.03368	deposit	2.5308e-05

Note: "e-05" represents 10^{-5}.

Achler has the data ready for the model training process. Rivera asks Achler to include start-up failure rates as a feature. Achler notices that the number of start-ups that fail (majority class) is significantly larger than the number of the start-ups that are successful (minority class). Achler is concerned that because of class imbalance, the model will not be able to discriminate between start-ups that fail and start-ups that are successful.

Achler splits the DTM into training, cross-validation, and test datasets. Achler uses a supervised learning approach to train the logistic regression model in predicting sentiment. Applying the receiver operating characteristics (ROC) technique and area under the curve (AUC) metrics, Achler evaluates model performance on both the training and the cross-validation datasets. The trained model performance for three different logistic regressions' threshold p-values is presented in Exhibit 3.

EXHIBIT 3   AUC for Different Threshold p-values

Threshold p-Value	Training Set	Cross-Validation Set
$p = 0.57$	56.7%	57.3%
$p = 0.79$	91.3%	89.7%
$p = 0.84$	98.4%	87.1%

Rivera suggests adjusting the model's hyperparameters to improve performance. Achler runs a grid search that compares the difference between the prediction error on both the training and the cross-validation datasets for various combinations of hyperparameter values. For the current values of hyperparameters, Achler observes that the prediction error on the training dataset is small, whereas the prediction error on the cross-validation dataset is significantly larger.

23. Which of Rivera's statements about differences in ML model building steps is correct?
     A. Only Statement 1
     B. Only Statement 2
     C. Both Statement 1 and Statement 2

24. Based on the source of the data, as part of the data cleansing and wrangling process, Achler *most likely* needs to remove:
     A. html tags and perform scaling.
     B. numbers and perform lemmatization.
     C. white spaces and perform winsorization.

25. Based on Exhibit 1, which token group has *most likely* undergone the text preparation and wrangling process?
     A. Token Group 1
     B. Token Group 2
     C. Token Group 3

26. The visual text representation technique that Achler recommends to Rivera is a:
     A. word cloud.
     B. bag of words.
     C. collection frequency.

27. Based on Exhibit 2, Achler should exclude from further analysis words in:
     A. only Group 1.
     B. only Group 2.
     C. both Group 1 and Group 2.

28. Achler's model training concern related to the model's ability to discriminate could be addressed by randomly:
    A. oversampling the failed start-up data.
    B. oversampling the successful start-up data.
    C. undersampling the successful start-up data.

29. Based on Exhibit 3, which threshold *p*-value indicates the *best* fitting model?
    A. 0.57
    B. 0.79
    C. 0.84

30. Based on Exhibit 3, if Achler wants to improve model performance at the threshold *p*-value of 0.84, he should:
    A. tune the model to lower the AUC.
    B. adjust model parameters to decrease ROC convexity.
    C. apply LASSO regularization to the logistic regression.

31. Based on Achler's grid search analysis, the current model can be characterized as:
    A. underfitted.
    B. having low variance.
    C. exhibiting slight regularization.

CHAPTER 12

USING MULTIFACTOR MODELS

LEARNING OUTCOMES

The candidate should be able to:

- describe arbitrage pricing theory (APT), including its underlying assumptions and its relation to multifactor models;
- define arbitrage opportunity and determine whether an arbitrage opportunity exists;
- calculate the expected return on an asset given an asset's factor sensitivities and the factor risk premiums;
- describe and compare macroeconomic factor models, fundamental factor models, and statistical factor models;
- explain sources of active risk and interpret tracking risk and the information ratio;
- describe uses of multifactor models and interpret the output of analyses based on multifactor models;
- describe the potential benefits for investors in considering multiple risk dimensions when modeling asset returns.

SUMMARY

In our coverage of multifactor models, we have presented concepts, models, and tools that are key ingredients to quantitative portfolio management and are used to both construct portfolios and to attribute sources of risk and return.

- Multifactor models permit a nuanced view of risk that is more granular than the single-factor approach allows.

- Multifactor models describe the return on an asset in terms of the risk of the asset with respect to a set of factors. Such models generally include systematic factors, which explain the average returns of a large number of risky assets. Such factors represent priced risk—risk for which investors require an additional return for bearing.
- The arbitrage pricing theory (APT) describes the expected return on an asset (or portfolio) as a linear function of the risk of the asset with respect to a set of factors. Like the CAPM, the APT describes a financial market equilibrium; however, the APT makes less strong assumptions.
- The major assumptions of the APT are as follows:
  - Asset returns are described by a factor model.
  - With many assets to choose from, asset-specific risk can be eliminated.
  - Assets are priced such that there are no arbitrage opportunities.

- Multifactor models are broadly categorized according to the type of factor used:
  - Macroeconomic factor models
  - Fundamental factor models
  - Statistical factor models

- In *macroeconomic* factor models, the factors are surprises in macroeconomic variables that significantly explain asset class (equity in our examples) returns. Surprise is defined as actual minus forecasted value and has an expected value of zero. The factors can be understood as affecting either the expected future cash flows of companies or the interest rate used to discount these cash flows back to the present and are meant to be uncorrelated.
- In *fundamental* factor models, the factors are attributes of stocks or companies that are important in explaining cross-sectional differences in stock prices. Among the fundamental factors are book-value-to-price ratio, market capitalization, price-to-earnings ratio, and financial leverage.
- In contrast to macroeconomic factor models, in fundamental models the factors are calculated as returns rather than surprises. In fundamental factor models, we generally specify the factor sensitivities (attributes) first and then estimate the factor returns through regressions. In macroeconomic factor models, however, we first develop the factor (surprise) series and then estimate the factor sensitivities through regressions. The factors of most fundamental factor models may be classified as company fundamental factors, company share-related factors, or macroeconomic factors.
- In *statistical* factor models, statistical methods are applied to a set of historical returns to determine portfolios that explain historical returns in one of two senses. In factor analysis models, the factors are the portfolios that best explain (reproduce) historical return covariances. In principal components models, the factors are portfolios that best explain (reproduce) the historical return variances.
- Multifactor models have applications to return attribution, risk attribution, portfolio construction, and strategic investment decisions.
- A factor portfolio is a portfolio with unit sensitivity to a factor and zero sensitivity to other factors.
- Active return is the return in excess of the return on the benchmark.
- Active risk is the standard deviation of active returns. Active risk is also called tracking error or tracking risk. Active risk squared can be decomposed as the sum of active factor risk and active specific risk.

- The information ratio (IR) is mean active return divided by active risk (tracking error). The IR measures the increment in mean active return per unit of active risk.
- Factor models have uses in constructing portfolios that track market indexes and in alternative index construction.
- Traditionally, the CAPM approach would allocate assets between the risk-free asset and a broadly diversified index fund. Considering multiple sources of systematic risk may allow investors to improve on that result by tilting away from the market portfolio. Generally, investors would gain from accepting above average (below average) exposures to risks that they have a comparative advantage (comparative disadvantage) in bearing.

PRACTICE PROBLEMS

1. Compare the assumptions of the arbitrage pricing theory (APT) with those of the capital asset pricing model (CAPM).
2. Last year the return on Harry Company stock was 5 percent. The portion of the return on the stock not explained by a two-factor macroeconomic factor model was 3 percent. Using the data given below, calculate Harry Company stock's expected return.

Macroeconomic Factor Model for Harry Company Stock

Variable	Actual Value (%)	Expected Value (%)	Stock's Factor Sensitivity
Change in interest rate	2.0	0.0	−1.5
Growth in GDP	1.0	4.0	2.0

3. Assume that the following one-factor model describes the expected return for portfolios:

$$E(R_p) = 0.10 + 0.12\beta_{p,1}$$

Also assume that all investors agree on the expected returns and factor sensitivity of the three highly diversified Portfolios A, B, and C given in the following table:

Portfolio	Expected Return	Factor Sensitivity
A	0.20	0.80
B	0.15	1.00
C	0.24	1.20

Assuming the one-factor model is correct and based on the data provided for Portfolios A, B, and C, determine if an arbitrage opportunity exists and explain how it might be exploited.

4. Which type of factor model is most directly applicable to an analysis of the style orientation (for example, growth vs. value) of an active equity investment manager? Justify your answer.

5. Suppose an active equity manager has earned an active return of 110 basis points, of which 80 basis points is the result of security selection ability. Explain the likely source of the remaining 30 basis points of active return.

6. Address the following questions about the information ratio.
   A. What is the information ratio of an index fund that effectively meets its investment objective?
   B. What are the two types of risk an active investment manager can assume in seeking to increase his information ratio?

7. A wealthy investor has no other source of income beyond her investments and that income is expected to reliably meet all her needs. Her investment advisor recommends that she tilt her portfolio to cyclical stocks and high-yield bonds. Explain the advisor's advice in terms of comparative advantage in bearing risk.

The following information relates to Questions 8–13

Carlos Altuve is a manager-of-managers at an investment company that uses quantitative models extensively. Altuve seeks to construct a multi-manager portfolio using some of the funds managed by portfolio managers within the firm. Maya Zapata is assisting him.

Altuve uses arbitrage pricing theory (APT) as a basis for evaluating strategies and managing risks. From his earlier analysis, Zapata knows that Funds A and B in Exhibit 1 are well diversified. He has not previously worked with Fund C and is puzzled by the data because it is inconsistent with APT. He asks Zapata gather additional information on Fund C's holdings and to determine if an arbitrage opportunity exists among these three investment alternatives. Her analysis, using the data in Exhibit 1, confirms that an arbitrage opportunity does exist.

EXHIBIT 1   Expected Returns and Factor Sensitivities (One-Factor Model)

Fund	Expected Return	Factor Sensitivity
A	0.02	0.5
B	0.04	1.5
C	0.03	0.9

Using a two-factor model, Zapata now estimates the three funds' sensitivity to inflation and GDP growth. That information is presented in Exhibit 2. Zapata assumes a zero value for the error terms when working with the selected two-factor model.

EXHIBIT 2   Expected Returns and Factor Sensitivities (Two-Factor Model)

Fund	Expected Return	Factor Sensitivity	
		Inflation	GDP Growth
A	0.02	0.5	1.0
B	0.04	1.6	0.0
C	0.03	1.0	1.1

Altuve asks Zapata to calculate the return for Portfolio AC, composed of a 60 percent allocation to Fund A and 40 percent allocation to Fund C, using the surprises in inflation and GDP growth in Exhibit 3.

EXHIBIT 3   Selected Data on Factors

Factor	Research Staff Forecast	Actual Value
Inflation	2.0%	2.2%
GDP Growth	1.5%	1.0%

Finally, Altuve asks Zapata about the return sensitivities of Portfolios A, B, and C given the information provided in Exhibit 3.

8. Which of the following is *not* a key assumption of APT, which is used by Altuve to evaluate strategies and manage risks?
   A. A factor model describes asset returns.
   B. Asset-specific risk can be eliminated through diversification.
   C. Arbitrage opportunities exist among well-diversified portfolios.

9. The arbitrage opportunity identified by Zapata can be exploited with:
   A. Strategy 1: Buy $50,000 Fund A and $50,000 Fund B; sell short $100,000 Fund C.
   B. Strategy 2: Buy $60,000 Fund A and $40,000 Fund B; sell short $100,000 Fund C.
   C. Strategy 3: Sell short $60,000 of Fund A and $40,000 of Fund B; buy $100,000 Fund

10. The two-factor model Zapata uses is a:
    A. statistical factor model.
    B. fundamental factor model.
    C. macroeconomic factor model.

11. Based on the data in Exhibits 2 and 3, the return for Portfolio AC, given the surprises in inflation and GDP growth, is *closest* to:
    A. 2.02 percent.
    B. 2.40 percent.
    C. 4.98 percent.

12. The surprise in which of the following had the greatest effect on fund returns?
    A. Inflation on Fund B
    B. GDP growth on Fund A
    C. GDP growth on Fund C

13. Based on the data in Exhibit 2, which fund is most sensitive to the combined surprises in inflation and GDP growth in Exhibit 3?
    A. Fund A
    B. Fund B
    C. Fund C

The following information relates to Questions 14–19

Hui Cheung, a portfolio manager, asks her assistant, Ronald Lam, to review the macroeconomic factor model currently in use and to consider a fundamental factor model as an alternative.

The current macroeconomic factor model has four factors:

$$R_i = a_i + b_{i1}F_{GDP} + b_{i2}F_{CAP} + b_{i3}F_{CON} + b_{i4}F_{UNEM} + \varepsilon_i$$

where F_{GDP}, F_{CAP}, F_{CON}, and F_{UNEM} represent unanticipated changes in four factors: gross domestic product, manufacturing capacity utilization, consumer spending, and the rate of unemployment, respectively. Lam assumes the error term is equal to zero when using this model.

Lam estimates the current model using historical monthly returns for three portfolios for the most recent five years. The inputs used in and estimates derived from the macroeconomic factor model are presented in Exhibit 1. The US Treasury bond rate of 2.5 percent is used as a proxy for the risk-free rate of interest.

EXHIBIT 1   Inputs for and Estimates from the Current Macroeconomic Model

Factor	Factor Sensitivities and Intercept Coefficients				Factor Surprise (%)
	Portfolio 1	Portfolio 2	Portfolio 3	Benchmark	
Intercept (%)	2.58	3.20	4.33		
F_{GDP}	0.75	1.00	0.24	0.50	0.8
F_{CAP}	−0.23	0.00	−1.45	−1.00	0.5
F_{CON}	1.23	0.00	0.50	1.10	2.5
F_{UNEM}	−0.14	0.00	−0.05	−0.10	1.0
Annual Returns, Most Recent Year					
Return (%)	6.00	4.00	5.00	4.50	

Lam uses the macroeconomic model to calculate the tracking error and the mean active return for each portfolio. He presents these statistics in Exhibit 2.

EXHIBIT 2   Macroeconomic Factor Model Tracking Error and Mean Active Return

Portfolio	Tracking Error	Mean Active Return
Portfolio 1	1.50%	1.50%
Portfolio 2	1.30%	−0.50%
Portfolio 3	1.00%	0.50%

Lam considers a fundamental factor model with four factors:

$$R_i = a_j + b_{j1}F_{LIQ} + b_{j2}F_{LEV} + b_{j3}F_{EGR} + b_{j4}F_{VAR} + \varepsilon_j$$

where F_{LIQ}, F_{LEV}, F_{EGR}, and F_{VAR} represent liquidity, financial leverage, earnings growth, and the variability of revenues, respectively.

Lam and Cheung discuss similarities and differences between macroeconomic factor models and fundamental factor models, and Lam offers a comparison of those models to statistical factor models. Lam makes the following statements.

Statement 1.   The factors in fundamental factor models are based on attributes of stocks or companies, whereas the factors in macroeconomic factor models are based on surprises in economic variables.

Statement 2.   The factor sensitivities are generally determined first in fundamental factor models, whereas the factor sensitivities are estimated last in macroeconomic factor models.

Lam also tells Cheung: "An advantage of statistical factor models is that they make minimal assumptions, and therefore, statistical factor model estimation lends itself to easier interpretation than macroeconomic and fundamental factor models."

Lam tells Cheung that multifactor models can be useful in active portfolio management, but not in passive management. Cheung disagrees; she tells Lam that multifactor models can be useful in both active and passive management.

14. Based on the information in Exhibit 1, the expected return for Portfolio 1 is *closest* to:
    A.   2.58 percent.
    B.   3.42 percent.
    C.   6.00 percent.

15. Based on Exhibit 1, the active risk for Portfolio 2 is explained by surprises in:
    A.   GDP.
    B.   consumer spending.
    C.   all four model factors.

16. Based on Exhibit 2, which portfolio has the best information ratio?
    A.   Portfolio 1
    B.   Portfolio 2
    C.   Portfolio 3

17. Which of Lam's statements regarding macroeconomic factor models and fundamental factor models is correct?
    A.   Only Statement 1
    B.   Only Statement 2
    C.   Both Statements 1 and 2

18. Is Lam's comment regarding statistical factor models correct?
    A.   Yes
    B.   No, because he is incorrect with respect to interpretation of the models' results
    C.   No, because he is incorrect with respect to the models' assumptions

19. Whose statement regarding the use of multifactor models in active and passive portfolio management is correct?
    A.   Lam only
    B.   Cheung only
    C.   Both Lam and Cheung

CHAPTER 13

MEASURING AND MANAGING MARKET RISK

LEARNING OUTCOMES

The candidate should be able to:

- explain the use of value at risk (VaR) in measuring portfolio risk;
- compare the parametric (variance–covariance), historical simulation, and Monte Carlo simulation methods for estimating VaR;
- estimate and interpret VaR under the parametric, historical simulation, and Monte Carlo simulation methods;
- describe advantages and limitations of VaR;
- describe extensions of VaR;
- describe sensitivity risk measures and scenario risk measures and compare these measures to VaR;
- demonstrate how equity, fixed-income, and options exposure measures may be used in measuring and managing market risk and volatility risk;
- describe the use of sensitivity risk measures and scenario risk measures;
- describe advantages and limitations of sensitivity risk measures and scenario risk measures;
- explain constraints used in managing market risks, including risk budgeting, position limits, scenario limits, and stop-loss limits;
- explain how risk measures may be used in capital allocation decisions;
- describe risk measures used by banks, asset managers, pension funds, and insurers.

SUMMARY

This chapter on market risk management models covers various techniques used to manage the risk arising from market fluctuations in prices and rates. The key points are summarized as follows:

- Value at risk (VaR) is the minimum loss in either currency units or as a percentage of portfolio value that would be expected to be incurred a certain percentage of the time over a certain period of time given assumed market conditions.
- VaR requires the decomposition of portfolio performance into risk factors.
- The three methods of estimating VaR are the parametric method, the historical simulation method, and the Monte Carlo simulation method.
- The parametric method of VaR estimation typically provides a VaR estimate from the left tail of a normal distribution, incorporating the expected returns, variances, and covariances of the components of the portfolio.
- The parametric method exploits the simplicity of the normal distribution but provides a poor estimate of VaR when returns are not normally distributed, as might occur when a portfolio contains options.
- The historical simulation method of VaR estimation uses historical return data on the portfolio's current holdings and allocation.
- The historical simulation method has the advantage of incorporating events that actually occurred and does not require the specification of a distribution or the estimation of parameters, but it is only useful to the extent that the future resembles the past.
- The Monte Carlo simulation method of VaR estimation requires the specification of a statistical distribution of returns and the generation of random outcomes from that distribution.
- The Monte Carlo simulation method is extremely flexible but can be complex and time consuming to use.
- There is no single right way to estimate VaR.
- The advantages of VaR include the following: It is a simple concept; it is relatively easy to understand and easily communicated, capturing much information in a single number. It can be useful in comparing risks across asset classes, portfolios, and trading units and, as such, facilitates capital allocation decisions. It can be used for performance evaluation and can be verified by using backtesting. It is widely accepted by regulators.
- The primary limitations of VaR are that it is a subjective measure and highly sensitive to numerous discretionary choices made in the course of computation. It can underestimate the frequency of extreme events. It fails to account for the lack of liquidity and is sensitive to correlation risk. It is vulnerable to trending or volatility regimes and is often misunderstood as a worst-case scenario. It can oversimplify the picture of risk and focuses heavily on the left tail.
- There are numerous variations and extensions of VaR, including conditional VaR (CVaR), incremental VaR (IVaR), and marginal VaR (MVaR), that can provide additional useful information.
- Conditional VaR is the average loss conditional on exceeding the VaR cutoff.
- Incremental VaR measures the change in portfolio VaR as a result of adding or deleting a position from the portfolio or if a position size is changed relative to the remaining positions.
- MVaR measures the change in portfolio VaR given a small change in the portfolio position. In a diversified portfolio, MVaRs can be summed to determine the contribution of each asset to the overall VaR.
- *Ex ante* tracking error measures the degree to which the performance of a given investment portfolio might deviate from its benchmark.
- Sensitivity measures quantify how a security or portfolio will react if a single risk factor changes. Common sensitivity measures are beta for equities; duration and convexity for bonds; and delta, gamma, and vega for options. Sensitivity measures do not indicate which portfolio has greater loss potential.

- Risk managers can use deltas, gammas, vegas, durations, convexities, and betas to get a comprehensive picture of the sensitivity of the entire portfolio.
- Stress tests apply extreme negative stress to a particular portfolio exposure.
- Scenario measures, including stress tests, are risk models that evaluate how a portfolio will perform under certain high-stress market conditions.
- Scenario measures can be based on actual historical scenarios or on hypothetical scenarios.
- Historical scenarios are scenarios that measure the portfolio return that would result from a repeat of a particular period of financial market history.
- Hypothetical scenarios model the impact of extreme movements and co-movements in different markets that have not previously occurred.
- Reverse stress testing is the process of stressing the portfolio's most significant exposures.
- Sensitivity and scenario risk measures can complement VaR. They do not need to rely on history, and scenarios can be designed to overcome an assumption of normal distributions.
- Limitations of scenario measures include the following: Historical scenarios are unlikely to re-occur in exactly the same way. Hypothetical scenarios may incorrectly specify how assets will co-move and thus may get the magnitude of movements wrong. And, it is difficult to establish appropriate limits on a scenario analysis or stress test.
- Constraints are widely used in risk management in the form of risk budgets, position limits, scenario limits, stop-loss limits, and capital allocation.
- Risk budgeting is the allocation of the total risk appetite across sub-portfolios.
- A scenario limit is a limit on the estimated loss for a given scenario, which, if exceeded, would require corrective action in the portfolio.
- A stop-loss limit either requires a reduction in the size of a portfolio or its complete liquidation (when a loss of a particular size occurs in a specified period).
- Position limits are limits on the market value of any given investment.
- Risk measurements and constraints in and of themselves are not restrictive or unrestrictive; it is the limits placed on the measures that drive action.
- The degree of leverage, the mix of risk factors to which the business is exposed, and accounting or regulatory requirements influence the types of risk measures used by different market participants.
- Banks use risk tools to assess the extent of any liquidity and asset/liability mismatch, the probability of losses in their investment portfolios, their overall leverage ratio, interest rate sensitivities, and the risk to economic capital.
- Asset managers' use of risk tools focuses primarily on volatility, probability of loss, or the probability of underperforming a benchmark.
- Pension funds use risk measures to evaluate asset/liability mismatch and surplus at risk.
- Property and casualty insurers use sensitivity and exposure measures to ensure exposures remain within defined asset allocation ranges. They use economic capital and VaR measures to estimate the impairment in the event of a catastrophic loss. They use scenario analysis to stress the market risks and insurance risks simultaneously.
- Life insurers use risk measures to assess the exposures of the investment portfolio and the annuity liability, the extent of any asset/liability mismatch, and the potential stress losses based on the differences between the assets in which they have invested and the liabilities resulting from the insurance contracts they have written.

PRACTICE PROBLEMS

The following information relates to Questions 1–5.

Randy Gorver, chief risk officer at Eastern Regional Bank, and John Abell, assistant risk officer, are currently conducting a risk assessment of several of the bank's independent investment functions. These reviews include the bank's fixed-income investment portfolio and an equity fund managed by the bank's trust department. Gorver and Abell are also assessing Eastern Regional's overall risk exposure.

Eastern Regional Bank Fixed-Income Investment Portfolio
The bank's proprietary fixed-income portfolio is structured as a barbell portfolio: About half of the portfolio is invested in zero-coupon Treasuries with maturities in the 3- to 5-year range (Portfolio P_1), and the remainder is invested in zero-coupon Treasuries with maturities in the 10- to 15-year range (Portfolio P_2). Georges Montes, the portfolio manager, has discretion to allocate between 40 percent and 60 percent of the assets to each maturity bucket. He must remain fully invested at all times. Exhibit 1 shows details of this portfolio.

EXHIBIT 1   US Treasury Barbell Portfolio

	Maturity	
	P_1	P_2
	3–5 Years	10–15 Years
Average duration	3.30	11.07
Average yield to maturity	1.45%	2.23%
Market value	$50.3 million	$58.7 million

Trust Department's Equity Fund
a. **Use of Options:** The trust department of Eastern Regional Bank manages an equity fund called the Index Plus Fund, with $325 million in assets. This fund's objective is to track the S&P 500 Index price return while producing an income return 1.5 times that of the S&P 500. The bank's chief investment officer (CIO) uses put and call options on S&P 500 stock index futures to adjust the risk exposure of certain client accounts that have an investment in this fund. The portfolio of a 60-year-old widow with a below-average risk tolerance has an investment in this fund, and the CIO has asked his assistant, Janet Ferrell, to propose an options strategy to bring the portfolio's delta to 0.90.
b. **Value at Risk:** The Index Plus Fund has a value at risk (VaR) of $6.5 million at 5 percent for one day. Gorver asks Abell to write a brief summary of the portfolio VaR for the report he is preparing on the fund's risk position.

Combined Bank Risk Exposures

The bank has adopted a new risk policy, which requires forward-looking risk assessments in addition to the measures that look at historical risk characteristics. Management has also become very focused on tail risk since the subprime crisis and is evaluating the bank's capital allocation to certain higher-risk lines of business. Gorver must determine what additional risk metrics to include in his risk reporting to address the new policy. He asks Abell to draft a section of the risk report that will address the risk measures' adequacy for capital allocation decisions.

1. If Montes is expecting a 50 bp increase in yields at all points along the yield curve, which of the following trades is he *most likely* to execute to minimize his risk?
   A. Sell $35 million of P_2 and reinvest the proceeds in three-year bonds
   B. Sell $15 million of P_2 and reinvest the proceeds in three-year bonds
   C. Reduce the duration of P_2 to 10 years and reduce the duration of P_1 to 3 years

2. Which of the following options strategies is Ferrell *most likely* to recommend for the client's portfolio?
   A. Long calls
   B. Short calls
   C. Short puts

3. Which of the following statements regarding the VaR of the Index Plus Fund is correct?
   A. The expected maximum loss for the portfolio is $6.5 million.
   B. Five percent of the time, the portfolio can be expected to experience a loss of at least $6.5 million.
   C. Ninety-five percent of the time, the portfolio can be expected to experience a one-day loss of no more than $6.5 million.

4. To comply with the new bank policy on risk assessment, which of the following is the *best* set of risk measures to add to the chief risk officer's risk reporting?
   A. Conditional VaR, stress test, and scenario analysis
   B. Monte Carlo VaR, incremental VaR, and stress test
   C. Parametric VaR, marginal VaR, and scenario analysis

5. Which of the following statements should *not* be included in Abell's report to management regarding the use of risk measures in capital allocation decisions?
   A. VaR measures capture the increased liquidity risk during stress periods.
   B. Stress tests and scenario analysis can be used to evaluate the effect of outlier events on each line of business.
   C. VaR approaches that can accommodate a non-normal distribution are critical to understand relative risk across lines of business.

The following information relates to Questions 6–11.

Hiram Life (Hiram), a large multinational insurer located in Canada, has received permission to increase its ownership in an India-based life insurance company, LICIA, from 26 percent to 49 percent. Before completing this transaction, Hiram wants to complete a risk assessment of LICIA's investment portfolio. Judith Hamilton, Hiram's chief financial officer, has been asked to brief the management committee on investment risk in its India-based insurance operations.

LICIA's portfolio, which has a market value of CAD260 million, is currently structured as shown in Exhibit 1. Despite its more than 1,000 individual holdings, the portfolio is invested predominantly in India. The Indian government bond market is highly liquid, but the country's mortgage and infrastructure loan markets, as well as the corporate bond market, are relatively illiquid. Individual mortgage and corporate bond positions are large relative to the normal trading volumes in these securities. Given the elevated current and fiscal account deficits, Indian investments are also subject to above-average economic risk.

Hamilton begins with a summary of the India-based portfolio. Exhibit 1 presents the current portfolio composition and the risk and return assumptions used to estimate value at risk (VaR).

EXHIBIT 1   Selected Assumptions for LICIA's Investment Portfolio

	Allocation	Average Daily Return	Daily Standard Deviation
India government securities	50%	0.015%	0.206%
India mortgage/infrastructure loans	25%	0.045%	0.710%
India corporate bonds	15%	0.025%	0.324%
India equity	10%	0.035%	0.996%

Infrastructure is a rapidly growing asset class with limited return history; the first infrastructure loans were issued just 10 years ago.

Hamilton's report to the management committee must outline her assumptions and provide support for the methods she used in her risk assessment. If needed, she will also make recommendations for rebalancing the portfolio to ensure its risk profile is aligned with that of Hiram.

Hamilton develops the assumptions shown in Exhibit 2, which will be used for estimating the portfolio VaR.

EXHIBIT 2   VaR Input Assumptions for Proposed CAD260 Million Portfolio

Method	Average Return Assumption	Standard Deviation Assumption
Monte Carlo simulation	0.026%	0.501%
Parametric approach	0.026%	0.501%
Historical simulation	0.023%	0.490%

Hamilton elects to apply a one-day, 5 percent VaR limit of CAD2 million in her risk assessment of LICIA's portfolio. This limit is consistent with the risk tolerance the committee has specified for the Hiram portfolio.

The markets' volatility during the last 12 months has been significantly higher than the historical norm, with increased frequency of large daily losses, and Hamilton expects the next 12 months to be equally volatile.

She estimates the one-day 5 percent portfolio VaR for LICIA's portfolio using three different approaches:

EXHIBIT 3   VaR Results over a One-Day Period for Proposed Portfolio

Method	5% VaR
Monte Carlo simulation	CAD2,095,565
Parametric approach	CAD2,083,610
Historical simulation	CAD1,938,874

The committee is likely to have questions in a number of key areas—the limitations of the VaR report, potential losses in an extreme adverse event, and the reliability of the VaR numbers if the market continues to exhibit higher-than-normal volatility. Hamilton wants to be certain that she has thoroughly evaluated the risks inherent in the LICIA portfolio and compares them with the risks in Hiram's present portfolio.

Hamilton believes the possibility of a ratings downgrade on Indian sovereign debt is high and not yet fully reflected in securities prices. If the rating is lowered, many of the portfolio's holdings will no longer meet Hiram's minimum ratings requirement. A downgrade's effect is unlikely to be limited to the government bond portfolio. All asset classes can be expected to be affected to some degree. Hamilton plans to include a scenario analysis that reflects this possibility to ensure that management has the broadest possible view of the risk exposures in the India portfolio.

6. Given Hamilton's expectations, which of the following models is *most appropriate* to use in estimating portfolio VaR?
    A. Parametric method
    B. Historical simulation method
    C. Monte Carlo simulation method

7. Which risk measure is Hamilton *most likely* to present when addressing the committee's concerns regarding potential losses in extreme stress events?
    A. Relative VaR
    B. Incremental VaR
    C. Conditional VaR

8. The scenario analysis that Hamilton prepares for the committee is *most likely* a:
    A. stress test.
    B. historical scenario.
    C. hypothetical scenario.

9. The scenario analysis that Hamilton prepares for the committee is a valuable tool to supplement VaR *because* it:
    A. incorporates historical data to evaluate the risk in the tail of the VaR distribution.
    B. enables Hamilton to isolate the risk stemming from a single risk factor—the ratings downgrade.
    C. allows the committee to assess the effect of low liquidity in the event of a ratings downgrade.

10. Using the data in Exhibit 2, the portfolio's annual 1% parametric VaR is *closest* to:
    A. CAD17 million.
    B. CAD31 million.
    C. CAD48 million.

11. What additional risk measures would be most appropriate to add to Hamilton's risk assessment?
     A. Delta
     B. Duration
     C. Tracking error

The following information relates to Questions 12–19.

Tina Ming is a senior portfolio manager at Flusk Pension Fund (Flusk). Flusk's portfolio is composed of fixed-income instruments structured to match Flusk's liabilities. Ming works with Shrikant McKee, Flusk's risk analyst.

Ming and McKee discuss the latest risk report. McKee calculated value at risk (VaR) for the entire portfolio using the historical method and assuming a lookback period of five years and 250 trading days per year. McKee presents VaR measures in Exhibit 1.

EXHIBIT 1   Flusk Portfolio VaR (in $ millions)

Confidence Interval	Daily VaR	Monthly VaR
95%	1.10	5.37

After reading McKee's report, Ming asks why the number of daily VaR breaches over the last year is zero even though the portfolio has accumulated a substantial loss.

Next, Ming requests that McKee perform the following two risk analyses on Flusk's portfolio:

Analysis 1. Use scenario analysis to evaluate the impact on risk and return of a repeat of the last financial crisis.

Analysis 2. Estimate over one year, with a 95 percent level of confidence, how much Flusk's assets could underperform its liabilities.

Ming recommends purchasing newly issued emerging market corporate bonds that have embedded options. Prior to buying the bonds, Ming wants McKee to estimate the effect of the purchase on Flusk's VaR. McKee suggests running a stress test using a historical period specific to emerging markets that encompassed an extreme change in credit spreads.

At the conclusion of their conversation, Ming asks the following question about risk management tools: "What are the advantages of VaR compared with other risk measures?"

12. Based on Exhibit 1, Flusk's portfolio is expected to experience:
     A. a minimum daily loss of $1.10 million over the next year.
     B. a loss over one month equal to or exceeding $5.37 million 5 percent of the time.
     C. an average daily loss of $1.10 million 5 percent of the time during the next 250 trading days.

13. The number of Flusk's VaR breaches most likely resulted from:
     A. using a standard normal distribution in the VaR model.
     B. using a 95 percent confidence interval instead of a 99 percent confidence interval.
     C. lower market volatility during the last year compared with the lookback period.

14. To perform Analysis 1, McKee should use historical bond:
    A. prices.
    B. yields.
    C. durations.

15. The limitation of the approach requested for Analysis 1 is that it:
    A. omits asset correlations.
    B. precludes incorporating portfolio manager actions.
    C. assumes no deviation from historical market events.

16. The estimate requested in Analysis 2 is *best* described as:
    A. liquidity gap.
    B. surplus at risk.
    C. maximum drawdown.

17. Which measure should McKee use to estimate the effect on Flusk's VaR from Ming's portfolio recommendation?
    A. Relative VaR
    B. Incremental VaR
    C. Conditional VaR

18. When measuring the portfolio impact of the stress test suggested by McKee, which of the following is *most likely* to produce an accurate result?
    A. Marginal VaR
    B. Full revaluation of securities
    C. The use of sensitivity risk measures

19. The risk management tool referenced in Ming's question:
    A. is widely accepted by regulators.
    B. takes into account asset liquidity.
    C. usually incorporates right-tail events.

The following information relates to questions 20–26.

Carol Kynnersley is the chief risk officer at Investment Management Advisers (IMA). Kynnersley meets with IMA's portfolio management team and investment advisers to discuss the methods used to measure and manage market risk and how risk metrics are presented in client reports.

The three most popular investment funds offered by IMA are the Equity Opportunities, the Diversified Fixed Income, and the Alpha Core Equity. The Equity Opportunities Fund is composed of two exchange-traded funds: a broadly diversified large-cap equity product and one devoted to energy stocks. Kynnersley makes the following statements regarding the risk management policies established for the Equity Opportunities portfolio:

Statement 1. IMA's preferred approach to model value at risk (VaR) is to estimate expected returns, volatilities, and correlations under the assumption of a normal distribution.

Statement 2. In last year's annual client performance report, IMA stated that a hypothetical $6 million Equity Opportunities Fund account had a daily 5 percent VaR of approximately 1.5 percent of portfolio value.

Kynnersley informs the investment advisers that the risk management department recently updated the model for estimating the Equity Opportunities Fund VaR based on the information presented in Exhibit 1.

EXHIBIT 1   Equity Opportunities Fund—VaR Model Input Assumptions

	Large-Cap ETF	Energy ETF	Total Portfolio
Portfolio weight	65.0%	35.0%	100.0%
Expected annual return	12.0%	18.0%	14.1%
Standard deviation	20.0%	40.0%	26.3%
Correlation between ETFs: 0.90			
Number of trading days/year: 250			

For clients interested in fixed-income products, IMA offers the Diversified Fixed-Income Fund. Kynnersley explains that the portfolio's bonds are all subject to interest rate risk. To demonstrate how fixed-income exposure measures can be used to identify and manage interest rate risk, Kynnersley distributes two exhibits featuring three hypothetical Treasury coupon bonds (Exhibit 2) under three interest rate scenarios (Exhibit 3).

EXHIBIT 2   Fixed-Income Risk Measure

Hypothetical Bond	Duration
Bond 1	1.3
Bond 2	3.7
Bond 3	10.2

EXHIBIT 3   Interest Rate Scenarios

Scenario	Interest Rate Environment
Scenario 1	Rates increase 25 bps
Scenario 2	Rates increase 10 bps
Scenario 3	Rates decrease 20 bps

One of the investment advisers comments that a client recently asked about the performance of the Diversified Fixed-Income Fund relative to its benchmark, a broad fixed-income index. Kynnersley informs the adviser as follows:

Statement 3.   The Diversified Fixed-Income Fund manager monitors the historical deviation between portfolio returns and benchmark returns. The fund prospectus stipulates a target deviation from the benchmark of no more than 5 bps.

Kynnersley concludes the meeting by reviewing the constraints IMA imposes on securities included in the Alpha Core Equity Fund. The compliance department conducts daily oversight using numerous risk screens and, when indicated, notifies portfolio managers to make adjustments. Kynnersley makes the following statement:

Statement 4.   It is important that all clients investing in the fund be made aware of IMA's compliance measures. The Alpha Core Equity Fund restricts the exposure of individual securities to 1.75 percent of the total portfolio.

20. Based on Statement 1, IMA's VaR estimation approach is *best* described as the:
    A. parametric method.
    B. historical simulation method.
    C. Monte Carlo simulation method.

21. In Statement 2, Kynnersley implies that the portfolio:
    A. is at risk of losing $4,500 each trading day.
    B. value is expected to decline by $90,000 or more once in 20 trading days.
    C. has a 5 percent chance of falling in value by a maximum of $90,000 on a single trading day.

22. Based *only* on Statement 2, the risk measurement approach:
    A. ignores right-tail events in the return distribution.
    B. is similar to the Sharpe ratio because it is backward looking.
    C. provides a relatively accurate risk estimate in both trending and volatile regimes.

23. Based on Exhibit 1, the daily 5 percent VaR estimate is *closest* to:
    A. 1.61 percent.
    B. 2.42 percent.
    C. 2.69 percent.

24. Based *only* on Exhibits 2 and 3, it is *most likely* that under:
    A. Scenario 1, Bond 2 outperforms Bond 1.
    B. Scenario 2, Bond 1 underperforms Bond 3.
    C. Scenario 3, Bond 3 is the best performing security.

25. The risk measure referred to in Statement 3 is:
    A. active share.
    B. beta sensitivity
    C. *ex post* tracking error.

26. In Statement 4, Kynnersley describes a constraint associated with a:
    A. risk budget.
    B. position limit.
    C. stop-loss limit.

CHAPTER 14

BACKTESTING AND SIMULATION

LEARNING OUTCOMES

The candidate should be able to:

- describe objectives in backtesting an investment strategy;
- describe and contrast steps and procedures in backtesting an investment strategy;
- interpret metrics and visuals reported in a backtest of an investment strategy;
- identify problems in a backtest of an investment strategy;
- describe different ways to construct multifactor models;
- compare methods of modeling randomness;
- evaluate and interpret a scenario analysis;
- contrast Monte Carlo and historical simulation;
- explain inputs and decisions in simulation and interpret a simulation; and
- demonstrate the use of sensitivity analysis.

SUMMARY

In this chapter, we have discussed on how to perform rolling window backtesting—a widely used technique in the investment industry. Next, we described how to use scenario analysis and simulation along with sensitivity analysis to supplement backtesting, so investors can better account for the randomness in data that may not be fully captured by backtesting.

- The main objective of backtesting is to understand the risk–return trade-off of an investment strategy, by approximating the real-life investment process.
- The basic steps in a rolling window backtesting include specifying the investment hypothesis and goals, determining the rules and processes behind an investment strategy, forming

an investment portfolio according to the rules, rebalancing the portfolio periodically, and computing the performance and risk profiles of the strategy.

- In the rolling window backtesting methodology, researchers use a rolling window (or walk-forward) framework, fit/calibrate factors or trade signals based on the rolling window, rebalance the portfolio periodically, and then track the performance over time. Thus, rolling window backtesting is a proxy for actual investing.

- There are two commonly used approaches in backtesting—long/short hedged portfolio and Spearman rank IC. The two approaches often give similar results, but results can be quite different at times. Choosing the right approach depends on the model building and portfolio construction process.

- In assessing backtesting results, in addition to traditional performance measurements (e.g., Sharpe ratio, maximum drawdown), analysts need to take into account data coverage, return distribution, factor efficacy, factor turnover, and decay.

- There are several behavioral issues in backtesting to which analysts need to pay particular attention, including survivorship bias and look-ahead bias.

- Risk parity is a popular portfolio construction technique that takes into account the volatility of each factor (or asset) and the correlations of returns between all factors (or assets) to be combined in the portfolio. The objective is for each factor (or asset) to make an equal (hence "parity") risk contribution to the overall or targeted risk of the portfolio.

- Asset (and factor) returns are often negatively skewed and exhibit excess kurtosis (fat tails) and tail dependence compared with normal distribution. As a result, standard rolling window backtesting may not be able to fully account for the randomness in asset returns, particularly on downside risk.

- Financial data often face structural breaks. Scenario analysis can help investors understand the performance of an investment strategy in different structural regimes.

- Historical simulation is relatively straightforward to perform but shares pros and cons similar to those of rolling window backtesting. For example, a key assumption these methods share is that the distribution pattern from the historical data is sufficient to represent the uncertainty in the future. Bootstrapping (or random draws with replacement) is often used in historical simulation.

- Monte Carlo simulation is a more sophisticated technique than historical simulation is. In Monte Carlo simulation, the most important decision is the choice of functional form of the statistical distribution of decision variables/return drivers. Multivariate normal distribution is often used in investment research, owing to its simplicity. However, a multivariate normal distribution cannot account for negative skewness and fat tails observed in factor and asset returns.

- The Monte Carlo simulation technique makes use of the inverse transformation method—the process of converting a randomly generated uniformly distributed number into a simulated value of a random variable of a desired distribution.

- Sensitivity analysis, a technique for exploring how a target variable and risk profiles are affected by changes in input variables, can further help investors understand the limitations of conventional Monte Carlo simulation (which typically assumes a multivariate normal distribution as a starting point). A multivariate skewed t-distribution takes into account skewness and kurtosis but requires estimation of more parameters and thus is more likely to suffer from larger estimation errors.

PRACTICE PROBLEMS

The following information relates to Questions 1–8.

Emily Yuen is a senior analyst for a consulting firm that specializes in assessing equity strategies using backtesting and simulation techniques. She is working with an assistant, Cameron Ruckey, to develop multifactor portfolio strategies based on nine factors common to the growth style of investing. To do so, Yuen and Ruckey plan to construct nine separate factor portfolios and then use them to create factor-weighted allocation portfolios.

Yuen tasks Ruckey with specifying the investment universe and determining the availability of appropriate reporting data in vendor databases. Ruckey selects a vendor database that does not provide point-in-time data, then makes adjustments to include point-in-time constituent stocks and assumes a reporting lag of four months.

Next, Yuen and Ruckey run initial backtests by creating a stock portfolio and calculating performance statistics and key metrics for each of the nine factors based on a Spearman rank information coefficient (IC) approach. For backtesting purposes, the factor portfolios are each rebalanced monthly over a 30-year time horizon using a rolling-window procedure.

Yuen and Ruckey consider a variety of metrics to assess the results of the factor portfolio backtests. Yuen asks Ruckey what can be concluded from the data for three of the factor strategies in Exhibit 1:

EXHIBIT 1   Backtest Metrics for Factor Strategies

	Factor 1	Factor 2	Factor 3
Thirty-year average signal autocorrelation	90%	80%	85%
Spearman rank IC: Month 1 (IC_1)	5%	4%	3%
Spearman rank IC decay speed	Fast	Slow	Modest

Yuen and Ruckey then run multifactor model backtests by combining the factor portfolios into two factor-weighted multifactor portfolios: an equally weighted benchmark portfolio (Portfolio A) and a risk parity portfolio (Portfolio B). Ruckey tells Yuen the following:

Statement 1:   A risk parity multifactor model is constructed by equally weighting the risk contribution of each factor.

Statement 2:   The process of creating Portfolios A and B requires a second rolling-window procedure in order to avoid model selection bias.

To gain a more complete picture of the investment strategy performance, Yuen and Ruckey design and then run two simulation methods to generate investment performance data for the underlying factor portfolios, assuming 1,000 simulation trials for each approach:

Approach 1:   Historical simulation
Approach 2:   Monte Carlo simulation

Yuen and Ruckey discuss the differences between the two approaches and then design the simulations, making key decisions at various steps. During the process, Yuen expresses a number of concerns:

Concern 1: Returns from six of the nine factors are clearly correlated.

Concern 2: The distribution of Factor 1 returns exhibits excess kurtosis and negative skewness.

Concern 3: The number of simulations needed for Approach 1 is larger than the size of the historical dataset.

For each approach, Yuen and Ruckey run 1,000 trials to obtain 1,000 returns for Portfolios A and B. To help understand the effect of the skewness and excess kurtosis observed in the Factor 1 returns on the performance of Portfolios A and B, Ruckey suggests simulating an additional 1,000 factor returns using a multivariate skewed Student's t-distribution, then repeating the Approach 2 simulation.

1. Following Ruckey's adjustments to the initial vendor database, backtested returns will *most likely* be subject to:
    A. stale data.
    B. look-ahead bias.
    C. survivorship bias.

2. Based on Exhibit 1, Ruckey should conclude that:
    A. Factor Strategy 1 portfolios experience the highest turnover.
    B. Factor Strategy 2 provides the strongest predictive power in the long term.
    C. Factor Strategy 3 provides the strongest predictive power in the first month.

3. Which of Ruckey's statements about constructing multifactor portfolios is correct?
    A. Only Statement 1
    B. Only Statement 2
    C. Both Statement 1 and Statement 2

4. Approach 1 differs from Approach 2 in that:
    A. it is deterministic.
    B. a functional form of the statistical distribution for each decision variable needs to be specified.
    C. it assumes that sampling the returns from the actual data provides sufficient guidance about future asset returns.

5. To address Concern 1 when designing Approach 2, Yuen should:
    A. model each factor or asset on a standalone basis.
    B. calculate the 15 covariance matrix elements needed to calibrate the model.
    C. simulate future factor returns using a joint cumulative probability distribution function.

6. Based on Concern 2, the Factor 1 strategy is *most likely* to:
    A. be favored by risk-averse investors.
    B. generate surprises in the form of negative returns.
    C. have return data that line up tightly around a trend line.

7. To address Concern 3 when designing Approach 1, Yuen should:
    A. bootstrap additional returns using a walk-forward framework.
    B. randomly sample from the historical returns with replacement.
    C. choose the multivariate normal distribution as the initial functional form.

8. The process Ruckey suggests to better understand how the performance of Portfolios A and B using Approach 2 is affected by the distribution of Factor 1 returns is *best* described as:

   A. data snooping.

   B. sensitivity analysis.

   C. inverse transformation.

The following information relates to Questions 9–16.

Kata Rom is an equity analyst working for Gimingham Wealth Partners (GWP), a large investment advisory company. Rom meets with Goran Galic, a Canadian private wealth client, to explain investment strategies used by GWP to generate portfolio alpha for its clients.

Rom describes how GWP creates relevant investment strategies and then explains GWP's backtesting process. Rom notes the following:

Statement 1:   Using historical data, backtesting approximates a real-life investment process to illustrate the risk–return tradeoff of a particular proposed investment strategy.

Statement 2:   Backtesting is used almost exclusively by quantitative investment managers and rarely by fundamental investment managers, who are more concerned with information such as forward estimates of company earnings, macroeconomic factors, and intrinsic values.

Rom states that GWP is recognized in the Canadian investment industry as a value manager and that it uses traditional value parameters to build and backtest portfolios designed to outperform benchmarks stipulated in each client's investment policy statement. Galic, who is 62 years old, decides to allocate C\$2 million (representing 10% of his net worth) to an account with GWP and stipulates that portfolio assets be restricted exclusively to domestic securities. Rom creates Value Portfolio I for Galic based on value factors analyzed in a series of backtests.

At a subsequent meeting with Galic, Rom explains the long–short hedged portfolio approach for implementing factor-based portfolios that GWP used to create Value Portfolio I and the steps involved in the backtesting procedure. One specific step in the process concerns Galic, who states the following:

Statement 3:   I have never sold a stock that I did not own, and I really do not like the notion of giving the banks almost all of the income earned on the cash proceeds from the stock dispositions. On top of the forgone interest income, I think it could be really difficult to avoid high turnover and transaction costs, which would also negatively affect my risk-adjusted performance.

In an effort to relieve the concern raised by Galic, Rom suggests using an alternative backtesting approach to evaluate Value Portfolio I. This method uses the correlation between the prior-period ranked factor scores and the ranked current-period returns to evaluate the model's effectiveness. The approach generates a measure of the predictive power of a given factor relative to future stock returns.

Rom explains that the two backtesting approaches discussed so far have a weakness embedded in them. The approaches generally do not capture the dynamic nature of financial markets and in particular may not capture extreme downside risk. In an attempt to remedy this issue, Rom suggests considering different methods of modeling randomness. Rom states that GWP recently performed a statistical study of value and momentum factors, which found that both distributions were negatively skewed with fat tails. Additionally, the joint distribution of the returns for the factors had two peaks in the tails, and the peaks were higher than that from a normal distribution.

The study also investigated the return distributions of a number of individual value and momentum factors and found that they were non-normal based on their negative skewness, excess kurtosis, and tail dependence. Rom indicated that investment strategies based on this type of data are prone to significantly higher downside risk. Exhibit 1 compares downside risk measures for three model factors.

EXHIBIT 1   Downside Risk Measures for Model Factors

Risk Measure	Factor 1	Factor 2	Factor 3
Value at risk (VaR) (95%)	(6.49%)	(0.77%)	(2.40%)
Conditional VaR (CVaR) (95%)	(15.73%)	(4.21%)	(3.24%)
Maximum drawdown	35.10%	38.83%	45.98%

Rom explains that many of the examples used so far have incorporated the rolling-window backtesting approach. When comparing GWP's studies with those performed by Fastlane Wealth Managers for the same data and factors, Rom finds that the results are quite different. Rom discovers that Fastlane uses various modeling techniques, backtests each of them, and then picks the best-performing models. This discovery leads Rom to believe that Fastlane's modeling approach may exhibit selection bias.

Finally, after evaluating financial data that has periods of structural breaks, Rom informs Galic that GWP uses a technique commonly referred to as scenario analysis. This technique helps investment managers understand the performance of an investment strategy in different structural regimes. Exhibit 2 compares the performance of two factor allocation strategies under varying macroeconomic conditions.

EXHIBIT 2   Scenario Analysis Using the Sharpe Ratio

Strategy/Regime	High Volatility	Low Volatility	Recession	Non-recession
Strategy I	0.88	0.64	0.20	1.00
Strategy II	1.56	1.60	1.76	1.52

9. Which of Rom's statements concerning backtesting is correct?
    A. Only Statement 1
    B. Only Statement 2
    C. Both Statement 1 and Statement 2

10. The key parameter *most likely* to be incorporated in the analysis of Value Portfolio I is:
    A. monthly rebalancing.
    B. the MSCI World equity index.
    C. hedged returns into domestic currency.

11. In Statement 3, Galic expresses the *most* concern about the backtesting step that involves:
    A. strategy design.
    B. analysis of backtesting output.
    C. historical investment simulation.

12. The alternative approach to evaluate the backtesting of Value Portfolio I suggested by Rom is *most likely*:
    A. the Pearson information coefficient.
    B. the Spearman rank information coefficient.
    C. a cross-sectional regression.

13. Based on the statistical study performed by GWP, the tail dependence coefficient is *most likely*:
    A. low and negative.
    B. high and negative.
    C. high and positive.

14. Based on Exhibit 1, the factor with the smallest downside risk as measured by the weighted average of all losses that exceed a threshold is:
    A. Factor 1.
    B. Factor 2.
    C. Factor 3

15. The approach used by Fastlane Wealth Managers *most likely* incorporates:
    A. risk parity.
    B. data snooping.
    C. cross-validation.

16. Comparing the two strategies in Exhibit 2, the *best* risk-adjusted performance is demonstrated by:
    A. Strategy II in periods of low volatility and recession.
    B. Strategy I in periods of high volatility and non-recession.
    C. Strategy II in periods of high volatility and non-recession.

SOLUTIONS

CHAPTER 1

THE TIME VALUE OF MONEY

SOLUTIONS

1. A. Investment 2 is identical to Investment 1 except that Investment 2 has low liquidity. The difference between the interest rate on Investment 2 and Investment 1 is 0.5 percentage point. This amount represents the liquidity premium, which represents compensation for the risk of loss relative to an investment's fair value if the investment needs to be converted to cash quickly.

   B. To estimate the default risk premium, find the two investments that have the same maturity but different levels of default risk. Both Investments 4 and 5 have a maturity of eight years. Investment 5, however, has low liquidity and thus bears a liquidity premium. The difference between the interest rates of Investments 5 and 4 is 2.5 percentage points. The liquidity premium is 0.5 percentage point (from Part A). This leaves $2.5 - 0.5 = 2.0$ percentage points that must represent a default risk premium reflecting Investment 5's high default risk.

   C. Investment 3 has liquidity risk and default risk comparable to Investment 2, but with its longer time to maturity, Investment 3 should have a higher maturity premium. The interest rate on Investment 3, r_3, should thus be above 2.5 percent (the interest rate on Investment 2). If the liquidity of Investment 3 were high, Investment 3 would match Investment 4 except for Investment 3's shorter maturity. We would then conclude that Investment 3's interest rate should be less than the interest rate on Investment 4, which is 4 percent. In contrast to Investment 4, however, Investment 3 has low liquidity. It is possible that the interest rate on Investment 3 exceeds that of Investment 4 despite 3's shorter maturity, depending on the relative size of the liquidity and maturity premiums. However, we expect r_3 to be less than 4.5 percent, the expected interest rate on Investment 4 if it had low liquidity. Thus 2.5 percent $< r_3 <$ 4.5 percent.

2. i. Draw a time line.

   ii. Identify the problem as the future value of an annuity.

iii. Use the formula for the future value of an annuity.

$$FV_N = A\left[\frac{(1+r)^N - 1}{r}\right]$$

$$= \$20,000\left[\frac{(1+0.07)^{20} - 1}{0.07}\right]$$

$$= \$819,909.85$$

FV = $819,909.85

iv. Alternatively, use a financial calculator.

Notation Used on Most Calculators	Numerical Value for This Problem
N	20
%i	7
PV	n/a (= 0)
FV **compute**	X
PMT	$20,000

Enter 20 for N, the number of periods. Enter 7 for the interest rate and 20,000 for the payment size. The present value is not needed, so enter 0. Calculate the future value. Verify that you get $819,909.85 to make sure you have mastered your calculator's keystrokes.

In summary, if the couple sets aside $20,000 each year (starting next year), they will have $819,909.85 in 20 years if they earn 7 percent annually.

3. i. Draw a time line.

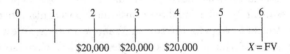

ii. Recognize the problem as the future value of a delayed annuity. Delaying the payments requires two calculations.

iii. Use the formula for the future value of an annuity (Equation 7).

$$FV_N = A\left[\frac{(1+r)^N - 1}{r}\right]$$

to bring the three $20,000 payments to an equivalent lump sum of $65,562.00 four years from today.

Notation Used on Most Calculators	Numerical Value for This Problem
N	3
$\%i$	9
PV	n/a (= 0)
FV **compute**	X
PMT	$20,000

iv. Use the formula for the future value of a lump sum (Equation 2), $FV_N = PV(1 + r)^N$, to bring the single lump sum of \$65,562.00 to an equivalent lump sum of \$77,894.21 six years from today.

Notation Used on Most Calculators	Numerical Value for This Problem
N	2
$\%i$	9
PV	$65,562.00
FV **compute**	X
PMT	n/a (= 0)

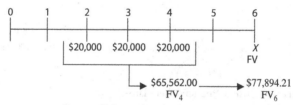

In summary, your client will have \$77,894.21 in six years if she receives three yearly payments of \$20,000 starting in Year 2 and can earn 9 percent annually on her investments.

4. i. Draw a time line.

  ii. Identify the problem as the present value of a lump sum.
  iii. Use the formula for the present value of a lump sum.

$$PV = FV_N(1 + r)^{-N}$$
$$= \$75,000(1 + 0.06)^{-5}$$
$$= \$56,044.36$$

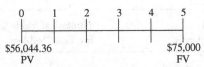

In summary, the father will need to invest $56,044.36 today in order to have $75,000 in five years if his investments earn 6 percent annually.

5.   i.   Draw a time line for the 10 annual payments.

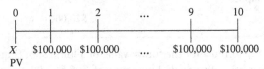

ii.   Identify the problem as the present value of an annuity.
iii.   Use the formula for the present value of an annuity.

$$PV = A \left[\frac{1 - \frac{1}{(1+r)^N}}{r} \right]$$

$$= \$100,000 \left[\frac{1 - \frac{1}{(1+0.05)^{10}}}{0.05} \right]$$

$$= \$772,173.49$$

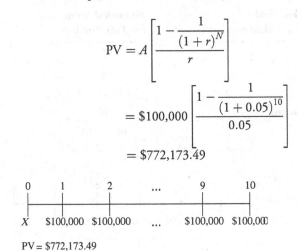

iv.   Alternatively, use a financial calculator.

Notation Used on Most Calculators	Numerical Value for This Problem
N	10
%i	5
PV **compute**	X
FV	n/a (= 0)
PMT	$100,000

In summary, the present value of 10 payments of $100,000 is $772,173.49 if the first payment is received in one year and the rate is 5 percent compounded annually. Your client should accept no less than this amount for his lump sum payment.

6.   A.   To evaluate the first instrument, take the following steps:
        i.   Draw a time line.

ii.

$$PV_3 = A \left[\frac{1 - \frac{1}{(1+r)^N}}{r} \right]$$

$$= \$20,000 \left[\frac{1 - \frac{1}{(1+0.08)^4}}{0.08} \right]$$

$$= \$66,242.54$$

iii.

$$PV_0 = \frac{PV_3}{(1+r)^N} = \frac{\$66,242.54}{1.08^3} = \$52,585.46$$

You should be willing to pay $52,585.46 for this instrument.

B. To evaluate the second instrument, take the following steps:
    i. Draw a time line.

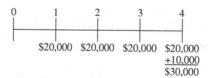

The time line shows that this instrument can be analyzed as an ordinary annuity of $20,000 with four payments (valued in Step ii below) and a $10,000 payment to be received at $t = 4$ (valued in Step iii below).

ii.

$$PV = A \left[\frac{1 - \frac{1}{(1+r)^N}}{r} \right]$$

$$= \$20,000 \left[\frac{1 - \frac{1}{(1+0.08)^4}}{0.08} \right]$$

$$= \$66,242.54$$

iii.
$$PV = \frac{FV_4}{(1+r)^N} = \frac{\$10,000}{(1+0.08)^4} = \$7,350.30$$

iv. Total $= \$66,242.54 + \$7,350.30 = \$73,592.84$
You should be willing to pay \$73,592.84 for this instrument.

7.   i.   Draw a time line.

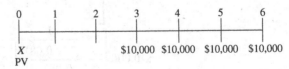

ii.   Recognize the problem as a delayed annuity. Delaying the payments requires two calculations.

iii.   Use the formula for the present value of an annuity (Equation 11).

$$PV = A\left[\frac{1 - \frac{1}{(1+r)^N}}{r}\right]$$

to bring the four payments of \$10,000 back to a single equivalent lump sum of \$33,121.27 at $t = 2$. Note that we use $t = 2$ because the first annuity payment is then one period away, giving an ordinary annuity.

Notation Used on Most Calculators	Numerical Value for This Problem
N	4
%i	8
PV compute	X
PMT	\$10,000

iv.   Then use the formula for the present value of a lump sum (Equation 8), $PV = FV_N(1 + r)^{-N}$, to bring back the single payment of \$33,121.27 (at $t = 2$) to an equivalent single payment of \$28,396.15 (at $t = 0$).

Notation Used on Most Calculators	Numerical Value for This Problem
N	2
%i	8
PV compute	X
FV	\$33,121.27
PMT	n/a (= 0)

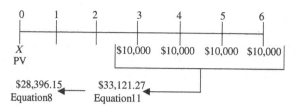

In summary, you should set aside $28,396.15 today to cover four payments of $10,000 starting in three years if your investments earn a rate of 8 percent annually.

8.   i.   Draw a time line.

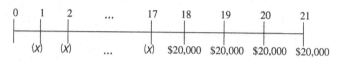

ii.   Recognize that you need to equate the values of two annuities.

iii.   Equate the value of the four $20,000 payments to a single payment in Period 17 using the formula for the present value of an annuity (Equation 11), with $r = 0.05$. The present value of the college costs as of $t = 17$ is $70,919.

$$PV = \$20,000 \left[\frac{1 - \frac{1}{(1.05)^4}}{0.05} \right] = \$70,919$$

Notation Used on Most Calculators	Numerical Value for This Problem
N	4
%i	5
PV **compute**	X
FV	n/a (= 0)
PMT	$20,000

iv.   Equate the value of the 17 investments of X to the amount calculated in Step iii, college costs as of $t = 17$, using the formula for the future value of an annuity (Equation 7). Then solve for X.

$$\$70,919 = \left[\frac{(1.05)^{17} - 1}{0.05} \right] = 25.840366X$$

$$X = \$2,744.50$$

Notation Used on Most Calculators	Numerical Value for This Problem
N	17
$\%i$	5
PV	n/a (= 0)
FV	$70,919
PMT compute	X

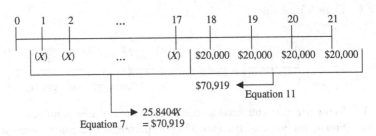

In summary, your client will have to save $2,744.50 each year if she starts next year and makes 17 payments into a savings account paying 5 percent annually.

9. i. Draw a time line.

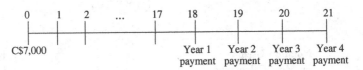

ii. Recognize that the payments in Years 18, 19, 20, and 21 are the future values of a lump sum of C$7,000 in Year 0.

iii. With $r = 5\%$, use the formula for the future value of a lump sum (Equation 2), $FV_N = PV\ (1 + r)^N$, four times to find the payments. These future values are shown on the time line below.

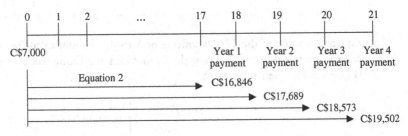

iv. Using the formula for the present value of a lump sum ($r = 6\%$), equate the four college payments to single payments as of $t = 17$ and add them together. C$16,846(1.06)^{-1} + C\$17,689(1.06)^{-2} + C\$18,573(1.06)^{-3} + C\$19,502(1.06)^{-4}$ = C$62,677

v.   Equate the sum of C\$62,677 at $t = 17$ to the 17 payments of X, using the formula for the future value of an annuity (Equation 7). Then solve for X.

$$C\$62,677 = X\left[\frac{(1.06)^{17} - 1}{0.06}\right] = 28.21288X$$
$$X = C\$2,221.58$$

Notation Used on Most Calculators	Numerical Value for This Problem
N	17
%i	6
PV	n/a (= 0)
FV	C\$62,677
PMT compute	X

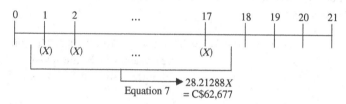

In summary, the couple will need to put aside C\$2,221.58 each year if they start next year and make 17 equal payments.

10.   C is correct. The sum of the real risk-free interest rate and the inflation premium is the nominal risk-free rate.

11.   C is correct. US Treasury bonds are highly liquid, whereas the bonds of small issuers trade infrequently and the interest rate includes a liquidity premium. This liquidity premium reflects the relatively high costs (including the impact on price) of selling a position.

12.   A is correct. The effective annual rate (EAR) when compounded daily is 4.08%.

$$\text{EAR} = (1 + \text{Periodic interest rate})^m - 1$$
$$\text{EAR} = (1 + 0.04/365)^{365} - 1$$
$$\text{EAR} = (1.0408) - 1 = 0.04081 \approx 4.08\%.$$

13.   C is correct, as shown in the following (where FV is future value and PV is present value):

$$FV = PV\left(1 + \frac{r_s}{m}\right)^{mN}$$
$$FV_6 = \$75,000\left(1 + \frac{0.07}{4}\right)^{(4\times6)}$$
$$FV_6 = \$113,733.21.$$

14. B is correct because £97,531 represents the present value (PV) of £100,000 received one year from today when today's deposit earns a stated annual rate of 2.50% and interest compounds weekly, as shown in the following equation (where FV is future value):

$$PV = FV_N \left(1 + \frac{r_s}{m}\right)^{-mN}$$

$$PV = £100,000 \left(1 + \frac{0.025}{52}\right)^{-52}$$

$$PV = £97,531.58.$$

15. A is correct. The effective annual rate (EAR) is calculated as follows:

$$EAR = (1 + \text{Periodic interest rate})^m - 1$$
$$EAR = (1 + 0.03/365)^{365} - 1$$
$$EAR = (1.03045) - 1 = 0.030453 \approx 3.0453\%.$$

Solving for N on a financial calculator results in (where FV is future value and PV is present value):

$$(1 + 0.030453)^N = FV_N/PV = ¥1,000,000/¥250,000$$
$$= 46.21 \text{ years, which multiplied by 12 to convert}$$
$$\text{to months results in } 554.5, \text{ or} \approx 555 \text{ months.}$$

16. B is correct. The difference between continuous compounding and daily compounding is

€127,496.85 − €127,491.29 = €5.56, or ≈ €6, as shown in the following calculations. With continuous compounding, the investment earns (where PV is present value)

$$PVe^{r_s N} - PV$$
$$= €1,127,496.85 - €1,000,000$$
$$= €127,496.85$$

With daily compounding, the investment earns:
$$€1,000,000(1 + 0.03/365)^{365(4)} - €1,000,000 = €1,127,491.29 - €1,000,000$$
$$= €127,491.29.$$

17. B is correct, as shown in the following calculation for an annuity (A) due:

$$PV = A \left[\frac{1 - \frac{1}{(1+r)^N}}{r}\right](1 + r),$$

where A = €300, r = 0.04, and N = 5.

$$PV = €300 \left[\frac{1 - \frac{1}{(1+.04)^5}}{.04} \right] (1.04)$$

$$PV = €1{,}388.97, \text{ or} \approx €1{,}389.$$

18. B is correct. The value of the perpetuity one year from now is calculated as:
    $PV = A/r$, where PV is present value, A is annuity, and r is expressed as a quarterly required rate of return because the payments are quarterly.

$$PV = \$2.00/(0.06/4)$$
$$PV = \$133.33.$$

   The value today is (where FV is future value)

$$PV = FV_N(1 + r)^{-N}$$
$$PV = \$133.33(1 + 0.015)^{-4}$$
$$PV = \$125.62 \approx \$126.$$

19. B is correct. To solve for the future value of unequal cash flows, compute the future value of each payment as of Year 4 at the semiannual rate of 2%, and then sum the individual future values, as follows:

Year	End-of-Year Deposits ($)	Factor	Future Value ($)
1	4,000	$(1.02)^6$	4,504.65
2	8,000	$(1.02)^4$	8,659.46
3	7,000	$(1.02)^2$	7,282.80
4	10,000	$(1.02)^0$	10,000.00
		Sum =	30,446.91

20. C is correct, as shown in the following (where FV is future value and PV is present value):
    If:

$$FV_N = PV \left(1 + \frac{r_s}{m}\right)^{mN},$$

   Then:

$$\left(\frac{FV_N}{PV}\right)^{\frac{1}{mN}} - 1 = \frac{r_s}{m}$$

$$\left(\frac{800{,}000}{500{,}000}\right)^{\frac{1}{2\times6}} - 1 = \frac{r_s}{2}$$

$$r_s = 0.07988 \text{ (rounded to 8.0\%)}.$$

21. C is correct. As shown below, the present value (PV) of a £2,000 per month perpetuity is worth approximately £400,000 at a 6% annual rate compounded monthly. Thus, the

present value of the annuity (A) is worth more than the lump sum offers.

$$A = £2,000$$
$$r = (6\%/12) = 0.005$$
$$PV = (A/r)$$
$$PV = (£2,000/0.005)$$
$$PV = £400,000$$

22. B is correct.
The present value of a 10-year annuity (A) due with payments of $2,000 at a 5% discount rate is calculated as follows:

$$PV = A \left[\frac{1 - \frac{1}{(1+r)^N}}{r} \right] + \$2,000$$

$$PV = \$2,000 \left[\frac{1 - \frac{1}{(1+0.05)^9}}{0.05} \right] + \$2,000$$

$$PV = \$16,215.64.$$

Alternatively, the PV of a 10-year annuity due is simply the PV of the ordinary annuity multiplied by 1.05:

$$PV = \$15,443.47 \times 1.05$$
$$PV = \$16,215.64.$$

23. B is correct. First, find the present value (PV) of an ordinary annuity in Year 17 that represents the tuition costs:

$$\$50,000 \left[\frac{1 - \frac{1}{(1+0.06)^4}}{0.06} \right]$$

$$= \$50,000 \times 3.4651$$
$$= \$173,255.28.$$

Then, find the PV of the annuity in today's dollars (where FV is future value):

$$PV_0 = \frac{FV}{(1 + 0.06)^{17}}$$

$$PV_0 = \frac{\$173,255.28}{(1 + 0.06)^{17}}$$
$$PV_0 = \$64,340.85 \approx \$64,341.$$

24. B is correct, as shown in the following table.

Year	Cash Flow (€)	Formula CF × $(1 + r)^t$	PV at Year 0
1	100,000	$100,000(1.12)^{-1} =$	89,285.71
2	150,000	$150,000(1.12)^{-2} =$	119,579.08

Year	Cash Flow (€)	Formula $CF \times (1 + r)^t$	PV at Year 0
5	−10,000	$-10{,}000(1.12)^{-5} =$	−5,674.27
			203,190.52

25. B is correct, calculated as follows (where A is annuity and PV is present value):

$$A = (\text{PV of annuity}) / \left[\dfrac{1 - \dfrac{1}{(1 + r_s/m)^{mN}}}{r_s/m} \right]$$

$$= (£200{,}000) / \left[\dfrac{1 - \dfrac{1}{(1 + r_s/m)^{mN}}}{r_s/m} \right]$$

$$(£200{,}000) / \left[\dfrac{1 - \dfrac{1}{(1 + 0.06/12)^{12(5)}}}{0.06/12} \right]$$

$$= (£200{,}000)/51.72556$$

$$= £3{,}866.56$$

26. A is correct. To solve for an annuity (A) payment, when the future value (FV), interest rate, and number of periods is known, use the following equation:

$$FV = A \left[\dfrac{\left(1 + \frac{r}{m}\right)^{mN} - 1}{\frac{r}{m}} \right]$$

$$£25{,}000 = A \left[\dfrac{\left(1 + \frac{0.06}{4}\right)^{4 \times 10} - 1}{\frac{0.06}{4}} \right]$$

$$A = £460.68$$

27. B is correct. The PV in Year 5 of a $50,000 lump sum paid in Year 20 is $27,763.23 (where FV is future value):

$$PV = FV_N(1 + r)^{-N}$$
$$PV = \$50{,}000(1 + 0.04)^{-15}\backslash$$
$$PV = \$27{,}763.23$$

28. B is correct, as the following cash flows show:

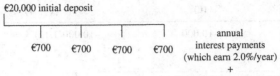

€20,000 initial deposit

€700   €700   €700   €700   annual interest payments (which earn 2.0%/year)
+
€20,000 (return of principal)

The four annual interest payments are based on the CD's 3.5% annual rate.
The first payment grows at 2.0% compounded monthly for three years (where FV is future value):

$$FV_N = €700\left(1 + \frac{0.02}{12}\right)^{3 \times 12}$$

$$FV_N = 743.25$$

The second payment grows at 2.0% compounded monthly for two years:

$$FV_N = €700\left(1 + \frac{0.02}{12}\right)^{2 \times 12}$$

$$FV_N = 728.54$$

The third payment grows at 2.0% compounded monthly for one year:

$$FV_N = €700\left(1 + \frac{0.02}{12}\right)^{1 \times 12}$$

$$FV_N = 714.13$$

The fourth payment is paid at the end of Year 4. Its future value is €700.
The sum of all future value payments is as follows:

€20,000.00	CD
€743.25	First payment's *FV*
€728.54	Second payment's *FV*
€714.13	Third payment's *FV*
€700.00	Fourth payment's *FV*
€22,885.92	Total *FV*

CHAPTER 2

ORGANIZING, VISUALIZING, AND DESCRIBING DATA

SOLUTIONS

1. A is correct. Ordinal scales sort data into categories that are ordered with respect to some characteristic and may involve numbers to identify categories but do not assure that the differences between scale values are equal. The buy rating scale indicates that a stock ranked 5 is expected to perform better than a stock ranked 4, but it tells us nothing about the performance difference between stocks ranked 4 and 5 compared with the performance difference between stocks ranked 1 and 2, and so on.

2. C is correct. Nominal data are categorical values that are not amenable to being organized in a logical order. A is incorrect because ordinal data are categorical data that can be logically ordered or ranked. B is incorrect because discrete data are numerical values that result from a counting process; thus, they can be ordered in various ways, such as from highest to lowest value.

3. B is correct. Categorical data (or qualitative data) are values that describe a quality or characteristic of a group of observations and therefore can be used as labels to divide a dataset into groups to summarize and visualize. The two types of categorical data are nominal data and ordinal data. Nominal data are categorical values that are not amenable to being organized in a logical order, while ordinal data are categorical values that can be logically ordered or ranked. A is incorrect because discrete data would be classified as numerical data (not categorical data). C is incorrect because continuous data would be classified as numerical data (not categorical data).

4. C is correct. Continuous data are data that can be measured and can take on any numerical value in a specified range of values. In this case, the analyst is estimating bankruptcy probabilities, which can take on any value between 0 and 1. Therefore, the set of bankruptcy probabilities estimated by the analyst would likely be characterized as continuous data. A is incorrect because ordinal data are categorical values that can be logically ordered or ranked. Therefore, the set of bankruptcy probabilities would not be characterized as ordinal data. B is incorrect because discrete data are numerical values

that result from a counting process, and therefore the data are limited to a finite number of values. The proprietary model used can generate probabilities that can take any value between 0 and 1; therefore, the set of bankruptcy probabilities would not be characterized as discrete data.

5. A is correct. Ordinal data are categorical values that can be logically ordered or ranked. In this case, the classification of sentences in the earnings call transcript into three categories (negative, neutral, or positive) describes ordinal data, as the data can be logically ordered from positive to negative. B is incorrect because discrete data are numerical values that result from a counting process. In this case, the analyst is categorizing sentences (i.e., unstructured data) from the earnings call transcript as having negative, neutral, or positive sentiment. Thus, these categorical data do not represent discrete data. C is incorrect because nominal data are categorical values that are not amenable to being organized in a logical order. In this case, the classification of unstructured data (i.e., sentences from the earnings call transcript) into three categories (negative, neutral, or positive) describes ordinal (not nominal) data, as the data can be logically ordered from positive to negative.

6. B is correct. Time-series data are a sequence of observations of a specific variable collected over time and at discrete and typically equally spaced intervals of time, such as daily, weekly, monthly, annually, and quarterly. In this case, each column is a time series of data that represents annual total return (the specific variable) for a given country index, and it is measured annually (the discrete interval of time). A is incorrect because panel data consist of observations through time on one or more variables for multiple observational units. The entire table of data is an example of panel data showing annual total returns (the variable) for three country indexes (the observational units) by year. C is incorrect because cross-sectional data are a list of the observations of a specific variable from multiple observational units at a given point in time. Each row (not column) of data in the table represents cross-sectional data.

7. C is correct. Cross-sectional data are observations of a specific variable from multiple observational units at a given point in time. Each row of data in the table represents cross-sectional data. The specific variable is annual total return, the multiple observational units are the three countries' indexes, and the given point in time is the time period indicated by the particular row. A is incorrect because panel data consist of observations through time on one or more variables for multiple observational units. The entire table of data is an example of panel data showing annual total returns (the variable) for three country indexes (the observational units) by year. B is incorrect because time-series data are a sequence of observations of a specific variable collected over time and at discrete and typically equally spaced intervals of time, such as daily, weekly, monthly, annually, and quarterly. In this case, each column (not row) is a time series of data that represents annual total return (the specific variable) for a given country index, and it is measured annually (the discrete interval of time).

8. A is correct. Panel data consist of observations through time on one or more variables for multiple observational units. A two-dimensional rectangular array, or data table, would be suitable here as it is comprised of columns to hold the variable(s) for the observational units and rows to hold the observations through time. B is incorrect because a one-dimensional (not a two-dimensional rectangular) array would be most suitable for organizing a collection of data of the same data type, such as the time-series data from a single variable. C is incorrect because a one-dimensional (not a

two-dimensional rectangular) array would be most suitable for organizing a collection of data of the same data type, such as the same variable for multiple observational units at a given point in time (cross-sectional data).

9.   B is correct. In a frequency distribution, the absolute frequency, or simply the raw frequency, is the actual number of observations counted for each unique value of the variable. A is incorrect because the relative frequency, which is calculated as the absolute frequency of each unique value of the variable divided by the total number of observations, presents the absolute frequencies in terms of percentages. C is incorrect because the relative (not absolute) frequency provides a normalized measure of the distribution of the data, allowing comparisons between datasets with different numbers of total observations.

10.   A is correct. The relative frequency is the absolute frequency of each bin divided by the total number of observations. Here, the relative frequency is calculated as: $(12/60) \times 100 = 20\%$. B is incorrect because the relative frequency of this bin is $(23/60) \times 100 = 38.33\%$. C is incorrect because the cumulative relative frequency of the last bin must equal 100%.

11.   C is correct. The cumulative relative frequency of a bin identifies the fraction of observations that are less than the upper limit of the given bin. It is determined by summing the relative frequencies from the lowest bin up to and including the given bin. The following exhibit shows the relative frequencies for all the bins of the data from the previous exhibit:

Lower Limit (%)	Upper Limit (%)	Absolute Frequency	Relative Frequency	Cumulative Relative Frequency
$-9.19\leq$	<-5.45	1	0.083	0.083
$-5.45\leq$	<-1.71	2	0.167	0.250
$-1.71\leq$	<2.03	4	0.333	0.583
$2.03\leq$	<5.77	3	0.250	0.833
$5.77\leq$	≤9.47	2	0.167	1.000

The bin $-1.71\% \leq x < 2.03\%$ has a cumulative relative frequency of 0.583.

12.   C is correct. The marginal frequency of energy sector bonds in the portfolio is the sum of the joint frequencies across all three levels of bond rating, so $100 + 85 + 30 = 215$. A is incorrect because 27 is the relative frequency for energy sector bonds based on the total count of 806 bonds, so $215/806 = 26.7\%$, not the marginal frequency. B is incorrect because 85 is the joint frequency for AA rated energy sector bonds, not the marginal frequency.

13.   A is correct. The relative frequency for any value in the table based on the total count is calculated by dividing that value by the total count. Therefore, the relative frequency for AA rated energy bonds is calculated as $85/806 = 10.5\%$.

B is incorrect because 31.5% is the relative frequency for AA rated energy bonds, calculated based on the marginal frequency for all AA rated bonds, so $85/(32 + 25 + 85 + 100 + 28)$, not based on total bond counts. C is incorrect because 39.5% is the relative frequency for AA rated energy bonds, calculated based on the marginal frequency for all energy bonds, so $85/(100 + 85 + 30)$, not based on total bond counts.

14. C is correct. Because 50 data points are in the histogram, the median return would be the mean of the 50/2 = 25th and (50 + 2)/2 = 26th positions. The sum of the return bin frequencies to the left of the 13% to 18% interval is 24. As a result, the 25th and 26th returns will fall in the 13% to 18% interval.

15. C is correct. The mode of a distribution with data grouped in intervals is the interval with the highest frequency. The three intervals of 3% to 8%, 18% to 23%, and 28% to 33% all have a high frequency of 7.

16. A is correct. Twenty observations lie in the interval "0.0 to 2.0," and six observations lie in the "2.0 to 4.0" interval. Together, they represent 26/48, or 54.17%, of all observations, which is more than 50%.

17. A is correct. A bar chart that orders categories by frequency in descending order and includes a line displaying cumulative relative frequency is called a Pareto Chart. A Pareto Chart is used to highlight dominant categories or the most important groups. B is incorrect because a grouped bar chart or clustered bar chart is used to present the frequency distribution of two categorical variables. C is incorrect because a frequency polygon is used to display frequency distributions.

18. C is correct. A word cloud, or tag cloud, is a visual device for representing unstructured, textual data. It consists of words extracted from text with the size of each word being proportional to the frequency with which it appears in the given text. A is incorrect because a tree-map is a graphical tool for displaying and comparing categorical data, not for visualizing unstructured, textual data. B is incorrect because a scatter plot is used to visualize the joint variation in two numerical variables, not for visualizing unstructured, textual data.

19. C is correct. A tree-map is a graphical tool used to display and compare categorical data. It consists of a set of colored rectangles to represent distinct groups, and the area of each rectangle is proportional to the value of the corresponding group. A is incorrect because a line chart, not a tree-map, is used to display the change in a data series over time. B is incorrect because a scatter plot, not a tree-map, is used to visualize the joint variation in two numerical variables.

20. B is correct. An important benefit of a line chart is that it facilitates showing changes in the data and underlying trends in a clear and concise way. Often a line chart is used to display the changes in data series over time. A is incorrect because a scatter plot, not a line chart, is used to visualize the joint variation in two numerical variables. C is incorrect because a heat map, not a line chart, is used to visualize the values of joint frequencies among categorical variables.

21. B is correct. A heat map is commonly used for visualizing the degree of correlation between different variables. A is incorrect because a word cloud, or tag cloud, not a heat map, is a visual device for representing textual data with the size of each distinct word being proportional to the frequency with which it appears in the given text. C is incorrect because a histogram, not a heat map, depicts the shape, center, and spread of the distribution of numerical data.

22. B is correct. A bubble line chart is a version of a line chart where data points are replaced with varying-sized bubbles to represent a third dimension of the data. A line chart is very effective at visualizing trends in three or more variables over time. A is incorrect because a heat map differentiates high values from low values and reflects the correlation between variables but does not help in making comparisons of variables over time. C is incorrect because a scatterplot matrix is a useful tool for organizing

scatterplots between pairs of variables, making it easy to inspect all pairwise relationships in one combined visual. However, it does not help in making comparisons of these variables over time.

23. C is correct. The median of Portfolio R is 0.8% higher than the mean for Portfolio R.

24. C is correct. The portfolio return must be calculated as the weighted mean return, where the weights are the allocations in each asset class:

$$(0.20 \times 8\%) + (0.40 \times 12\%) + (0.25 \times -3\%) + (0.15 \times 4\%) = 6.25\%, \text{ or} \approx 6.3\%.$$

25. A is correct. The geometric mean return for Fund Y is found as follows:

$$\text{Fund Y} = [(1 + 0.195) \times (1 - 0.019) \times (1 + 0.197) \times (1 + 0.350) \times (1 + 0.057)]^{(1/5)} - 1$$
$$= 14.9\%.$$

26. A is correct. The harmonic mean is appropriate for determining the average price per unit. It is calculated by summing the reciprocals of the prices, then averaging that sum by dividing by the number of prices, then taking the reciprocal of the average:

$$4/[(1/62.00) + (1/76.00) + (1/84.00) + (1/90.00)] = 76.48.$$

27. B is correct. Quintiles divide a distribution into fifths, with the fourth quintile occurring at the point at which 80% of the observations lie below it. The fourth quintile is equivalent to the 80th percentile. To find the yth percentile (P_y), we first must determine its location. The formula for the location (L_y) of a yth percentile in an array with n entries sorted in ascending order is $L_y = (n + 1) \times (y/100)$. In this case, $n = 10$ and $y = 80\%$, so

$$L_{80} = (10 + 1) \times (80/100) = 11 \times 0.8 = 8.8.$$

With the data arranged in ascending order (−40.33%, −5.02%, 9.57%, 10.02%, 12.34%, 15.25%, 16.54%, 20.65%, 27.37%, and 30.79%), the 8.8th position would be between the 8th and 9th entries, 20.65% and 27.37%, respectively. Using linear interpolation, $P_{80} = X_8 + (L_y - 8) \times (X_9 - X_8)$,
$P_{80} = 20.65 + (8.8 - 8) \times (27.37 - 20.65)$
$= 20.65 + (0.8 \times 6.72) = 20.65 + 5.38$
$= 26.03\%.$

28. A is correct. The formula for mean absolute deviation (MAD) is

$$\text{MAD} = \frac{\sum_{i=1}^{n} |X_i \bar{X}|}{n}.$$

Column 1: Sum annual returns and divide by n to find the arithmetic mean ($\bar{X}$) of 16.40%.

Column 2: Calculate the absolute value of the difference between each year's return and the mean from Column 1. Sum the results and divide by n to find the MAD.

These calculations are shown in the following exhibit:

Year	Column 1 Return		Column 2 $\|X_i - \bar{X}\|$
Year 6	30.79%		14.39%
Year 7	12.34%		4.06%
Year 8	-5.02%		21.42%
Year 9	16.54%		0.14%
Year 10	27.37%		10.97%
Sum:	82.02%	Sum:	50.98%
n:	5	n:	5
$\bar{X}$:	16.40%	MAD:	10.20%

29. C is correct. The mean absolute deviation (MAD) of Fund ABC's returns is greater than the MAD of both of the other funds.

$$\text{MAD} = \frac{\sum_{i=1}^{n} |X_i - \bar{X}|}{n}, \text{ where } \bar{X} \text{ is the arithmetic mean of the series.}$$

MAD for Fund ABC

$$= \frac{|-20-(-4)|+|23-(-4)|+|-14-(-4)|+|5-(-4)|+|-14-(-4)|}{5}$$

$$= 14.4\%.$$

MAD for Fund XYZ

$$= \frac{\begin{array}{c}|-33-(-10.8)|+|-12-(-10.8)|+|-12-(-10.8)|\\+|-8-(-10.8)|+|11-(-10.8)|\end{array}}{5} = 9.8\%.$$

MAD for Fund PQR

$$= \frac{|-14-(-5)|+|-18-(-5)|+|6-(-5)|+|-2-(-5)|+|3-(-5)|}{5}$$

$$= 8.8\%.$$

A and B are incorrect because the range and variance of the three funds are as follows:

	Fund ABC	Fund XYZ	Fund PQR
Range	43%	44%	24%
Variance	317	243	110

The numbers shown for variance are understood to be in "percent squared" terms so that when taking the square root, the result is standard deviation in percentage terms. Alternatively, by expressing standard deviation and variance in decimal form, one can avoid the issue of units. In decimal form, the variances for Fund ABC, Fund XYZ, and Fund PQR are 0.0317, 0.0243, and 0.0110, respectively.

30. B is correct. The coefficient of variation (CV) is the ratio of the standard deviation to the mean, where a higher CV implies greater risk per unit of return.

$$CV_{UTIL} = s\bar{X} = \frac{1.23\%}{2.10\%} = 0.59.$$

$$CV_{MATR} = s\bar{X} = \frac{1.35\%}{1.25\%} = 1.08.$$

$$CV_{INDU} = s\bar{X} = \frac{1.52\%}{3.01\%} = 0.51.$$

31. A is correct. The more disperse a distribution, the greater the difference between the arithmetic mean and the geometric mean.
32. B is correct. The distribution is thin-tailed relative to the normal distribution because the excess kurtosis is less than zero.
33. B is correct. The geometric mean compounds the periodic returns of every period, giving the investor a more accurate measure of the terminal value of an investment.
34. B is correct. The sum of the returns is 30.0%, so the arithmetic mean is 30.0%/10 = 3.0%.
35. B is correct.

Year	Return	1+ Return
1	4.5%	1.045
2	6.0%	1.060
3	1.5%	1.015
4	–2.0%	0.980
5	0.0%	1.000
6	4.5%	1.045
7	3.5%	1.035
8	2.5%	1.025
9	5.5%	1.055
10	4.0%	1.040

The product of the 1 + Return is 1.3402338.

Therefore, $\bar{X}_G = \sqrt[10]{1.3402338} - 1 = 2.9717\%$.

36. A is correct.

Year	Return	1+ Return	1/(1+Return)
1	4.5%	1.045	0.957
2	6.0%	1.060	0.943
3	1.5%	1.015	0.985
4	-2.0%	0.980	1.020
5	0.0%	1.000	1.000
6	4.5%	1.045	0.957
7	3.5%	1.035	0.966
8	2.5%	1.025	0.976
9	5.5%	1.055	0.948
10	4.0%	1.040	0.962
Sum			9.714

The harmonic mean return = (n/Sum of reciprocals) – 1 = (10 / 9.714) – 1.

The harmonic mean return = 2.9442%.

37. B is correct.

Year	Return	Deviation	Deviation Squared
1	4.5%	0.0150	0.000225
2	6.0%	0.0300	0.000900
3	1.5%	-0.0150	0.000225
4	-2.0%	-0.0500	0.002500
5	0.0%	-0.0300	0.000900
6	4.5%	0.0150	0.000225
7	3.5%	0.0050	0.000025
8	2.5%	-0.0050	0.000025
9	5.5%	0.0250	0.000625
10	4.0%	0.0100	0.000100
Sum		0.0000	0.005750

The standard deviation is the square root of the sum of the squared deviations divided by $n - 1$:

$$s = \sqrt{\frac{0.005750}{9}} = 2.5276\%.$$

38. B is correct.

Year	Return	Deviation Squared below Target of 2%
1	4.5%	
2	6.0%	
3	1.5%	0.000025
4	–2.0%	0.001600
5	0.0%	0.000400
6	4.5%	
7	3.5%	
8	2.5%	
9	5.5%	
10	4.0%	
Sum		0.002025

The target semi-deviation is the square root of the sum of the squared deviations from the target, divided by $n - 1$:

$$s_{Target} = \sqrt{\frac{0.002025}{9}} = 1.5\%.$$

39. B is correct. The correlation coefficient is positive, indicating that the two series move together.

40. C is correct. Both outliers and spurious correlation are potential problems with interpreting correlation coefficients.

41. C is correct. The correlation coefficient is positive because the covariation is positive.

42. A is correct. The correlation coefficient is negative because the covariation is negative.

43. C is correct. The correlation coefficient is positive because the covariance is positive. The fact that one or both variables have a negative mean does not affect the sign of the correlation coefficient.

44. B is correct. The median is indicated within the box, which is the 100.49 in this diagram.

45. C is correct. The interquartile range is the difference between 114.25 and 79.74, which is 34.51.

46. B is correct. The coefficient of variation is the ratio of the standard deviation to the arithmetic average, or $\sqrt{0.001723}/0.09986 = 0.416$.

47. C is correct. The skewness is positive, so it is right-skewed (positively skewed).

48. C is correct. The excess kurtosis is positive, indicating that the distribution is "fat-tailed"; therefore, there is more probability in the tails of the distribution relative to the normal distribution.

CHAPTER 3

PROBABILITY CONCEPTS

SOLUTIONS

1. Use Equation 1 to find this conditional probability: *P(stock is dividend paying | telecom stock that meets criteria)* = *P(stock is dividend paying and telecom stock that meet\s criteria)/ P(telecom stock that meets criteria)* = 0.01/0.05 = 0.20.

2. According to the multiplication rule for independent events, the probability of a company meeting all three criteria is the product of the three probabilities. Labeling the event that a company passes the first, second, and third criteria, *A*, *B*, and *C*, respectively *P(ABC)* = *P(A)P(B)P(C)* = (0.20)(0.45)(0.78) = 0.0702. As a consequence, (0.0702)(500) = 35.10, so 35 companies pass the screen.

3. Use Equation 2, the multiplication rule for probabilities *P(AB)* = *P(A | B)P(B)*, defining *A* as the event that *a stock meets the financial strength criteria* and defining *B* as the event that *a stock meets the valuation criteria.* Then *P(AB)* = *P(A | B)P(B)* = 0.40 × 0.25 = 0.10. The probability that a stock meets both the financial and valuation criteria is 0.10.

4. A. *Outcomes associated with Scenario 1:* With a 0.45 probability of a $0.90 recovery per $1 principal value, given Scenario 1, and with the probability of Scenario 1 equal to 0.75, the probability of recovering $0.90 is 0.45 (0.75) = 0.3375. By a similar calculation, the probability of recovering $0.80 is 0.55(0.75) = 0.4125. *Outcomes associated with Scenario 2:* With a 0.85 probability of a $0.50 recovery per $1 principal value, given Scenario 2, and with the probability of Scenario 2 equal to 0.25, the probability of recovering $0.50 is 0.85(0.25) = 0.2125. By a similar calculation, the probability of recovering $0.40 is 0.15(0.25) = 0.0375.

   B. *E(recovery | Scenario 1)* = 0.45($0.90) + 0.55($0.80) = $0.845

   C. *E(recovery | Scenario 2)* = 0.85($0.50) + 0.15($0.40) = $0.485

   D. *E(recovery)* = 0.75($0.845) + 0.25($0.485) = $0.755

E.

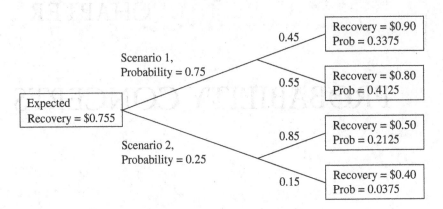

5. A. We can set up the equation using the total probability rule:

$$P(pass\ test) = P(pass\ test|survivor)P(survivor)$$
$$+ P(pass\ test|nonsurvivor)P(nonsurvivor)$$

We know that $P(survivor) = 1 - P(nonsurvivor) = 1 - 0.40 = 0.60$. Therefore, $P(pass\ test) = 0.55 = 0.85(0.60) + P(pass\ test\ |\ nonsurvivor)(0.40)$. Thus $P(pass\ test\ |\ nonsurvivor) = [0.55 - 0.85(0.60)]/0.40 = 0.10$.

B. $P(survivor|pass\ test) = [P(pass\ test|survivor)/P(pass\ test)]P(survivor)$
    $$= (0.85/0.55)0.60 = 0.927273$$

The information that a company passes the test causes you to update your probability that it is a survivor from 0.60 to approximately 0.927.

C. According to Bayes' formula, $P(nonsurvivor\ |\ fail\ test) = [P(fail\ test\ |\ nonsurvivor)/P(fail\ test)]P(nonsurvivor) = [P(fail\ test\ |\ nonsurvivor)/0.45]0.40$.
We can set up the following equation to obtain $P(fail\ test\ |\ nonsurvivor)$:

$$P(fail\ test) = P(fail\ test|nonsurvivor)P(nonsurvivor)$$
$$+ P(fail\ test|survivor)P(survivor)$$
$$0.45 = P(fail\ test|nonsurvivor)0.40 + 0.15(0.60)$$

where $P(fail\ test\ |\ survivor) = 1 - P(pass\ test\ |\ survivor) = 1 - 0.85 = 0.15$. So $P(fail\ test\ |\ nonsurvivor) = [0.45 - 0.15(0.60)]/0.40 = 0.90$. Using this result with the formula above, we find $P(nonsurvivor\ |\ fail\ test) = (0.90/0.45)0.40 = 0.80$. Seeing that a company fails the test causes us to update the probability that it is a nonsurvivor from 0.40 to 0.80.

D. A company passing the test greatly increases our confidence that it is a survivor. A company failing the test doubles the probability that it is a nonsurvivor. Therefore, the test appears to be useful.

6. C is correct. The term "exhaustive" means that the events cover all possible outcomes.

7. C is correct. A subjective probability draws on personal or subjective judgment that may be without reference to any particular data.

8. A is correct. Given odds for E of a to b, the implied probability of $E = a/(a + b)$. Stated in terms of odds a to b with $a = 1$, $b = 5$, the probability of $E = 1/(1 + 5) = 1/6 = 0.167$. This result confirms that a probability of 0.167 for beating sales is odds of 1 to 5.

9. C is correct. A conditional probability is the probability of an event given that another event has occurred.

10. B is correct. Because the events are independent, the multiplication rule is most appropriate for forecasting their joint probability. The multiplication rule for independent events states that the joint probability of both A and B occurring is P (AB) = P(A)P(B).

11. B is correct. The probability of the occurrence of one is related to the occurrence of the other. If we are trying to forecast one event, information about a dependent event may be useful.

12. C is correct. The total probability rule for expected value is used to estimate an expected value based on mutually exclusive and exhaustive scenarios.

13. B is correct. If Scenario 1 occurs, the expected recovery is 60% ($50,000) + 40% ($30,000) = $42,000, and if Scenario 2 occurs, the expected recovery is 90% ($80,000) + 10%($60,000) = $78,000. Weighting by the probability of each scenario, the expected recovery is 40%($42,000) + 60%($78,000) = $63,600. Alternatively, first calculating the probability of each amount occurring, the expected recovery is (40%) (60%)($50,000) + (40%)(40%)($30,000) + (60%)(90%)($80,000) + (60%)(10%) ($60,000) = $63,600.

14. A is correct. The covariance is the product of the standard deviations and correlation using the formula Cov(US bond returns, Spanish bond returns) = σ(US bonds) $\times \sigma$ (Spanish bonds) $\times \rho$(US bond returns, Spanish bond returns) = 0.64 $\times$ 0.56 $\times$ 0.24 = 0.086.

15. C is correct. The covariance of returns is positive when the returns on both assets tend to be on the same side (above or below) their expected values at the same time, indicating an average positive relationship between returns.

16. B is correct. Correlations near +1 exhibit strong positive linearity, whereas correlations near −1 exhibit strong negative linearity. A correlation of 0 indicates an absence of any linear relationship between the variables. The closer the correlation is to 0, the weaker the linear relationship.

17. C is correct. The correlation between two random variables R_i and R_j is defined as $\rho(R_i,R_j)$ = Cov$(R_i,R_j)/[\sigma(R_i)\sigma(R_j)]$. Using the subscript i to represent hedge funds and the subscript j to represent the market index, the standard deviations are $\sigma(R_i) = 256^{1/2} = 16$ and $\sigma(R_j) = 81^{1/2} = 9$. Thus, $\rho(R_i,R_j) = $ Cov$(R_i,R_j)/[\sigma(R_i) \sigma(R_j)] = 110/(16 \times 9) = 0.764$.

18. A is correct. As the correlation between two assets approaches +1, diversification benefits decrease. In other words, an increasingly positive correlation indicates an increasingly strong positive linear relationship and fewer diversification benefits.

19. A is correct. A covariance matrix for five stocks has 5 $\times$ 5 = 25 entries. Subtracting the 5 diagonal variance terms results in 20 off-diagonal entries. Because a covariance matrix is symmetrical, only 10 entries are unique (20/2 = 10).

20. A is correct. The analyst must first calculate expected sales as 0.05 $\times$ $70 + 0.70 $\times$ $40 + 0.25 $\times$ $25 = $3.50 million + $28.00 million + $6.25 million = $37.75 million.

After calculating expected sales, we can calculate the variance of sales:

$$= \sigma^2 \text{ (Sales)}$$

$$= P(\$70)[\$70 - E(\text{Sales})]^2 + P(\$40)[\$40 - E(\text{Sales})]^2 + P(\$25)[\$25 - E(\text{Sales})]^2$$

$$= 0.05(\$70 - 37.75)^2 + 0.70(\$40 - 37.75)^2 + 0.25(\$25 - 37.75)^2$$

$$= \$52.00 \text{ million} + \$3.54 \text{ million} + \$40.64 \text{ million} = \$96.18 \text{ million}.$$

The standard deviation of sales is thus $\sigma = (\$96.18)^{1/2} = \$9.81$ million.

21. C is correct. The covariance of returns is positive when the returns on both assets tend to be on the same side (above or below) their expected values at the same time.

22. B is correct. The covariance is 26.56, calculated as follows. First, expected returns are

$$E(R_{FI}) = (0.25 \times 25) + (0.50 \times 15) + (0.25 \times 10)$$

$$= 6.25 + 7.50 + 2.50 = 16.25 \text{ and}$$

$$E(R_{DI}) = (0.25 \times 30) + (0.50 \times 25) + (0.25 \times 15)$$

$$= 7.50 + 12.50 + 3.75 = 23.75.$$

Covariance is

$$\text{Cov}(R_{FI}, R_{DI}) = \sum_i \sum_j P(R_{FI,i}, R_{DI,j})(R_{FI,i} - ER_{FI})(R_{DI,j} - ER_{DI})$$

$$= 0.25[(25 - 16.25)(30 - 23.75)] + 0.50[(15 - 16.25)(25 - 23.75)] + 0.25$$
$$[(10 - 16.25)(15 - 23.75)]$$

$$= 13.67 + (-0.78) + 13.67 = 26.56.$$

23. C is correct. The combination formula provides the number of ways that r objects can be chosen from a total of n objects, when the order in which the r objects are listed does not matter. The order of the bonds within the portfolio does not matter.

24. A is correct. The answer is found using the combination formula

$$_nC_r = \binom{n}{r} = \frac{n!}{(n-r)!r!}$$

Here, $n = 4$ and $r = 2$, so the answer is $4!/[(4-2)!2!] = 24/[(2) \times (2)] = 6$. This result can be verified by assuming there are four vice presidents, VP1–VP4. The six possible additions to the investment committee are VP1 and VP2, VP1 and VP3, VP1 and VP4, VP2 and VP3, VP2 and VP4, and VP3 and VP4.

25. A is correct. The permutation formula is used to choose r objects from a total of n objects when order matters. Because the portfolio manager is trying to rank the four funds from most recommended to least recommended, the order of the funds matters; therefore, the permutation formula is most appropriate.

CHAPTER 4

COMMON PROBABILITY DISTRIBUTIONS

SOLUTIONS

1. A. The put's minimum value is $0. The put's value is $0 when the stock price is at or above $100 at the maturity date of the option. The put's maximum value is $100 = $100 (the exercise price) – $0 (the lowest possible stock price). The put's value is $100 when the stock is worthless at the option's maturity date. The put's minimum price increments are $0.01. The possible outcomes of terminal put value are thus $0.00, $0.01, $0.02, ..., $100.

   B. The price of the underlying has minimum price fluctuations of $0.01: These are the minimum price fluctuations for terminal put value. For example, if the stock finishes at $98.20, the payoff on the put is $100 – $98.20 = $1.80. We can specify that the nearest values to $1.80 are $1.79 and $1.81. With a continuous random variable, we cannot specify the nearest values. So, we must characterize terminal put value as a discrete random variable.

   C. The probability that terminal put value is less than or equal to $24 is $P(Y \leq 24)$ or $F(24)$, in standard notation, where F is the cumulative distribution function for terminal put value.

2. A binomial random variable is defined as the number of successes in n Bernoulli trials (a trial that produces one of two outcomes). The binomial distribution is used to make probability statements about a record of successes and failures or about anything with binary (twofold) outcomes.

3. B is correct. The value of the cumulative distribution function lies between 0 and 1 for any x: $0 \leq F(x) \leq 1$.

4. C is correct. The binomial distribution is symmetric when the probability of success on a trial is 0.50, but it is asymmetric or skewed otherwise. Here it is given that $p = 0.50$

5. B is correct. The probability of any outcome is 0.05, $P(1) = 1/20 = 0.05$. The probability that X is greater than or equal to 3 but less than 6, which is expressed as $P(3 \leq X < 6) = P(3) + P(4) + P(5) = 0.05 + 0.05 + 0.05 = 0.15$

6.　A.　The probability of an earnings increase (success) in a year is estimated as 7/10 = 0.70 or 70 percent, based on the record of the past 10 years.

　　B.　The probability that earnings will increase in 5 out of the next 10 years is about 10.3 percent. Define a binomial random variable X, counting the number of earnings increases over the next 10 years. From Part A, the probability of an earnings increase in a given year is $p = 0.70$ and the number of trials (years) is $n = 10$. Equation 1 gives the probability that a binomial random variable has x successes in n trials, with the probability of success on a trial equal to p.

$$P(X = x) = \binom{n}{x} p^x (1 - p)^{n-x} = \frac{n!}{(n - x)!x!} p^x (1 - p)^{n-x}$$

For this example,

$$\binom{10}{5} 0.7^5 0.3^{10-5} = \frac{10!}{(10 - 5)!5!} 0.7^5 0.3^{10-5}$$
$$= 252 \times 0.16807 \times 0.00243 = 0.102919$$

　　　We conclude that the probability that earnings will increase in exactly 5 of the next 10 years is 0.1029, or approximately 10.3 percent.

　　C.　The expected number of yearly increases is $E(X) = np = 10 \times 0.70 = 7$.

　　D.　The variance of the number of yearly increases over the next 10 years is $\sigma^2 = np (1 - p) = 10 \times 0.70 \times 0.30 = 2.1$. The standard deviation is 1.449 (the positive square root of 2.1).

　　E.　You must assume that 1) the probability of an earnings increase (success) is constant from year to year and 2) earnings increases are independent trials. If current and past earnings help forecast next year's earnings, Assumption 2 is violated. If the company's business is subject to economic or industry cycles, neither assumption is likely to hold.

7.　B is correct. To calculate the probability of 4 years of outperformance, use the formula:

$$p(x) = P(X = x) = \binom{n}{x} p^x (1 - p)^{n-x} = \frac{n!}{(n - x)!x!} p^x (1 - p)^{n-x}$$

Using this formula to calculate the probability in 4 of 5 years, $n = 5$, $x = 4$ and $p = 0.60$. Therefore,

$$p(4) = \frac{5!}{(5 - 4)!4!} 0.6^4 (1 - 0.6)^{5-4} = [120/24](0.1296)(0.40) = 0.2592$$

$$p(5) = \frac{5!}{(5 - 5)!5!} 0.6^5 (1 - 0.6)^{5-5} = [120/120](0.0778)(1) = 0.0778$$

The probability of outperforming 4 or more times is $p(4) + p(5) = 0.2592 + 0.0778 = 0.3370$

8.　The observed success rate is 4/7 = 0.571, or 57.1 percent. The probability of four or fewer successes is $F(4) = p(4) + p(3) + p(2) + p(1) + p(0)$, where $p(4), p(3), p(2), p(1)$, and $p(0)$ are respectively the probabilities of 4, 3, 2, 1, and 0 successes, according to the binomial distribution with $n = 7$ and $p = 0.70$. We have

$$p(4) = (7!/4!3!)(0.70^4)(0.30^3) = 35(0.006483) = 0.226895$$

$$p(3) = (7!/3!4!)(0.70^3)(0.30^4) = 35(0.002778) = 0.097241$$

$$p(2) = (7!/2!5!)(0.70^2)(0.30^5) = 21(0.001191) = 0.025005$$

$$p(1) = (7!/1!6!)(0.70^1)(0.30^6) = 7(0.000510) = 0.003572$$

$$p(0) = (7!/0!7!)(0.70^0)(0.30^7) = 1(0.000219) = 0.000219$$

Summing all these probabilities, you conclude that $F(4) = 0.226895 + 0.097241 + 0.025005 + 0.003572 + 0.000219 = 0.352931$, or 35.3 percent.

9. A. The expected value of fourth-quarter sales is €14,500,000, calculated as (€14,000,000 + €15,000,000)/2. With a continuous uniform random variable, the mean or expected value is the midpoint between the smallest and largest values. (See Example 7.)

    B. The probability that fourth-quarter sales will be less than €14,125,000 is 0.125 or 12.5 percent, calculated as (€14,125,000 − €14,000,000)/(€15,000,000 − €14,000,000).

10. A. Approximately 68 percent of all outcomes of a normal random variable fall within plus or minus one standard deviation of the mean.

    B. Approximately 95 percent of all outcomes of a normal random variable fall within plus or minus two standard deviations of the mean.

    C. Approximately 99 percent of all outcomes of a normal random variable fall within plus or minus three standard deviations of the mean.

11. The area under the normal curve for $z = 0.36$ is 0.6406 or 64.06 percent. The following table presents an excerpt from the tables of the standard normal cumulative distribution function in the back of this volume. To locate $z = 0.36$, find 0.30 in the fourth row of numbers, then look at the column for 0.06 (the second decimal place of 0.36). The entry is 0.6406.

$P(Z \le x) = N(x)$ for $x \ge 0$ or $P(Z \le z) = N(z)$ for $z \ge 0$

x or z	0	0.01	0.02	0.03	0.04	0.05	0.06	0.07	0.08	0.09
0.00	0.5000	0.5040	0.5080	0.5120	0.5160	0.5199	0.5239	0.5279	0.5319	0.5359
0.10	0.5398	0.5438	0.5478	0.5517	0.5557	0.5596	0.5636	0.5675	0.5714	0.5753
0.20	0.5793	0.5832	0.5871	0.5910	0.5948	0.5987	0.6026	0.6064	0.6103	0.6141
0.30	0.6179	0.6217	0.6255	0.6293	0.6331	0.6368	**0.6406**	0.6443	0.6480	0.6517
0.40	0.6554	0.6591	0.6628	0.6664	0.6700	0.6736	0.6772	0.6808	0.6844	0.6879
0.50	0.6915	0.6950	0.6985	0.7019	0.7054	0.7088	0.7123	0.7157	0.7190	0.7224

The interpretation of 64.06 percent for $z = 0.36$ is that 64.06 percent of observations on a standard normal random variable are smaller than or equal to the value 0.36. (So 100% − 64.06% = 35.94% of the values are greater than 0.36.)

12. C is correct. The probability that the performance is at or below the expectation is calculated by finding $F(3) = p(3) + p(2) + p(1)$ using the formula:

$$p(x) = P(X = x) = \binom{n}{x} p^x (1-p)^{n-x} = \frac{n!}{(n-x)!x!} p^x (1-p)^{n-x}$$

Using this formula,

$$p(3) = \frac{4!}{(4-3)!3!} 0.75^3 (1 - 0.75)^{4-3} = [24/6](0.42)(0.25) = 0.42$$

$$p(2) = \frac{4!}{(4-2)!2!} 0.75^2 (1 - 0.75)^{4-2} = [24/4](0.56)(0.06) = 0.20$$

$$p(1) = \frac{4!}{(4-1)!1!} 0.75^1 (1 - 0.75)^{4-1} = [24/6](0.75)(0.02) = 0.06$$

$$p(0) = \frac{4!}{(4-0)!0!} 0.75^0 (1 - 0.75)^{4-0} = [24/24](1)(0.004) = 0.004$$

Therefore,

$F(3) = p(3) + p(2) + p(1) + p(0) = 0.42 + 0.20 + 0.06 + 0.004 = 0.684$ or approximately 68 percent

13. A. The probability of exhausting the liquidity pool is 4.7 percent. First calculate $x = \lambda/(\sigma\sqrt{T}) = 2,000/(450\sqrt{5}) = 1.987616$. We can round this value to 1.99 to use the standard normal tables in the back of this book. Using those tables, we find that $N(1.99) = 0.9767$. Thus, the probability of exhausting the liquidity pool is $2[1 - N(1.99)] = 2(1 - 0.9767) = 0.0466$ or about 4.7 percent.

     B. The probability of exhausting the liquidity pool is now 32.2 percent. The calculation follows the same steps as those in Part A. We calculate $x = \lambda/(\sigma\sqrt{T}) = 2,000/(450\sqrt{20}) = 0.993808$. We can round this value to 0.99 to use the standard normal tables in the back of this book. Using those tables, we find that $N(0.99) = 0.8389$. Thus, the probability of exhausting the liquidity pool is $2[1 - N(0.99)] = 2(1 - 0.8389) = 0.3222$ or about 32.2 percent. This is a substantial probability that you will run out of funds to meet mark to market.
     In their paper, Kolb et al. call the probability of exhausting the liquidity pool the probability of ruin, a traditional name for this type of calculation.

14. B is correct. The normal distribution has a skewness of 0, a kurtosis of 3, and a mean, median and mode that are all equal.

15. B is correct. Multivariate distributions specify the probabilities for a group of related random variables. A portfolio of technology stocks represents a group of related assets. Accordingly, statistical interrelationships must be considered, resulting in the need to use a multivariate normal distribution.

16. C is correct. A bivariate normal distribution (two stocks) will have two means, two variances and one correlation. A multivariate normal distribution for the returns on n stocks will have n means, n variances and $n(n - 1)/2$ distinct correlations.

17. A. Because £50,000/£1,350,000 is 3.7 percent, for any return less than 3.7 percent the client will need to invade principal if she takes out £50,000. So R_L = 3.7 percent.

     B. To decide which of the allocations is safety-first optimal, select the alternative with the highest ratio $[E(R_P) - R_L]/\sigma_P$.

Allocation A: 0.5125 = (16 − 3.7)/24

Allocation B: 0.488235 = (12 − 3.7)/17

Allocation C: 0.525 = (10 − 3.7)/12

Allocation D: 0.481818 = (9 − 3.7)/11

Allocation C, with the largest ratio (0.525), is the best alternative according to the safety-first criterion.

C. To answer this question, note that $P(R_C < 3.7) = N(-0.525)$. We can round 0.525 to 0.53 for use with tables of the standard normal cdf. First, we calculate $N(-0.53)$ = 1 − $N(0.53)$ = 1 − 0.7019 = 0.2981 or about 30 percent. The safety-first optimal portfolio has a roughly 30 percent chance of not meeting a 3.7 percent return threshold.

18. A is correct. $P(8\% \leq$ Portfolio return $\leq 11\%) = N(Z$ corresponding to 11%$) − N(Z$ corresponding to 8%$)$. For the first term, $Z = (11\% − 8\%)/14\% = 0.21$ approximately, and using the table of cumulative normal distribution given in the problem, $N(0.21)$ = 0.5832. To get the second term immediately, note that 8 percent is the mean, and for the normal distribution 50 percent of the probability lies on either side of the mean. Therefore, $N(Z$ corresponding to 8%$)$ must equal 50 percent. So $P(8\% \leq$ Portfolio return $\leq 11\%)$ = 0.5832 − 0.50 = 0.0832 or approximately 8.3 percent.

19. B is correct. There are three steps, which involve standardizing the portfolio return: First, subtract the portfolio mean return from each side of the inequality: $P($Portfolio return − 7%$) \leq 4\% − 7\%)$. Second, divide each side of the inequality by the standard deviation of portfolio return: $P[($Portfolio return − 7%$)/13\% \leq (4\% − 7\%)/13\%] = P(Z \leq −0.2308) = N(-0.2308)$. Third, recognize that on the left-hand side we have a standard normal variable, denoted by Z and $N(-x) = 1 − N(x)$. Rounding −0.2308 to −0.23 for use with the cumulative distribution function (cdf) table, we have $N(-0.23)$ = 1 − $N(0.23)$ = 1 − 0.5910 = 0.409, approximately 41 percent. The probability that the portfolio will underperform the target is about 41 percent.

20. A. Elements that should appear in a definition of Monte Carlo simulation are that it makes use of a computer; that it is used to represent the operation of a complex system, or in some applications, to find an approximate solution to a problem; and that it involves the generation of a large number of random samples from a specified probability distribution. The exact wording can vary, but one definition follows:

Monte Carlo simulation in finance involves the use of a computer to represent the operation of a complex financial system. In some important applications, Monte Carlo simulation is used to find an approximate solution to a complex financial problem. An integral part of Monte Carlo simulation is the generation of a large number of random samples from a probability distribution.

B. *Strengths*. Monte Carlo simulation can be used to price complex securities for which no analytic expression is available, particularly European-style options.

Weaknesses. Monte Carlo simulation provides only statistical estimates, not exact results. Analytic methods, when available, provide more insight into cause-and-effect relationships than does Monte Carlo simulation.

21. C is correct. The rate of return is a random variable because the future outcomes are uncertain, and it is continuous because it can take on an unlimited number of outcomes.

22. B is correct. The function $g(x)$ satisfies the conditions of a probability function. All of the values of $g(x)$ are between 0 and 1, and the values of $g(x)$ all sum to 1.

23. A is correct. The probability that X will take on a value of 4 or less is: $F(4) = P(X \leq 4) = p(1) + p(2) + p(3) + p(4) = 0.60$. The probability that X will take on a value of 3 or less is: $F(3) = P(X \leq 3) = p(1) + p(2) + p(3) = 0.50$. So, the probability that X will take on a value of 4 is: $F(4) - F(3) = p(4) = 0.10$. The probability of $X = 2$ can be found using the same logic: $F(2) - F(1) = p(2) = 0.25 - 0.15 = 0.10$. The probability of X taking on a value of 2 or 4 is: $p(2) + p(4) = 0.10 + 0.10 = 0.20$.

24. A is correct. A trial, such as a coin flip, will produce one of two outcomes. Such a trial is a Bernoulli trial.

25. A is correct. The continuously compounded return of an asset over a period is equal to the natural log of period's change. In this case:

$$\ln(120/112) = 6.90\%$$

26. C is correct. The probability of an up move (p) can be found by solving the equation: $(p)uS + (1 - p)dS = (p)105 + (1 - p)97 = 102$. Solving for p gives $8p = 5$, so that $p = 0.625$.

27. A is correct. Only the top node value of $219.9488 exceeds $200.

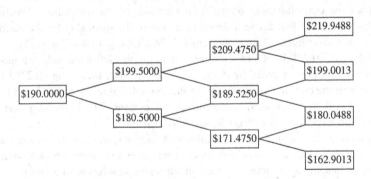

28. A is correct. The probability of generating a random number equal to any fixed point under a continuous uniform distribution is zero.

29. C is correct. A characteristic feature of Monte Carlo simulation is the generation of a large number of random samples from a specified probability distribution or distributions to represent the role of risk in the system.

30. C is correct. Monte Carlo simulation is a complement to analytical methods. Monte Carlo simulation provides statistical estimates and not exact results. Analytical methods, when available, provide more insight into cause-and-effect relationships

31. B is correct. A normal distribution has a skewness of zero (it is symmetrical around the mean). A non-zero skewness implies asymmetry in a distribution.

32. A is correct. The chance of a negative return falls in the area to the left of 0% under a standard normal curve. By standardizing the returns and standard deviations of the two

assets, the likelihood of either asset experiencing a negative return may be determined: Z-score (standardized value) $= (X - \mu)/\sigma$

$$\text{Z-score for a bond return of } 0\% = (0 - 2)/5 = -0.40.$$

$$\text{Z-score for a stock return of } 0\% = (0 - 10)/15 = -0.67.$$

For bonds, a 0% return falls 0.40 standard deviations below the mean return of 2%. In contrast, for stocks, a 0% return falls 0.67 standard deviations below the mean return of 10%. A standard deviation of 0.40 is less than a standard deviation of 0.67. Negative returns thus occupy more of the left tail of the bond distribution than the stock distribution. Thus, bonds are more likely than stocks to experience a negative return.

33.   B is correct. Allocation B has the highest safety-first ratio. The threshold return level R_L for the portfolio is £90,000/£2,000,000 = 4.5%, thus any return less than R_L = 4.5% will invade the portfolio principal. To compute the allocation that is safety-first optimal, select the alternative with the highest ratio:

$$\frac{[E(R_P - R_L)]}{\sigma_P}$$

$$\text{Allocation A} = \frac{6.5 - 4.5}{8.35} = 0.240$$

$$\text{Allocation B} = \frac{7.5 - 4.5}{10.21} = 0.294$$

$$\text{Allocation C} = \frac{8.5 - 4.5}{14.34} = 0.279$$

34.   B is correct. By definition, lognormal random variables cannot have negative values.

35.   C is correct. A lognormal distributed variable has a lower bound of zero. The lognormal distribution is also right skewed, which is a useful property in describing asset prices.

36.   A is correct. The continuously compounded return from $t = 0$ to $t = 1$ is $r_{0,1} = \ln(S_1/S_0)$ = $\ln(186.75/208.25) = -0.10897 = -10.90\%$.

SAMPLING AND ESTIMATION

SOLUTIONS

1. **A.** The standard deviation or standard error of the sample mean is $\sigma\bar{X} = \sigma/\sqrt{n}$. Substituting in the values for $\sigma\bar{X}$ and σ, we have $1\% = 6\%/\sqrt{n}$, or $\sqrt{n} = 6$. Squaring this value, we get a random sample of $n = 36$.

   B. As in Part A, the standard deviation of sample mean is $\sigma\bar{X} = \sigma/\sqrt{n}$. Substituting in the values for $\sigma\bar{X}$ and σ, we have $0.25\% = 6\%/\sqrt{n}$, or $\sqrt{n} = 24$. Squaring this value, we get a random sample of $n = 576$, which is substantially larger than for Part A of this question.

2. **A.** Assume the sample size will be large and thus the 95 percent confidence interval for the mean of a sample of manager returns is $\bar{X} \pm 1.96s\bar{X}$, where $s\bar{X} = s/\sqrt{n}$. Munzi wants the distance between the upper limit and lower limit in the confidence interval to be 1 percent, which is

$$(\bar{X} + 1.96s\bar{X}) - (\bar{X} - 1.96s\bar{X}) = 1\%$$

   Simplifying this equation, we get $2(1.96s\bar{X}) = 1\%$. Finally, we have $3.92s\bar{X} = 1\%$, which gives us the standard deviation of the sample mean, $s\bar{X} = 0.255\%$. The distribution of sample means is $s\bar{X} = s/\sqrt{n}$. Substituting in the values for $s\bar{X}$ and s, we have $0.255\% = 4\%/\sqrt{n}$, or $\sqrt{n} = 15.69$. Squaring this value, we get a random sample of $n = 246$.

   B. With her budget, Munzi can pay for a sample of up to 100 observations, which is far short of the 246 observations needed. Munzi can either proceed with her current budget and settle for a wider confidence interval or she can raise her budget (to around $2,460) to get the sample size for a 1 percent width in her confidence interval.

3. **A.** This is a small-sample problem in which the sample comes from a normal population with a known standard deviation; thus we use the z-distribution in the solution. For a 95 percent confidence interval (and 2.5 percent in each tail), the

critical z-value is 1.96. For returns that are normally distributed, a 95 percent confidence interval is of the form

$$\mu + 1.96\frac{\sigma}{\sqrt{n}}$$

The lower limit is $X_1 = \mu - 1.96\frac{\sigma}{\sqrt{n}} = 6\% - 1.96\frac{18\%}{\sqrt{4}} = 6\% - 1.96(9\%) =$ −11.64%.

The upper limit is $X_u = \mu + 1.96\frac{\sigma}{\sqrt{n}} = 6\% + 1.96\frac{18\%}{\sqrt{4}} = 6\% + 1.96(9\%) =$ 23.64%.

There is a 95 percent probability that four-year average returns will be between −11.64 percent and +23.64 percent.

B. The critical z-value associated with the −2.0 percent return is

$$Z = \frac{\bar{X} - \mu}{\sigma/\sqrt{n}} = \frac{-2\% - 6\%}{18\%/\sqrt{4}} = \frac{-8\%}{9\%} = -0.89$$

Using a normal table, the probability of a z-value less than −0.89 is P $(Z < -0.89) = 0.1867$. Unfortunately, although your client is unhappy with the investment result, a four-year average return of −2.0 percent or lower should occur 18.67 percent of the time.

4. (Refer to Figure 1 to help visualize the answer to this question.) Basically, only one standard normal distribution exists, but many t-distributions exist—one for every different number of degrees of freedom. The normal distribution and the t-distribution for a large number of degrees of freedom are practically the same. The lower the degrees of freedom, the flatter the t-distribution becomes. The t-distribution has less mass (lower probabilities) in the center of the distribution and more mass (higher probabilities) out in both tails. Therefore, the confidence intervals based on t-values will be wider than those based on the normal distribution. Stated differently, the probability of being within a given number of standard deviations (such as within ± 1 standard deviation or ± 2 standard deviations) is lower for the t-distribution than for the normal distribution.

5. A. For a 99 percent confidence interval, the reliability factor we use is $t_{0.005}$; for df $= 20$, this factor is 2.845.

   B. For a 90 percent confidence interval, the reliability factor we use is $t_{0.05}$; for df $= 20$, this factor is 1.725.

   C. Degrees of freedom equals $n - 1$, or in this case $25 - 1 = 24$. For a 95 percent confidence interval, the reliability factor we use is $t_{0.025}$; for df $= 24$, this factor is 2.064.

   D. Degrees of freedom equals $16 - 1 = 15$. For a 95 percent confidence interval, the reliability factor we use is $t_{0.025}$; for df $= 15$, this factor is 2.131.

6. Because this is a small sample from a normal population and we have only the sample standard deviation, we use the following model to solve for the confidence interval of the population mean:

$$\bar{X} \pm t_{\alpha/2}\frac{s}{\sqrt{n}}$$

where we find $t_{0.025}$ (for a 95 percent confidence interval) for df $= n - 1 = 24 - 1$ $= 23$; this value is 2.069. Our solution is 1% $\pm$ 2.069(4%)/$\sqrt{24}$ = 1% $\pm$ 2.069 (0.8165) = 1% $\pm$ 1.69. The 95 percent confidence interval spans the range from -0.69 percent to $+2.69$ percent.

7. The following table summarizes the calculations used in the answers.

Forecast (X_i)	Number of Analysts (n_i)	$X_i n_i$	$(X_i - \bar{X})$	$(X_i - \bar{X})^2$	$(X_i - \bar{X})^2 n_i$
1.40	1	1.40	−0.05	0.0025	0.0025
1.43	1	1.43	−0.02	0.0004	0.0004
1.44	3	4.32	−0.01	0.0001	0.0003
1.45	2	2.90	0.00	0.0000	0.0000
1.47	1	1.47	0.02	0.0004	0.0004
1.48	1	1.48	0.03	0.0009	0.0009
1.50	1	1.50	0.05	0.0025	0.0025
Sums	10	14.50			0.0070

A. With $n = 10$, $\bar{X} = \sum_{i=1}^{10} X_i/n = 14.50/10 = 1.45$. The variance is $s^2 =$

$[\sum_{i=1}^{10}(X_i - \bar{X})^2]/(n-1) = 0.0070/9 = 0.0007778$. The sample standard deviation is $s = \sqrt{0.0007778} = 0.02789$.

B. The confidence interval for the mean can be estimated by using $\bar{X} \pm t_{\alpha/2}(s/\sqrt{n})$. For 9 degrees of freedom, the reliability factor, $t_{0.025}$, equals 2.262 and the confidence interval is

$$1.45 \pm 2.262 \times 0.02789/\sqrt{10} = 1.45 \pm 2.262(0.00882)$$
$$= 1.45 \pm 0.02$$

The confidence interval for the population mean ranges from 1.43 to 1.47.

8. The following table summarizes the calculations used in the answers.

Forecast (X_i)	Number of Analysts (n_i)	$X_i n_i$	$(X_i - \bar{X})$	$(X_i - \bar{X})^2$	$(X_i - \bar{X})^2 n_i$
0.70	2	1.40	−0.04	0.0016	0.0032
0.72	4	2.88	−0.02	0.0004	0.0016
0.74	1	0.74	0.00	0.0000	0.0000
0.75	3	2.25	0.01	0.0001	0.0003
0.76	1	0.76	0.02	0.0004	0.0004
0.77	1	0.77	0.03	0.0009	0.0009
0.82	1	0.82	0.08	0.0064	0.0064
Sums	13	9.62			0.0128

A. With $n = 13$, $\bar{X} = \sum_{i=1}^{13} X_i/n = 9.62/13 = 0.74$. The variance is $s^2 =$

$[\sum_{i=1}^{13}(X_i - \bar{X})^2] / (n-1) = 0.0128/12 = 0.001067$. The sample standard

deviation is $s = \sqrt{0.001067} = 0.03266$.

B. The sample is small, and the distribution appears to be bimodal. We cannot compute a confidence interval for the population mean because we have probably sampled from a distribution that is not normal.

9. If the population variance is known, the confidence interval is

$$\bar{X} \pm z_{\alpha/2}\frac{\sigma}{\sqrt{n}}$$

The confidence interval for the population mean is centered at the sample mean, $\bar{X}$. The population standard deviation is σ, and the sample size is n. The population standard deviation divided by the square root of n is the standard error of the estimate of the mean. The value of z depends on the desired degree of confidence. For a 95 percent confidence interval, $z_{0.025} = 1.96$ and the confidence interval estimate is

$$\bar{X} \pm 1.96\frac{\sigma}{\sqrt{n}}$$

If the population variance is not known, we make two changes to the technique used when the population variance is known. First, we must use the sample standard deviation instead of the population standard deviation. Second, we use the t-distribution instead of the normal distribution. The critical t-value will depend on degrees of freedom $n - 1$. If the sample size is large, we have the alternative of using the z-distribution with the sample standard deviation.

10. A. The probabilities can be taken from a normal table, in which the critical z-values are 2.00 or 3.00 and we are including the probabilities in both tails. The probabilities that the exchange rate will be at least 2 or 3 standard deviations away from the mean are

$$P(\mid X - \mu \mid \geq 2\sigma) = 0.0456$$
$$P(\mid X - \mu \mid \geq 3\sigma) = 0.0026$$

B. With Chebyshev's inequality, the maximum probability of the exchange rate being at least k standard deviations from the mean is $P(\mid X - \mu \mid \geq k\sigma) \leq (1/k)^2$. The maximum probabilities of the rate being at least 2 or 3 standard deviations away from the mean are

$$P(\mid X - \mu \mid \geq 2\sigma) \leq (1/2)^2 = 0.2500$$
$$P(\mid X - \mu \mid \geq 3\sigma) \leq (1/3)^2 = 0.1111$$

The probability of the rate being outside 2 or 3 standard deviations of the mean is much smaller with a known normal distribution than when the distribution is unknown and we are relying on Chebyshev's inequality.

11. No. First the conclusion on the limit of zero is wrong; second, the support cited for drawing the conclusion (i.e., the central limit theorem) is not relevant in this context.

12. In many instances, the distribution that describes the underlying population is not normal or the distribution is not known. The central limit theorem states that if the sample size is large, regardless of the shape of the underlying population, the distribution of the sample mean is approximately normal. Therefore, even in these instances, we can still construct confidence intervals (and conduct tests of inference) as long as the sample size is large (generally $n \geq 30$).

13. The statement makes the following mistakes:
    - Given the conditions in the statement, the distribution of $\bar{X}$ will be approximately normal only for large sample sizes.
    - The statement omits the important element of the central limit theorem that the distribution of $\bar{X}$ will have mean μ.

14. A is correct. The discrepancy arises from sampling error. Sampling error exists whenever one fails to observe every element of the population, because a sample statistic can vary from sample to sample. As stated in the reading, the sample mean is an unbiased estimator, a consistent estimator, and an efficient estimator of the population mean. Although the sample mean is an unbiased estimator of the population mean—the expected value of the sample mean equals the population mean—because of sampling error, we do not expect the sample mean to exactly equal the population mean in any one sample we may take.

15. No, we cannot say that Alcorn Mutual Funds as a group is superior to competitors. Alcorn Mutual Funds' advertisement may easily mislead readers because the advertisement does not show the performance of all its funds. In particular, Alcorn Mutual Funds is engaging in sample selection bias by presenting the investment results from its best-performing funds only.

16. Spence may be guilty of data mining. He has used so many possible combinations of variables on so many stocks, it is not surprising that he found some instances in which a model worked. In fact, it would have been more surprising if he had not found any. To decide whether to use his model, you should do two things: First, ask that the model be tested on out-of-sample data—that is, data that were not used in building the model. The model may not be successful with out-of-sample data. Second, examine his model to make sure that the relationships in the model make economic sense, have a story, and have a future.

17. C is correct. Stratified random sampling involves dividing a population into subpopulations based on one or more classification criteria. Then, simple random samples are drawn from each subpopulation in sizes proportional to the relative size of each subpopulation. These samples are then pooled to form a stratified random sample.

18. B is correct. Given a population described by any probability distribution (normal or non-normal) with finite variance, the central limit theorem states that the sampling distribution of the sample mean will be approximately normal, with the mean approximately equal to the population mean, when the sample size is large.

19. B is correct. Taking the square root of the known population variance to determine the population standard deviation (σ) results in: $\sigma = \sqrt{2.45} = 1.565$
     The formula for the standard error of the sample mean (σ_X), based on a known sample size (n), is:

$$\sigma_X = \frac{\sigma}{\sqrt{n}}$$

Therefore,

$$\sigma_X = \frac{1.565}{\sqrt{40}} = 0.247$$

20. B is correct. An unbiased estimator is one for which the expected value equals the parameter it is intended to estimate.

21. A is correct. A consistent estimator is one for which the probability of estimates close to the value of the population parameter increases as sample size increases. More specifically, a consistent estimator's sampling distribution becomes concentrated on the value of the parameter it is intended to estimate as the sample size approaches infinity.

22. A is correct. As the degree of confidence increases (e.g., from 95% to 99%), a given confidence interval will become wider. A confidence interval is a range for which one can assert with a given probability $1 - \alpha$, called the degree of confidence, that it will contain the parameter it is intended to estimate.

23. A is correct. A standard normal distribution has tails that approach zero faster than the t-distribution. As degrees of freedom increase, the tails of the t-distribution become less fat and the t-distribution begins to look more like a standard normal distribution. But as degrees of freedom decrease, the tails of the t-distribution become fatter.

24. B is correct. The confidence interval is calculated using the following equation:

$$\bar{X} \pm t_{\alpha/2}\frac{s}{\sqrt{n}}$$

Sample standard deviation (s) = $\sqrt{245.55} = 15.670$.
For a sample size of 17, degrees of freedom equal 16, so $t_{0.05} = 1.746$.
The confidence interval is calculated as

$$116.23 \pm 1.746\frac{15.67}{\sqrt{17}} = 116.23 \pm 6.6357$$

Therefore, the interval spans 109.5943 to 122.8656, meaning its width is equal to approximately 13.271. (This interval can be alternatively calculated as 6.6357 × 2).

25. A is correct. To solve, use the structure of Confidence interval = Point estimate $\pm$ Reliability factor × Standard error, which, for a normally distributed population with known variance, is represented by the following formula:

$$\bar{X} \pm z_{\alpha/2}\frac{\sigma}{\sqrt{n}}$$

For a 99% confidence interval, use $z_{0.005} = 2.58$.

Also, $\sigma = \sqrt{529} = 23$.

Therefore, the lower limit $= 31 - 2.58\frac{23}{\sqrt{65}} = 23.6398$.

26. B is correct. All else being equal, as the sample size increases, the standard error of the sample mean decreases and the width of the confidence interval also decreases.

27. B is correct. A report that uses a current list of stocks does not account for firms that failed, merged, or otherwise disappeared from the public equity market in previous years. As a consequence, the report is biased. This type of bias is known as survivorship bias.

28. B is correct. An out-of-sample test is used to investigate the presence of data-mining bias. Such a test uses a sample that does not overlap the time period of the sample on which a variable, strategy, or model was developed.

29. A is correct. A short time series is likely to give period-specific results that may not reflect a longer time period.

CHAPTER 6

HYPOTHESIS TESTING

SOLUTIONS

1. C is correct. Together, the null and alternative hypotheses account for all possible values of the parameter. Any possible values of the parameter not covered by the null must be covered by the alternative hypothesis (e.g., H_0: $\theta \leq 5$ versus H_a: $\theta > 5$).

2. A. The appropriate test statistic is a t-statistic with $n - 1 = 15 - 1 = 14$ degrees of freedom. A t-statistic is theoretically correct when the sample comes from a normally distributed population with unknown variance. When the sample size is also small, there is no practical alternative.

   B. The appropriate test statistic is a t-statistic with $40 - 1 = 39$ degrees of freedom. A t-statistic is theoretically correct when the sample comes from a normally distributed population with unknown variance. When the sample size is large (generally, 30 or more is a "large" sample), it is also possible to use a z-statistic, whether the population is normally distributed or not. A test based on a t-statistic is more conservative than a z-statistic test.

   C. The appropriate test statistic is a z-statistic because the sample comes from a normally distributed population with known variance. (The known population standard deviation is used to compute the standard error of the mean using Equation 2 in the text.)

   D. The appropriate test statistic is chi-square (χ^2) with $50 - 1 = 49$ degrees of freedom.

   E. The appropriate test statistic is the F-statistic (the ratio of the sample variances).

   F. The appropriate test statistic is a t-statistic for a paired observations test (a paired comparisons test), because the samples are correlated.

   G. The appropriate test statistic is a t-statistic using a pooled estimate of the population variance. The t-statistic has $25 + 30 - 2 = 53$ degrees of freedom. This statistic is appropriate because the populations are normally distributed with unknown variances; because the variances are assumed equal, the observations can be pooled to estimate the common variance. The requirement of independent samples for using this statistic has been met.

3. A. With degrees of freedom (DF) $n - 1 = 26 - 1 = 25$, the rejection point conditions for this two-sided test are $t > 2.060$ and $t < -2.060$. Because the significance level is 0.05, $0.05/2 = 0.025$ of the probability is in each tail. The tables give one-sided (one-tailed) probabilities, so we used the 0.025 column. Read across DF $= 25$ to the $\alpha = 0.025$ column to find 2.060, the rejection point for the right tail. By symmetry, -2.060 is the rejection point for the left tail.

    B. With DF $= 39$, the rejection point conditions for this two-sided test are $t > 2.708$ and $t < -2.708$. This is a two-sided test, so we use the $0.01/2 = 0.005$ column. Read across DF $= 39$ to the $\alpha = 0.005$ column to find 2.708, the rejection point for the right tail. By symmetry, -2.708 is the rejection point for the left tail.

    C. With DF $= 39$, the rejection point condition for this one-sided test is $t > 2.426$. Read across DF $= 39$ to the $\alpha = 0.01$ column to find 2.426, the rejection point for the right tail. Because we have a "greater than" alternative, we are concerned with only the right tail.

    D. With DF $= 20$, the rejection point condition for this one-sided test is $t > 1.725$. Read across DF $= 20$ to the $\alpha = 0.05$ column to find 1.725, the rejection point for the right tail. Because we have a "greater than" alternative, we are concerned with only the right tail.

    E. With DF $= 18$, the rejection point condition for this one-sided test is $t < -1.330$. Read across DF $= 18$ to the $\alpha = 0.10$ column to find 1.330, the rejection point for the right tail. By symmetry, the rejection point for the left tail is -1.330.

    F. With DF $= 49$, the rejection point condition for this one-sided test is $t < -1.677$. Read across DF $= 49$ to the $\alpha = 0.05$ column to find 1.677, the rejection point for the right tail. By symmetry, the rejection point for the left tail is -1.677.

4. Recall that with a z-test (in contrast to the t-test), we do not employ degrees of freedom. The standard normal distribution is a single distribution applicable to all z-tests. You should refer to "Rejection Points for a z-Test" in Section 3.1 to answer these questions.

    A. This is a two-sided test at a 0.01 significance level. In Part C of "Rejection Points for a z-Test," we find that the rejection point conditions are $z > 2.575$ and $z < -2.575$.

    B. This is a two-sided test at a 0.05 significance level. In Part B of "Rejection Points for a z-Test," we find that the rejection point conditions are $z > 1.96$ and $z < -1.96$.

    C. This is a two-sided test at a 0.10 significance level. In Part A of "Rejection Points for a z-Test," we find that the rejection point conditions are $z > 1.645$ and $z < -1.645$.

    D. This is a one-sided test at a 0.05 significance level. In Part B of "Rejection Points for a z-Test," we find that the rejection point condition for a test with a "greater than" alternative hypothesis is $z > 1.645$.

5. A. As stated in the text, we often set up the "hoped for" or "suspected" condition as the alternative hypothesis. Here, that condition is that the population value of Willco's mean annual net income exceeds \$24 million. Thus we have $H_0: \mu \leq 24$ versus $H_a: \mu > 24$.

    B. Given that net income is normally distributed with unknown variance, the appropriate test statistic is t with $n - 1 = 6 - 1 = 5$ degrees of freedom.

C.   In the *t*-distribution table in the back of the book, in the row for DF = 5 under $\alpha = 0.05$, we read the rejection point (critical value) of 2.015. We will reject the null if $t > 2.015$.

D.   The *t*-test is given by Equation 4:

$$t_5 = \frac{\bar{X} - \mu_0}{s/\sqrt{n}} = \frac{30 - 24}{10/\sqrt{6}} = \frac{6}{4.082483} = 1.469694$$

or 1.47. Because 1.47 does not exceed 2.015, we do not reject the null hypothesis. The difference between the sample mean of \$30 million and the hypothesized value of \$24 million under the null is not statistically significant.

6.   A. $H_0: \mu = 0$ versus $H_a: \mu \neq 0$.

B.   The *t*-test is based on $t = \frac{\bar{X} - \mu_0}{s/\sqrt{n}}$ with $n - 1 = 101 - 1 = 100$ degrees of freedom. At the 0.05 significance level, we reject the null if $t > 1.984$ or if $t < -1.984$. At the 0.01 significance level, we reject the null if $t > 2.626$ or if $t < -2.626$. For Analyst A, we have $t = (0.05 - 0)/(0.10/\sqrt{101}) = 0.05/0.00995 = 5.024938$ or 5.025. We clearly reject the null hypothesis at both the 0.05 and 0.01 levels.

The calculation of the *z*-statistic with unknown variance, as in this case, is the same as the calculation of the *t*-statistic. The rejection point conditions for a two-tailed test are as follows: $z > 1.96$ and $z < -1.96$ at the 0.05 level; and $z > 2.575$ and $z < -2.575$ at the 0.01 level. Note that the *z*-test is a less conservative test than the *t*-test, so when the *z*-test is used, the null is easier to reject. Because $z = 5.025$ is greater than 2.575, we reject the null at the 0.01 level; we also reject the null at the 0.05 level.

In summary, Analyst A's EPS forecasts appear to be biased upward—they tend to be too high.

C.   For Analyst B, the *t*-test is based on *t* with $121 - 1 = 120$ degrees of freedom. At the 0.05 significance level, we reject the null if $t > 1.980$ or if $t < -1.980$. At the 0.01 significance level, we reject the null if $t > 2.617$ or if $t < -2.617$. We calculate $t = (0.02 - 0)/(0.09/\sqrt{121}) = 0.02/0.008182 = 2.444444$ or 2.44. Because $2.44 > 1.98$, we reject the null at the 0.05 level. However, 2.44 is not larger than 2.617, so we do not reject the null at the 0.01 level.

For a *z*-test, the rejection point conditions are the same as given in Part B, and we come to the same conclusions as with the *t*-test. Because $2.44 > 1.96$, we reject the null at the 0.05 significance level; however, because 2.44 is not greater than 2.575, we do not reject the null at the 0.01 level.

The mean forecast error of Analyst B is only \$0.02; but because the test is based on a large number of observations, it is sufficient evidence to reject the null of mean zero forecast errors at the 0.05 level.

7.   A. Stating the suspected condition as the alternative hypothesis, we have

$$H_0: \mu_1 - \mu_2 \leq 0 \text{ versus } H_a: \mu_1 - \mu_2 > 0$$

where

μ_1 = the population mean value of Analyst A's forecast errors

μ_2 = the population mean value of Analyst B's forecast errors

B. We have two normally distributed populations with unknown variances. Based on the samples, it is reasonable to assume that the population variances are equal. The samples are assumed to be independent; this assumption is reasonable because the analysts cover quite different industries. The appropriate test statistic is t using a pooled estimate of the common variance. The number of degrees of freedom is

$$n_1 + n_2 - 2 = 101 + 121 - 2 = 222 - 2 = 220.$$

C. For DF = 200 (the closest value to 220), the rejection point for a one-sided test at the 0.05 significance level is 1.653.

D. We first calculate the pooled estimate of variance:

$$s_p^2 = \frac{(n_1 - 1)s_1^2 + (n_2 - 1)s_2^2}{n_1 + n_2 - 2} = \frac{(101 - 1)(0.10)^2 + (121 - 1)(0.09)^2}{101 + 121 - 2}$$

$$= \frac{1.972}{220} = 0.008964$$

Then

$$t = \frac{(\bar{X}_1 - \bar{X}_2) - (\mu_1 - \mu_2)}{\left(\dfrac{s_p^2}{n_1} + \dfrac{s_p^2}{n_2}\right)^{1/2}} = \frac{(0.05 - 0.02) - 0}{\left(\dfrac{0.008964}{101} + \dfrac{0.008964}{121}\right)^{1/2}}$$

$$= \frac{0.03}{0.01276} = 2.351018$$

or 2.35. Because 2.35 > 1.653, we reject the null hypothesis in favor of the alternative hypothesis that the population mean forecast error of Analyst A is greater than that of Analyst B.

8. A. We test H_0: $\mu_d = 0$ versus H_a: $\mu_d \neq 0$.

B. This is a paired comparisons t-test with $n - 1 = 480 - 1 = 479$ degrees of freedom. At the 0.05 significance level, we reject the null hypothesis if either $t > 1.96$ or $t < -1.96$. We use DF = ∞ in the t-distribution table under $\alpha = 0.025$ because we have a very large sample and a two-sided test.

$$t = \frac{\bar{d} - \mu_{d0}}{s_{\bar{d}}} = \frac{-0.258 - 0}{3.752/\sqrt{480}} = \frac{-0.258}{0.171255} = -1.506529 \quad \text{or} - 1.51$$

At the 0.05 significance level, because neither rejection point condition is met, we do not reject the null hypothesis that the mean difference between the returns on the S&P 500 and small-cap stocks during the entire sample period was 0.

C. This t-test now has $n - 1 = 240 - 1 = 239$ degrees of freedom. At the 0.05 significance level, we reject the null hypothesis if either $t > 1.972$ or $t < -1.972$, using DF = 200 in the t-distribution tables.

$$t = \frac{\bar{d} - \mu_{d0}}{s_{\bar{d}}} = \frac{-0.640 - 0}{4.096/\sqrt{240}} = \frac{-0.640}{0.264396} = -2.420615 \quad \text{or} - 2.42$$

Because $-2.42 < -1.972$, we reject the null hypothesis at the 0.05 significance level. During this subperiod, small-cap stocks significantly outperformed the S&P 500.

D.   This t-test has $n - 1 = 240 - 1 = 239$ degrees of freedom. At the 0.05 significance level, we reject the null hypothesis if either $t > 1.972$ or $t < -1.972$, using DF $= 200$ in the t-distribution tables.

$$t = \frac{\bar{d} - \mu_{d0}}{s_{\bar{d}}} = \frac{0.125 - 0}{3.339/\sqrt{240}} = \frac{0.125}{0.215532} = 0.579962 \quad \text{or } 0.58$$

At the 0.05 significance level, because neither rejection point condition is met, we do not reject the null hypothesis that for the second subperiod, the mean difference between the returns on the S&P 500 and small-cap stocks was zero.

9. A.   We have a "less than" alternative hypothesis, where σ^2 is the variance of return on the portfolio. The hypotheses are $H_0: \sigma^2 \geq 400$ versus $H_a: \sigma^2 < 400$, where 400 is the hypothesized value of variance, σ_0^2.

B.   The test statistic is chi-square with $10 - 1 = 9$ degrees of freedom.

C.   The rejection point is found across degrees of freedom of 9, under the 0.95 column (95 percent of probability above the value). It is 3.325. We will reject the null hypothesis if we find that $\chi^2 < 3.325$.

D.   The test statistic is calculated as

$$\chi^2 = \frac{(n-1)s^2}{\sigma_0^2} = \frac{9 \times 15^2}{400} = \frac{2{,}025}{400} = 5.0625 \quad \text{or} \quad 5.06$$

Because 5.06 is not less than 3.325, we do not reject the null hypothesis.

10. A.   We have a "not equal to" alternative hypothesis:

$$H_0 : \sigma^2_{Before} = \sigma^2_{After} \text{ versus } H_a : \sigma^2_{Before} \neq \sigma^2_{After}$$

B.   To test a null hypothesis of the equality of two variances, we use an F-test:

$$F = \frac{s_1^2}{s_2^2}$$

C.   The "before" sample variance is larger, so following a convention for calculating F-statistics, the "before" sample variance goes in the numerator. $F = 22.367/15.795 = 1.416$, with $120 - 1 = 119$ numerator and denominator degrees of freedom. Because this is a two-tailed test, we use F-tables for the 0.025 level (df $= 0.05/2$). Using the tables in the back of the volume, the closest value to 119 is 120 degrees of freedom. At the 0.05 level, the rejection point is 1.43. (Using the Insert/Function/Statistical feature on a Microsoft Excel spreadsheet, we would find FINV (0.025, 119, 119) $= 1.434859$ as the critical F-value.) Because 1.416 is not greater than 1.43, we do not reject the null hypothesis that the "before" and "after" variances are equal.

11. The critical t-value for $n - 2 = 34$ df, using a 5 percent significance level and a two-tailed test, is 2.032. First, take the smallest correlation in the table, the correlation between Fund 3 and Fund 4, and see if it is significantly different from zero. Its calculated t-value is

$$t = \frac{r\sqrt{n-2}}{\sqrt{1-r^2}} = \frac{0.3102\sqrt{36-2}}{\sqrt{1-0.3102^2}} = 1.903$$

This correlation is not significantly different from zero. If we take the next lowest correlation, between Fund 2 and Fund 3, this correlation of 0.4156 has a calculated t-value of 2.664. So this correlation is significantly different from zero at the 5 percent level of significance. All of the other correlations in the table (besides the 0.3102) are greater than 0.4156, so they too are significantly different from zero.

12. A is correct. The critical value in a decision rule is the rejection point for the test. It is the point with which the test statistic is compared to determine whether to reject the null hypothesis, which is part of the fourth step in hypothesis testing.

13. A is correct. The null hypothesis is the hypothesis to be tested. The null hypothesis is considered to be true unless the evidence indicates that it is false, in which case the alternative hypothesis is accepted.

14. A is correct. If the population sampled has unknown variance and the sample is large, a z-test may be used. Hypotheses involving "greater than" or "less than" postulations are one-sided (one-tailed). In this situation, the null and alternative hypotheses are stated as H_0: $\mu \leq 6\%$ and H_a: $\mu > 6\%$, respectively. A one-tailed t-test is also acceptable in this case.

15. C is correct. For a one-tailed hypothesis test, there is a 5 percent critical value rejection region in one tail of the distribution.

16. B is correct. One-tailed tests in which the alternative is "greater than" or "less than" represent the beliefs of the researcher more firmly than a "not equal to" alternative hypothesis.

17. A is correct. Calculated using a sample, a test statistic is a quantity whose value is the basis for deciding whether to reject the null hypothesis.

18. A is correct. The definition of a Type I error is when a true null hypothesis is rejected.

19. B is correct. A Type II error occurs when a false null hypothesis is not rejected.

20. B is correct. The level of significance is used to establish the rejection points of the hypothesis test.

21. A We have a "not equal to" alternative hypothesis:

$$H_0: \rho = 0 \text{ versus } H_a: \rho \neq 0$$

B. We would use the nonparametric Spearman rank correlation coefficient to conduct the test.

C. Mutual fund expense ratios are bounded from above and below, and in practice there is at least a lower bound on alpha (as any return cannot be less than −100 percent). These variables are markedly non-normally distributed, and the assumptions of a parametric test are not likely to be fulfilled. Thus a nonparametric test appears to be appropriate.

D.   The calculation of the Spearman rank correlation coefficient is given in the following table.

Mutual Fund	1	2	3	4	5	6	7	8	9
Alpha (X)	-0.52	-0.13	-0.60	-1.01	-0.26	-0.89	-0.42	-0.23	-0.60
Expense Ratio (Y)	1.34	0.92	1.02	1.45	1.35	0.50	1.00	1.50	1.45
X Rank	5	1	6.5	9	3	8	4	2	6.5
Y Rank	5	8	6	2.5	4	9	7	1	2.5
d_i	0	-7	0.5	6.5	-1	-1	-3	1	4
d_i^2	0	49	0.25	42.25	1	1	9	1	16

$$r_s = 1 - \frac{6\sum d_i^2}{n(n^2-1)} = 1 - \frac{6(119.50)}{9(81-1)} = 0.0042.$$

We use Table 11 to tabulate the rejection points for a test on the Spearman rank correlation. Given a sample size of 9 in a two-tailed test at a 0.05 significance level, the upper-tail rejection point is 0.6833 (we use the 0.025 column). Thus we reject the null hypothesis if the Spearman rank correlation coefficient is less than –0.6833 or greater than 0.6833. Because r_S is equal to 0.0042, we do not reject the null hypothesis.

22. B is correct. Specifying a smaller significance level decreases the probability of a Type I error (rejecting a true null hypothesis), but increases the probability of a Type II error (not rejecting a false null hypothesis). As the level of significance decreases, the null hypothesis is less frequently rejected.

23. B is correct. The power of a test is the probability of rejecting the null hypothesis when it is false.

24. B is correct. The power of a hypothesis test is the probability of correctly rejecting the null when it is false. Failing to reject the null when it is false is a Type II error. Thus, the power of a hypothesis test is the probability of not committing a Type II error.

25. C is correct. When a statistically significant result is also economically meaningful, one should further explore the logic of why the result might work in the future.

26. A is correct. The hypothesis is a two-tailed formulation. The t-statistic of 2.802 falls outside the critical rejection points of less than –2.756 and greater than 2.756, therefore the null hypothesis is rejected; the result is statistically significant. However, despite the statistical results, trying to profit on the strategy is not likely to be economically meaningful because the return is near zero after transaction costs

27. C is correct. When directly comparing the p-value with the level of significance, it can be used as an alternative to using rejection points to reach conclusions on hypothesis tests. If the p-value is smaller than the specified level of significance, the null hypothesis is rejected. Otherwise, the null hypothesis is not rejected.

28. C is correct. The p-value is the smallest level of significance at which the null hypothesis can be rejected for a given value of the test statistic. The null hypothesis is rejected when the p-value is less than the specified significance level.

29. A is correct. The p-value is the smallest level of significance (α) at which the null hypothesis can be rejected.

30. C is correct. The p-value is the smallest level of significance (α) at which the null hypothesis can be rejected. If the p-value is less than α, the null can be rejected. The smaller the p-value, the stronger the evidence is against the null hypothesis and in favor of the alternative hypothesis. Thus, the evidence for rejecting the null is strongest for Test 3.

31. B is correct. The z-test is theoretically the correct test to use in those limited cases when testing the population mean of a normally distributed population with known variance.

32. A is correct. A t-test is used if the sample is small and drawn from a normally or approximately normally distributed population.

33. B is correct. A t-statistic is the most appropriate for hypothesis tests of the population mean when the variance is unknown and the sample is small but the population is normally distributed.

34. A is correct. The t-statistic value of 0.4893 does not fall into the critical value rejection regions (≤ -1.984 or > 1.984). Instead it falls well within the acceptance region. Thus, H_0 cannot be rejected; the result is not statistically significant at the 0.05 level.

35. B is correct. The assumption that the variances are equal allows for the combining of both samples to obtain a pooled estimate of the common variance.

36. B is correct. A paired comparisons test is appropriate to test the mean differences of two samples believed to be dependent.

37. A is correct. The sample sizes for both the fund manager and the consultant's accounts consists of forty quarterly periods of returns. However, the consultant's client accounts are a subset of the fund manager's entire account base. As such, they are not independent samples. When samples are dependent, a paired comparisons test is appropriate to conduct tests of the differences in dependent items.

38. A is correct. A chi-square test is used for tests concerning the variance of a single normally distributed population.

39. B is correct. An F-test is used to conduct tests concerning the difference between the variances of two normally distributed populations with random independent samples.

40. B is correct. The calculated test statistic is

$$t = \frac{r\sqrt{n-2}}{\sqrt{1-r^2}}$$
$$= \frac{-0.1452\sqrt{248-2}}{\sqrt{1-(-0.1452)^2}} = -2.30177$$

Because the absolute value of $t = -2.30177$ is greater than 1.96, the correlation coefficient is statistically significant.

41. A is correct. A non-parametric test is used when the data are given in ranks.

42. B is correct. There are only 12 (monthly) observations over the one year of the sample and thus the samples are small. Additionally, the funds' returns are non-normally distributed. Therefore, the samples do not meet the distributional assumptions for a parametric test. The Mann–Whitney U test (a nonparametric test) could be used to test the differences between population means.

CHAPTER 7

INTRODUCTION TO LINEAR REGRESSION

SOLUTIONS

1. A. The coefficient of determination is

$$\frac{\text{Explained variation}}{\text{Total variation}} = \frac{60.16}{140.58} = 0.4279.$$

B. For a linear regression with one independent variable, the absolute value of correlation between the independent variable and the dependent variable equals the square root of the coefficient of determination, so the correlation is $\sqrt{0.4279} = 0.6542$. (The correlation will have the same sign as the slope coefficient.)

C. The standard error of the estimate is

$$\left[\sum_{i=1}^{n} \frac{(Y_i - \widehat{b}_0 - \widehat{b}_1 X_i)^2}{n-2} \right]^{1/2} = \left(\frac{\text{Unexplained variation}}{n-2} \right)^{1/2}$$

$$= \sqrt{\frac{80.42}{60-2}} = 1.178.$$

D. The sample variance of the dependent variable is

$$\sum_{i=1}^{n} \frac{(Y_i - \overline{Y})^2}{n-1} = \frac{\text{Total variation}}{n-1} = \frac{140.58}{60-1} = 2.3827.$$

The sample standard deviation is $\sqrt{2.3827} = 1.544$.

2. A. The degrees of freedom for the regression is the number of slope parameters in the regression, which is the same as the number of independent variables in the regression. Because regression DF = 1, we conclude that there is one independent variable in the regression.

    B. Total SS is the sum of the squared deviations of the dependent variable Y about its mean.

    C. The sample variance of the dependent variable is the total SS divided by its degrees of freedom ($n - 1 = 5 - 1 = 4$, as given). Thus, the sample variance of the dependent variable is $95.2/4 = 23.8$.

    D. The regression SS is the part of total sum of squares explained by the regression. Regression SS equals the sum of the squared differences between predicted values

    of the Y and the sample mean of Y: $\sum_{i=1}^{n} (\widehat{Y}_i - \overline{Y})^2$. In terms of other values in the

    table, regression SS is equal to total SS minus residual SS: $95.2 - 7.2 = 88$.

    E. The F-statistic tests whether all the slope coefficients in a linear regression are equal to 0.

    F. The calculated value of F in the table is equal to the regression MSS divided by the residual MSS: $88/2.4 = 36.667$.

    G. Yes. The significance of 0.00904 given in the table is the p-value of the test (the smallest level at which we can reject the null hypothesis). This value of 0.00904 is less than the specified significance level of 0.05, so we reject the null hypothesis. The regression equation has significant explanatory power.

3. The Month 2 data point is an outlier, lying far away from the other data values. Because this outlier was caused by a data entry error, correcting the outlier improves the validity and reliability of the regression. In this case, the true correlation is reduced from 0.996 to 0.824. The revised R^2 is substantially lower (0.678 versus 0.992). The significance of the regression is also lower, as can be seen in the decline of the F-value from 500.79 to 8.44 and the decline in the t-statistic of the slope coefficient from 22.379 to 2.905.

    The total sum of squares and regression sum of squares were greatly exaggerated in the incorrect analysis. With the correction, the slope coefficient changes from 1.069 to 0.623. This change is important. When the index moves up or down, the original model indicates that the portfolio return goes up or down by 1.069 times as much, and the revised model indicates that the portfolio return goes up or down by only 0.623 times as much. In this example, incorrect data entry caused the outlier. Had it been a valid observation, not caused by a data error, then the analyst would have had to decide whether the results were more reliable including or excluding the outlier.

4. B is correct. The coefficient of determination is the same as R^2.

5. C is correct. Deleting observations with small residuals will degrade the strength of the regression, resulting in an *increase* in the standard error and a *decrease* in R^2.

6. C is correct. For a regression with one independent variable, the correlation is the same as the multiple R with the sign of the slope coefficient. Because the slope coefficient is positive, the correlation is 0.8623.

7. B is correct. This answer describes the calculation of the F-statistic.

8. C is correct. To make a prediction using the regression model, multiply the slope coefficient by the forecast of the independent variable and add the result to the intercept.

9. C is correct. The p-value is the smallest level of significance at which the null hypotheses concerning the slope coefficient can be rejected. In this case, the p-value is less than

0.05, and thus the regression of the ratio of cash flow from operations to sales on the ratio of net income to sales is significant at the 5 percent level.

10. A is correct because the data are time series, and the expected value of the error term, $E(\epsilon)$, is 0.

11. C is correct. From the regression equation, Expected return $= 0.0138 + -0.6486$ $(-0.01) = 0.0138 + 0.006486 = 0.0203$, or 2.03%.

12. C is correct. R^2 is the coefficient of determination. In this case, it shows that 2.11% of the variability in Stellar's returns is explained by changes in CPIENG.

13. A is correct, because the standard error of the estimate is the standard deviation of the regression residuals.

14. C is the correct response, because it is a false statement. The slope and intercept are both statistically significant.

15. C is correct because the slope coefficient (Exhibit 2) and the cross-product (Exhibit 1) are negative.

16. B is correct. The sample covariance is calculated as

$$\frac{\sum_{i=1}^{n}(X_i - \overline{X})(Y_i - \overline{Y})}{n - 1} = -9.2430 \div 49 = -0.1886.$$

17. A is correct. For a regression with one independent variable, the correlation is the same as the multiple R with the sign of the slope coefficient. Because the slope coefficient is negative, the correlation is -0.3054.

18. C is correct. Conclusions cannot be drawn regarding causation; they can be drawn only about association.

19. C is correct. Liu explains the short interest ratio using the debt ratio.

20. A is correct. The degrees of freedom are the number of observations minus the number of parameters estimated, which equals 2 in this case (the intercept and the slope coefficient). The number of degrees of freedom is $50 - 2 = 48$.

21. B is correct. The calculation for the confidence interval is $-4.1589 \pm (2.011 \times 1.8718)$. The upper bound is -0.3947. The value of 2.011 is the critical t-value for the 5 percent level of significance (2.5 percent in one tail) for 48 degrees of freedom.

22. B is correct. The t-statistic is -2.2219, which is outside the bounds created by the critical t-values of ± 2.011 for a two-tailed test with a 5 percent significance level. The value of 2.011 is the critical t-value for the 5 percent level of significance (2.5% in one tail) for 48 degrees of freedom.

23. A is correct because Predicted value $= 5.4975 + (-4.1589 \times 0.40) = 5.4975 - 1.6636 = 3.8339$.

24. C is correct because $F = \dfrac{\text{Mean regression sum of squares}}{\text{Mean squared error}} = \dfrac{38.4404}{7.7867} = 4.9367.$

25. C is correct. The assumptions of the linear regression model are that (1) the relationship between the dependent variable and the independent variable is linear in the parameters b_0 and b_1, (2) the independent variable is not random, (3) the expected value of the error term is 0, (4) the variance of the error term is the same for all observations, (5) the error term is uncorrelated across observations, and (6) the error term is normally

distributed. Assumption 3 is incorrect because the expected value of the error term is assumed to be zero, not equal to the mean of the dependent variable.

26. B is correct. The standard error of the estimate (SEE) for a linear regression model with one independent variable is calculated as:

$$\text{SEE} = \sqrt{\frac{\sum_{i=1}^{n}(Y - \hat{b}_0 - \hat{b}_1 X_i)^2}{n-2}} = \sqrt{\frac{\sum_{i=1}^{n}(Y - \hat{Y})^2}{n-2}}$$

$$= \sqrt{\frac{0.071475}{34}}$$

$$= 0.045850.$$

27. C is correct. Crude oil returns explain the Amtex share returns if the slope coefficient is statistically different from zero. The slope coefficient is 0.2354 and is statistically different from zero because the absolute value of the t-statistic of 3.0974 is higher than the critical t-value of 2.032 (two-sided test for $n - 2 = 34$ degrees of freedom and a 5 percent significance level):

$$t\text{-statistic} = \frac{\hat{b}_1 - b_1}{s_{\hat{b}_1}} = \frac{0.2354 - 0.0000}{0.0760} = 3.0974.$$

Therefore, Vasileva should reject the null hypothesis that crude oil returns do not explain Amtex share returns because the slope coefficient is statistically different from zero.

28. C is correct. The confidence interval for the slope coefficient is calculated as

Confidence interval $= \hat{b}_1 \pm t_c s_{\hat{b}_1}$,
where $\hat{b}_1 = 0.2354$, $s_{\hat{b}_1} = 0.0760$, and $t_c = 2.032$.
The lower limit for the confidence interval $= 0.2354 - (2.032 \times 0.0760) = 0.0810$.
The upper limit for the confidence interval $= 0.2354 + (2.032 \times 0.0760) = 0.3898$.

A is incorrect because the lower limit for the confidence interval $= 0.2354 - (2.728 \times 0.0760) = 0.0281$ and the upper limit for the confidence interval $= 0.2354 + (2.728 \times 0.0760) = 0.4427$.

B is incorrect because the lower limit for the confidence interval $= 0.0095 - (2.032 \times 0.0078) = -0.0064$ and the upper limit for the confidence interval $= 0.0095 + (0.032 \times 0.0078) = 0.0254$.

29. B is correct. The predicted value of the dependent variable, Amtex share return, given the value of the independent variable, crude oil return, of -0.01, is calculated as

$$\hat{Y} = \hat{b}_0 + \hat{b}_1 X_i = 0.0095 + [0.2354 \times (-0.01)] = 0.0071.$$

30. A is correct. The 95 percent prediction interval for the dependent variable given a certain value of the independent variable is calculated as

Prediction interval $= \widehat{Y} \pm t_c s_f$,
where the predicted value is $\widehat{Y} = \widehat{b}_0 + \widehat{b}_1 X_i$.
Therefore,

$$\text{Predicted value} = 0.0095 + [0.2354 \times (-0.01)] = 0.0071.$$
$$s_f = (0.0022)^{0.5} = 0.0469.$$
$$t_c = 2.032.$$

The lower limit for the prediction interval $= 0.0071 - (2.032 \times 0.0469) = -0.0882$.
The upper limit for the prediction interval $= 0.0071 + (2.032 \times 0.0469) = 0.1025$.

31. A is correct. If the consensus inflation forecast is unbiased, then the intercept, b_0, should equal 0 and the slope coefficient, b_1, should equal 1. The t-statistic for the intercept coefficient is 0.5351, which is less than the critical t-value of 2.0, so the intercept coefficient is not statistically different than 0. To test whether the slope coefficient equals 1, the t-statistic is calculated as:

$$t = (\widehat{b}_1 - b_1)/s_{\widehat{b}_1} = (0.9830 - 1)/0.0155 = -1.0968.$$

Because the absolute value of the t-statistic of -1.0968 is less than the critical t-value of 2.0, the slope coefficient is not statistically different from 1. Therefore, Olabudo can conclude that the inflation forecasts are unbiased.

32. A is correct. The prediction interval for inflation is calculated in three steps:

Step 1. Make the prediction given the US CPI forecast of 2.8:

$$\widehat{Y} = b_0 + b_1 X$$
$$= 0.0001 + (0.9830 \times 2.8)$$
$$= 2.7525.$$

Step 2. Compute the variance of the prediction error:

$$s_f^2 = s^2\{1 + (1/n) + [(X - \overline{X})^2]/[(n-1) \times s_x^2]\}.$$
$$s_f^2 = 0.0009^2\{1 + (1/60) + [(2.8 - 1.3350)^2]/[(60-1) \times 0.7539^2]\}.$$
$$s_f^2 = 0.00000088.$$
$$s_f = 0.0009.$$

Step 3. Compute the prediction interval:

$$\widehat{Y} \pm t_c \times s_f$$

2.7525 $\pm$ (2.0 $\times$ 0.0009)

2.7525 $-$ (2.0 $\times$ 0.0009) = 2.7506—lower bound.

2.7525 $+$ (2.0 $\times$ 0.0009) = 2.7544—upper bound.

So, given the US CPI forecast of 2.8, the 95 percent prediction interval is 2.7506 to 2.7544.

33. C is correct. Public knowledge of regression relationships may negate their future usefulness in an investment context. Also, if regression assumptions are violated, hypothesis tests and predictions based on linear regression will not be valid.

CHAPTER 8

MULTIPLE REGRESSION

SOLUTIONS

1. A. $R_{it} = b_0 + b_1 R_{Mt} + b_2 \Delta X_t + \epsilon_{it}$

    B. We can test whether the coefficient on the S&P 500 Index returns is statistically significant. Our null hypothesis is that the coefficient is equal to 0 (H_0: $b_1 = 0$); our alternative hypothesis is that the coefficient is not equal to 0 (H_a: $b_1 \neq 0$). We construct the t-test of the null hypothesis as follows:

$$\frac{\widehat{b_1} - b_1}{s_{\widehat{b_1}}} = \frac{0.5373 - 0}{0.1332} = 4.0338$$

where

$\widehat{b_1}$ = regression estimate of b_1

b_1 = the hypothesized value of the coefficient (here, 0)

$s_{\widehat{b_1}}$ = the estimated standard error of $\widehat{b_1}$

Because this regression has 156 observations and three regression coefficients, the t-test has 156 – 3 = 153 degrees of freedom. At the 0.05 significance level, the critical value for the test statistic is between 1.98 and 1.97. The absolute value of the test statistic is 4.0338; therefore, we can reject the null hypothesis that $b_1 = 0$.

Similarly, we can test whether the coefficient on the change in the value of the US dollar is statistically significant in this regression. Our null hypothesis is that the coefficient is equal to 0 (H_0: $b_2 = 0$); our alternative hypothesis is that the coefficient is not equal to 0 (H_a: $b_2 \neq 0$). We construct the t-test as follows:

$$\frac{\widehat{b_2} - b_2}{s_{pt_{\widehat{b_2}}}} = \frac{-0.5768 - 0}{0.5121} = -1.1263$$

As before, the t-test has 153 degrees of freedom, and the critical value for the test statistic is between 1.98 and 1.97 at the 0.05 significance level. The absolute value of the test statistic is 1.1263; therefore, we cannot reject the null hypothesis that $b_2 = 0$. Based on the above t-tests, we conclude that S&P 500 Index returns do affect ADM's returns but that changes in the value of the US dollar do not affect ADM's returns.

C. The statement is not correct. To make it correct, we need to add the qualification "holding ΔX constant" to the end of the quoted statement.

2. A. $R_i = b_0 + b_1(B/M)_i + b_2 Size_i + \epsilon_i$

   B. We can test whether the coefficients on the book-to-market ratio and size are individually statistically significant using t-tests. For the book-to-market ratio, our null hypothesis is that the coefficient is equal to 0 (H_0: $b_1 = 0$); our alternative hypothesis is that the coefficient is not equal to 0 (H_a: $b_1 \neq 0$). We can test the null hypothesis using a t-test constructed as follows:

$$\frac{\widehat{b}_1 - b_1}{s_{\widehat{b}_1}} = \frac{-0.0541 - 0}{0.0588} = -0.9201$$

where

$\widehat{b}_1$ = regression estimate of b_1

b_1 = the hypothesized value of the coefficient (here, 0)

$s_{\widehat{b}_1}$ = the estimated standard error of $\widehat{b}_1$

This regression has 66 observations and three coefficients, so the t-test has $66 - 3 = 63$ degrees of freedom. At the 0.05 significance level, the critical value for the test statistic is about 2.0. The absolute value of the test statistic is 0.9201; therefore, we cannot reject the null hypothesis that $b_1 = 0$. We can conclude that the book-to-market ratio is not useful in explaining the cross-sectional variation in returns for this sample.

We perform the same analysis to determine whether size (as measured by the log of the market value of equity) can help explain the cross-sectional variation in asset returns. Our null hypothesis is that the coefficient is equal to 0 (H_0: $b_2 = 0$); our alternative hypothesis is that the coefficient is not equal to 0 (H_a: $b_2 \neq 0$). We can test the null hypothesis using a t-test constructed as follows:

$$\frac{\widehat{b}_2 - b_2}{s_{\widehat{b}_2}} = \frac{-0.0164 - 0}{0.0350} = -0.4686$$

where

$\widehat{b}_2$ = regression estimate of b_2

b_2 = the hypothesized value of the coefficient (here, 0)

$s_{\widehat{b}_2}$ = the estimated standard error of $\widehat{b}_2$

Again, because this regression has 66 observations and three coefficients, the t-test has $66 - 3 = 63$ degrees of freedom. At the 0.05 significance level, the critical value for the test statistic is about 2.0. The absolute value of the test statistic is 0.4686; therefore, we cannot reject the null hypothesis that $b_2 = 0$. We can conclude that asset size is not useful in explaining the cross-sectional variation of asset returns in this sample.

3. A. The estimated regression is (Analyst following)$_i$ = $-0.2845 + 0.3199$Size$_i$ - 0.1895 (D/E)$_i$ + ϵ_i. Therefore, the prediction for the first company is

$$\text{(Analyst following)}_i = -0.2845 + 0.3199(\ln 100) - 0.1895(0.75)$$
$$= -0.2845 + 1.4732 - 0.1421 = 1.0466$$

Recalling that (Analyst following)$_i$ is the natural log of $(1 + n_i)$, where n_i is the number of analysts following company i; it follows that $1 + n_1 = e^{1.0466} = 2.848$, approximately. Therefore, $n_1 = 2.848 - 1 = 1.848$, or about two analysts. Similarly, the prediction for the second company is as follows:

$$\text{(Analyst following)}_i = -0.2845 + 0.3199(\ln 1,000) - 0.1895(0.75)$$
$$= -0.2845 + 2.2098 - 0.1421$$
$$= 1.7832$$

Thus, $1 + n_2 = e^{1.7832} = 5.949$, approximately. Therefore, $n_2 = 5.949 - 1 = 4.949$, or about five analysts.

The model predicts that $5 - 2 = 3$ more analysts will follow the second company than the first company.

B. We would interpret the p-value of 0.00236 as the smallest level of significance at which we can reject a null hypothesis that the population value of the coefficient is 0, in a two-sided test. Clearly, in this regression the debt-to-equity ratio is a highly significant variable.

4. The estimated model is

Percentage decline in TSE spread of company i = $-0.45 + 0.05$Size$_i$ - 0.06(Ratio of spreads)$_i$ + 0.29(Decline in NASDAQ spreads)$_i$

Therefore, the prediction is

Percentage decline in TSE spread = $-0.45 + 0.05(\ln 900,000) - 0.06(1.3) + 0.29(1)$
$$= -0.45 + 0.69 - 0.08 + 0.29$$
$$= 0.45$$

The model predicts that for a company with average sample characteristics, the spread on the TSE declines by 0.45 percent for a 1 percent decline in NASDAQ spreads.

5. A. To test the null hypothesis that all the slope coefficients in the regression model are equal to 0 ($H_0: b_1 = b_2 = 0$) against the alternative hypothesis that at least one slope coefficient is not equal to 0, we must use an F-test.

B. To conduct the F-test, we need four inputs, all of which are found in the ANOVA section of the table in the statement of the problem:
  i.   total number of observations, n
  ii. total number of regression coefficients to be estimated, $k + 1$
  iii. sum of squared errors or residuals, $\sum_{i=1}^{n}(Y_i - \hat{Y}_i)^2$ abbreviated SSE, and
  iv. regression sum of squares, $\sum_{i=1}^{n}(\hat{Y}_i - \bar{Y})^2$ abbreviated RSS

C. The F-test formula is

$$F = \frac{RSS/k}{SSE/[n-(k+1)]} = \frac{0.0094/2}{0.6739/[66-(2+1)]} = 0.4394$$

The F-statistic has degrees of freedom $F\{k, [n-(k+1)]\} = F(2, 63)$. From the F-test table, for the 0.05 significance level, the critical value for $F(2, 63)$ is about 3.15, so we cannot reject the hypothesis that the slope coefficients are both 0. The two independent variables are jointly statistically unrelated to returns.

D. Adjusted R^2 is a measure of goodness of fit that takes into account the number of independent variables in the regression, in contrast to R^2. We can assert that adjusted R^2 is smaller than $R^2 = 0.0138$ without the need to perform any calculations. (However, adjusted R^2 can be shown to equal -0.0175 using an expression in the text on the relationship between adjusted R^2 and R^2.)

6. A. You believe that opening markets actually reduces return volatility; if that belief is correct, then the slope coefficient would be negative, $b_1 < 0$. The null hypothesis is that the belief is not true: $H_0: b_1 \geq 0$. The alternative hypothesis is that the belief is true: $H_a: b_1 < 0$.

   B. The critical value for the t-statistic with $95 - 2 = 93$ degrees of freedom at the 0.05 significance level in a one-sided test is about 1.66. For the one-sided test stated in Part A, we reject the null hypothesis if the t-statistic on the slope coefficient is less than -1.66. As the t-statistic of $-2.7604 < -1.66$, we reject the null. Because the dummy variable takes on a value of 1 when foreign investment is allowed, we can conclude that the volatility was lower with foreign investment.

   C. According to the estimated regression, average return volatility was 0.0133 (the estimated value of the intercept) before July 1993 and 0.0058 ($= 0.0133 - 0.0075$) after July 1993.

7. A. The appropriate regression model is $R_{Mt} = b_0 + b_1 \, \text{Party}_t + \epsilon_t$.

   B. The t-statistic reported in the table for the dummy variable tests whether the coefficient on Party_t is significantly different from 0. It is computed as follows:

$$\frac{\hat{b}_1 - b_1}{s_{\hat{b}_1}} = \frac{-0.0570 - 0}{0.0466} = -1.22$$

where

$\hat{b}_1$ = regression estimate of b_1
b_1 = the hypothesized value of the coefficient (here, 0)
$s_{\hat{b}_1}$ = the estimated standard error of $\hat{b}_1$

To two decimal places, this value is the same as the t-statistic reported in the table for the dummy variable, as expected. The problem specified two decimal places because the reported regression output reflects rounding; for this reason, we often cannot exactly reproduce reported t-statistics.

   C. Because the regression has 77 observations and two coefficients, the t-test has $77 - 2 = 75$ degrees of freedom. At the 0.05 significance level, the critical value for the two-tailed test statistic is about 1.99. The absolute value of the test statistic is 1.2242; therefore, we do not reject the null hypothesis that $b_1 = 0$. We can conclude that the political party in the White House does not, on average, affect the annual returns of the overall market as measured by the S&P 500.

8. A. The regression model is as follows:

$$\text{(Analyst following)}_i = b_0 + b_1 \text{Size}_i + b_2(\text{D/E})_i + b_3 \text{S\&P}_i + \epsilon_i$$

where $\text{(Analyst following)}_i$ is the natural log of $(1 + \text{number of analysts following company } i)$; Size_i is the natural log of the market capitalization of company i in millions of dollars; $(\text{D/E})_i$ is the debt-to-equity ratio for company i, and $\text{S\&P}_i$ is a dummy variable with a value of 1 if the company i belongs to the S&P 500 Index and 0 otherwise.

   B. The appropriate null and alternative hypotheses are $H_0: b_3 = 0$ and $H_a: b_3 \neq 0$, respectively.

   C. The t-statistic to test the null hypothesis can be computed as follows:

$$\frac{\hat{b}_3 - b_3}{s_{\hat{b}_3}} = \frac{0.4218 - 0}{0.0919} = 4.5898$$

This value is, of course, the same as the value reported in the table. The regression has 500 observations and 4 regression coefficients, so the t-test has $500 - 4 = 496$ degrees of freedom. At the 0.05 significance level, the critical value for the test statistic is between 1.96 and 1.97. Because the value of the test statistic is 4.5898 we can reject the null hypothesis that $b_3 = 0$. Thus a company's membership in the S&P 500 appears to significantly influence the number of analysts who cover that company.

   D. The estimated model is

$$\text{(Analyst following)}_i = -0.0075 + 0.2648\text{Size}_i - 0.1829(\text{D/E})_i + 0.4218\text{S\&P}_i + \epsilon_i$$

Therefore the prediction for number of analysts following the indicated company that is not part of the S&P 500 Index is

$$\begin{aligned}
\text{(Analyst following)}_i &= -0.0075 + 0.2648(\ln 10{,}000) - 0.1829(2/3) + 0.4218(0) \\
&= -0.0075 + 2.4389 - 0.1219 + 0 \\
&= 2.3095
\end{aligned}$$

Recalling that $\text{(Analyst following)}_i$ is the natural log of $(1 + n_i)$, where n_i is the number of analysts following company i; it ensues (coding the company under consideration as 1) that $1 + n_1 = e^{2.3095} = 10.069$, approximately. Therefore, the prediction is that $n_1 = 10.069 - 1 = 9.069$, or about nine analysts.

Similarly, the prediction for the company that is included in the S&P 500 Index is

$$\begin{aligned}
\text{(Analyst following)}_i &= -0.0075 + 0.2648(\ln 10{,}000) - 0.1829(2/3) + 0.4218(1) \\
&= -0.0075 + 2.4389 - 0.1219 + 0.4218
\end{aligned}$$

$$= 2.7313$$

Coding the company that does belong to the S&P 500 as 2, $1 + n_2 = e^{2.7313} = 15.353$. Therefore, the prediction is that $n_2 = 15.353 - 1 = 14.353$, or about 14 analysts.

E. There is no inconsistency in the coefficient on the size variable differing between the two regressions. The regression coefficient on an independent variable in a multiple regression model measures the expected net effect on the expected value of the dependent variable for a one-unit increase in that independent variable, after accounting for any effects of the other independent variables on the expected value of the dependent variable. The earlier regression had one fewer independent variable; after the effect of S&P 500 membership on the expected value of the dependent variable is taken into account, it is to be expected that the effect of the size variable on the dependent variable will change. What the regressions appear to indicate is that the net effect of the size variable on the expected analyst following diminishes when S&P 500 membership is taken into account.

9. A. In a well-specified regression, the differences between the actual and predicted relationship should be random; the errors should not depend on the value of the independent variable. In this regression, the errors seem larger for smaller values of the book-to-market ratio. This finding indicates that we may have conditional heteroskedasticity in the errors, and consequently, the standard errors may be incorrect. We cannot proceed with hypothesis testing until we test for and, if necessary, correct for heteroskedasticity.

B. A test for heteroskedasticity is to regress the squared residuals from the estimated regression equation on the independent variables in the regression. As seen in Section 4.1.2, Breusch and Pagan showed that, under the null hypothesis of no conditional heteroskedasticity, $n \times R^2$ (from the regression of the squared residuals on the independent variables from the original regression) will be a χ^2 random variable, with the number of degrees of freedom equal to the number of independent variables in the regression.

C. One method to correct for heteroskedasticity is to use robust standard errors. This method uses the parameter estimates from the linear regression model but corrects the standard errors of the estimated parameters to account for the heteroskedasticity. Many statistical software packages can easily compute robust standard errors.

10. The test statistic is nR^2, where n is the number of observations and R^2 is the R^2 of the regression of squared residuals. So, the test statistic is $52 \times 0.141 = 7.332$. Under the null hypothesis of no conditional heteroskedasticity, this test statistic is a χ^2 random variable. There are three degrees of freedom, the number of independent variables in the regression. Appendix C, at the end of this volume, shows that for a one-tailed test, the test statistic critical value for a variable from a χ^2 distribution with 3 degrees of freedom at the 0.05 significance level is 7.815. The test statistic from the Breusch–Pagan test is 7.332. So, we cannot reject the hypothesis of no conditional heteroskedasticity at the 0.05 level. Therefore, we do not need to correct for conditional heteroskedasticity.

11. A. The test statistic is nR^2, where n is the number of observations and R^2 is the R^2 of the regression of squared residuals. So, the test statistic is $750 \times 0.006 = 4.5$. Under the null hypothesis of no conditional heteroskedasticity, this test statistic is a χ^2 random variable. Because the regression has only one independent variable, the number of degrees of freedom is equal to 1. Appendix C, at the end of this volume, shows that for a one-tailed test, the test statistic critical value for a variable from a χ^2 distribution with one degree of freedom at the 0.05 significance level is 3.841. The test statistic is 4.5. So, we can reject the hypothesis of no conditional heteroskedasticity at the 0.05 level. Therefore, we need to correct for conditional heteroskedasticity.

   B. Two different methods can be used to correct for the effects of conditional heteroskedasticity in linear regression models. The first method involves computing robust standard errors. This method corrects the standard errors of the linear regression model's estimated parameters to account for the conditional heteroskedasticity. The second method is generalized least squares. This method modifies the original equation in an attempt to eliminate the heteroskedasticity. The new, modified regression equation is then estimated under the assumption that heteroskedasticity is no longer a problem.

   Many statistical software packages can easily compute robust standard errors (the first method), and we recommend using them.

12. A. Because the value of the Durbin–Watson statistic is less than 2, we can say that the regression residuals are positively correlated. Because this statistic is fairly close to 2, however, we cannot say without a statistical test if the serial correlation is statistically significant.

   B. From January 1987 through December 2002, there are 16 years, or $16 \times 12 = 192$ monthly returns. Thus the sample analyzed is quite large. Therefore, the Durbin–Watson statistic is approximately equal to $2(1 - r)$, where r is the sample correlation between the regression residuals from one period and those from the previous period.

$$DW = 1.8953 \approx 2(1 - r)$$

   So, $r \approx 1 - DW/2 = 1 - 1.8953/2 = 0.0524$. Consistent with our answer to Part A, the correlation coefficient is positive.

   C. Appendix E indicates that the critical values d_l and d_u for 100 observations when there is one independent variable are 1.65 and 1.69, respectively. Based on the information given in the problem, the critical values d_l and d_u for about 200 observations when there is one independent variable are about 1.74 and 1.78, respectively. Because the DW statistic of 1.8953 for our regression is above d_u, we fail to reject the null hypothesis of no positive serial correlation. Therefore, we conclude that there is no evidence of positive serial correlation for the error term.

13. A. This problem is known as multicollinearity. When some linear combinations of the independent variables in a regression model are highly correlated, the standard errors of the independent coefficient estimates become quite large, even though the regression equation may fit rather well.

B. The choice of independent variables presents multicollinearity concerns because market value of equity appears in both variables.

C. The classic symptom of multicollinearity is a high R^2 (and significant F-statistic) even though the t-statistics on the estimated slope coefficients are insignificant. Here a significant F-statistic does not accompany the insignificant t-statistics, so the classic symptom is not present.

14. A. To test the null hypothesis that all of the regression coefficients except for the intercept in the multiple regression model are equal to 0 (H_0: $b_1 = b_2 = b_3 = 0$) against the alternative hypothesis that at least one slope coefficient is not equal to 0, we must use an F-test.

$$F = \frac{RSS/k}{SSE/[n-(k+1)]} = \frac{0.1720/3}{0.8947/[156-(3+1)]} = 9.7403$$

The F-statistic has degrees of freedom $F\{k, [n-(k+1)]\} = F(3, 152)$. From the F-test table, the critical value for $F(3, 120) = 2.68$ and $F(3, 152)$ will be less than $F(3, 120)$, so we can reject at the 0.05 significance level the null hypothesis that the slope coefficients are all 0. Changes in the three independent variables are jointly statistically related to returns.

B. None of the t-statistics are significant, but the F-statistic is significant. This suggests the possibility of multicollinearity in the independent variables.

C. The apparent multicollinearity is very likely related to the inclusion of *both* the returns on the S&P 500 Index *and* the returns on a value-weighted index of all the companies listed on the NYSE, AMEX, and NASDAQ as independent variables. The value-weighting of the latter index, giving relatively high weights to larger companies such as those included in the S&P 500, may make one return series an approximate linear function of the other. By dropping one or the other of these two variables, we might expect to eliminate the multicollinearity.

15. A. Your colleague is indicating that you have omitted an important variable from the regression. This problem is called the omitted variable bias. If the omitted variable is correlated with an included variable, the estimated values of the regression coefficients would be biased and inconsistent. Moreover, the estimates of standard errors of those coefficients would also be inconsistent. So, we cannot use either the coefficient estimates or the estimates of their standard errors to perform statistical tests.

B. A comparison of the new estimates with the original estimates clearly indicates that the original model suffered from the omitted variable bias due to the exclusion of company size from that model. As the t-statistics of the new model indicate, company size is statistically significant. Further, for the debt-to-equity ratio, the absolute value of the estimated coefficient substantially increases from 0.1043 to 0.1829, while its standard error declines. Consequently, it becomes significant in the new model, in contrast to the original model, in which it is not significant at the 5 percent level. The value of the estimated coefficient of the S&P 500 dummy substantially declines from 1.2222 to 0.4218. These changes imply that size should be included in the model.

16. A. You need to use a qualitative dependent variable. You could give a value of 1 to this dummy variable for a listing in the United States and a value of 0 for not listing in the United States.

   B. Because you are using a qualitative dependent variable, linear regression is not the right technique to estimate the model. One possibility is to use either a probit or a logit model. Both models are identical, except that the logit model is based on logistic distribution while the probit model is based on normal distribution. Another possibility is to use discriminant analysis.

17. C is correct. The predicted initial return (IR) is:
   IR = 0.0477 + (0.0150 × 6) + (0.435 × 0.04) − (0.0009 × 40) + (0.05 × 0.70)
   = 0.1541

18. B is correct. The 95% confidence interval is 0.435 ± (0.0202 × 1.96) = (0.395, 0.475).

19. C is correct. To test Hansen's belief about the direction and magnitude of the initial return, the test should be a one-tailed test. The alternative hypothesis is H_1: $b_j < 0.5$, and the null hypothesis is H_0: $b_j \geq 0.5$. The correct test statistic is: $t = (0.435 - 0.50)/0.0202 = -3.22$, and the critical value of the t-statistic for a one-tailed test at the 0.05 level is −1.645. The test statistic is significant, and the null hypothesis can be rejected at the 0.05 level of significance.

20. C is correct. The multiple R-squared for the regression is 0.36; thus, the model explains 36 percent of the variation in the dependent variable. The correlation between the predicted and actual values of the dependent variable is the square root of the R-squared or $\sqrt{0.36} = 0.60$.

21. A is correct. Chang is correct because the presence of conditional heteroskedasticity results in consistent parameter estimates, but biased (up or down) standard errors, t-statistics, and F-statistics.

22. A is correct. Chang is correct because a correlated omitted variable will result in biased and inconsistent parameter estimates and inconsistent standard errors.

23. B is correct.
   The F-test is used to determine if the regression model as a whole is significant.

   $$F = \text{Mean square regression (MSR)} \div \text{Mean squared error (MSE)}$$

   $$\text{MSE} = \text{SSE}/[n - (k + 1)] = 19{,}048 \div 427 = 44.60$$

   $$\text{MSR} = \text{SSR}/k = 1071 \div 3 = 357$$

   $$F = 357 \div 44.60 = 8.004$$

   The critical value for degrees of freedom of 3 and 427 with $\alpha = 0.05$ (one-tail) is $F = 2.63$ from Exhibit 5. The calculated F is greater than the critical value, and Chiesa should reject the null hypothesis that all regression coefficients are equal to zero.

24. B is correct. The Durbin–Watson test used to test for serial correlation in the error term, and its value reported in Exhibit 1 is 1.65. For no serial correlation, DW is approximately equal to 2. If DW < d_l, *the error terms are positively serially correlated.* Because the DW = 1.65 is less than $d_l = 1.827$ for $n = 431$ (see Exhibit 2), Chiesa

should reject the null hypothesis of no serial correlation and conclude that there is evidence of positive serial correlation among the error terms.

25. B is correct. The coefficient for the Pres party dummy variable (3.17) represents the increment in the mean value of the dependent variable related to the Democratic Party holding the presidency. In this case, the excess stock market return is 3.17 percent greater in Democratic presidencies than in Republican presidencies.

26. B is correct. The confidence interval is computed as $a_1 \pm s(a_1) \times t(95\%,\infty)$. From Exhibit 1, $a_1 = 3.04$ and $t(a_1) = 4.52$, resulting in a standard error of $a_1 = s(a_1) = 3.04/4.52 = 0.673$. The critical value for t from Exhibit 3 is 1.96 for $p = 0.025$. The confidence interval for a_1 is $3.04 \pm 0.673 \times 1.96 = 3.04 \pm 1.31908$ or from 1.72092 to 4.35908.

27. C is correct. The default spread is typically larger when business conditions are poor, i.e., a greater probability of default by the borrower. The positive sign for default spread (see Exhibit 1) indicates that expected returns are positively related to default spreads, meaning that excess returns are greater when business conditions are poor.

28. C is correct. Predictions in a multiple regression model are subject to both parameter estimate uncertainty and regression model uncertainty.

29. C is correct. The F-statistic is

$$F = \frac{RSS/k}{SSE/[n-(k+1)]} = \frac{714.169/8}{1583.113/546} = \frac{89.2712}{2.8995} = 30.79$$

Because $F = 30.79$ exceeds the critical F of 1.96, the null hypothesis that the regression coefficients are all 0 is rejected at the 0.05 significance level.

30. B is correct. The estimated coefficients for the dummy variables show the estimated difference between the returns on different types of funds. The growth dummy takes the value of 1 for growth funds and 0 for the value fund. Exhibit 1 shows a growth dummy coefficient of 2.4368. The estimated difference between the return of growth funds and value funds is thus 2.4368.

31. B is correct. The R^2 is expected to increase, not decline, with a new independent variable. The other two potential consequences Honoré describes are correct.

32. C is correct. Using dummy variables to distinguish among n categories would best capture the ability of the Morningstar rating system to predict mutual fund performance. We need $n - 1$ dummy variables to distinguish among n categories. In this case, there are five possible ratings and we need four dummy variables. Adding an independent variable that has a value equal to the number of stars in the rating of each fund is not appropriate because if the coefficient for this variable is positive, this method assumes that the extra return for a two-star fund is twice that of a one-star fund, the extra return for a three-star fund is three times that of a one-star fund, and so forth, which is not a reasonable assumption.

33. A is correct. Heteroskedasticity causes the F-test for the overall significance of the regression to be unreliable. It also causes the t-tests for the significance of individual regression coefficients to be unreliable because heteroskedasticity introduces bias into estimators of the standard error of regression coefficients.

34. A is correct. The model in Exhibit 2 does not have a lagged dependent variable. Positive serial correlation will, for such a model, not affect the consistency of the estimated coefficients. Thus, the coefficients will not need to be corrected for serial correlation.

Positive serial correlation will, however, cause the standard errors of the regression coefficients to be understated; thus, the corresponding t-statistics will be inflated.

35. A is correct. The critical Durbin–Watson (D–W) values are $d_l = 1.63$ and $d_u = 1.72$. Because the estimated D–W value of 1.81 is greater than $d_u = 1.73$ (and less than 2), she fails to reject the null hypothesis of no serial correlation.

36. B is correct. Probit and logit models are used for models with qualitative dependent variables, such as models in which the dependent variable can have one of two discreet outcomes (i.e., 0 or 1). The analysis in the two exhibits are explaining security returns, which are continuous (not 0 or 1) variables.

37. A is correct. Varden expects to find that CEO tenure is positively related to the firm's ROE. If he is correct, the regression coefficient for tenure, b_2, will be greater than zero $(b_2 > 0)$ and statistically significant. The null hypothesis supposes that the "suspected" condition is not true, so the null hypothesis should state the variable is less than or equal to zero. The t-statistic for tenure is 2.308, significant at the 0.027 level, meeting Varden's 0.05 significance requirement. Varden should reject the null hypothesis.

38. C is correct. The t-statistic for tenure is 2.308, indicating significance at the 0.027 level but not the 0.01 level. The t-statistic for ESG is 1.201, with a p-value of 0.238, which means we fail to reject the null hypothesis for ESG at the 0.01 significance level.

39. B is correct. The t-statistic for tenure is 2.308, which is significant at the 0.027 level. The t-statistic for ESG is 1.201, with a p-value of 0.238. This result is not significant at the 0.05 level.

40. C is correct. The regression equation is as follows:

$$\widehat{Y}_i = 9.442 + 0.069X1i + 0.681X2i$$

$$ROE = 9.442 + 0.069(ESG) + 0.681(Tenure)$$

$$= 9.442 + 0.069(55) + 0.681(10.5)$$

$$= 9.442 + 3.795 + 7.151$$

$$= 20.388.$$

41. B is correct. When you add an additional independent variable to the regression model, the amount of unexplained variance will decrease, provided the new variable explains any of the previously unexplained variation. This result occurs as long as the new variable is even slightly correlated with the dependent variable. Exhibit 2 indicates the dividend growth rate is correlated with the dependent variable, ROE. Therefore, R^2 will increase.

Adjusted R^2, however, may not increase and may even decrease if the relationship is weak. This result occurs because in the formula for adjusted R^2, the new variable increases k (the number of independent variables) in the denominator, and the increase in R^2 may be insufficient to increase the value of the formula.

$$\text{adjusted } R^2 = 1 - \left(\frac{n-1}{n-k-1}\right)(1 - R^2)$$

42. C is correct. Exhibit 1 indicates that the F-statistic of 4.161 is significant at the 0.05 level. A significant F-statistic means at least one of the independent variables is significant.

43. C is correct. In a multiple linear regression (as compared with simple regression), R^2 is less appropriate as a measure of whether a regression model fits the data well. A high adjusted R^2 does not necessarily indicate that the regression is well specified in the sense of including the correct set of variables. The F-test is an appropriate test of a regression's overall significance in either simple or multiple regressions.

44. C is correct. Multiple linear regression assumes that the relationship between the dependent variable and each of the independent variables is linear. Varden believes that this is not true for dividend growth because he believes the relationship may be different in firms with a long-standing CEO. Multiple linear regression also assumes that the independent variables are not random. Varden states that he believes CEO tenure is a random variable.

45. B is correct. If we use adjusted R^2 to compare regression models, it is important that the dependent variable be defined the same way in both models and that the sample sizes used to estimate the models are the same. Varden's first model was based on 40 observations, whereas the second model was based on 500.

CHAPTER 9

TIME-SERIES ANALYSIS

SOLUTIONS

1. A. The estimated forecasting equation is $UER_t = 5.5098 - 0.0294(t)$. The data begin in January 2013, and July 2013 is Period 7. Thus the linear trend model predicts the unemployment rate to be $UER_7 = 7.2237 - 0.0510(7) = 6.8667$, or approximately 6.9 percent.

   B. The DW statistic is designed to detect positive serial correlation of the errors of a regression equation. Under the null hypothesis of no positive serial correlation, the DW statistic is 2.0. Positive serial correlation will lead to a DW statistic that is less than 2.0. From the table in Problem 1, we see that the DW statistic is 0.1878. To see whether this result is significantly less than 2.0, refer to the Durbin–Watson table in Appendix E at the end of this volume, in the column marked $k = 1$ (one independent variable) and the row corresponding to 60 observations. We see that $d_l = 1.61$. Because our DW statistic is clearly less than d_l, we reject the null hypothesis of no serial correlation at the 0.05 significance level.

   The presence of serial correlation in the error term violates one of the regression assumptions. The standard errors of the estimated coefficients will be biased downward, so we cannot conduct hypothesis testing on the coefficients.

2. The difference between UER and its forecast value, PRED, is the forecast error. In an appropriately specified regression model, the forecast errors are randomly distributed around the regression line and have a constant variance. We can see that the errors from this model specification are persistent. The errors tend first to be above the regression line, and then, starting in 2014, they tend to be below the regression line until 2017, when they again are persistently above the regression line. This persistence suggests that the errors are positively serially correlated. Therefore, we conclude that the model is not appropriate for making estimates.

3. A log-linear model captures growth at a constant rate. The log-linear model $\ln(Sales_t) = b_0 + b_1 t + \epsilon_t$ would be the simplest model consistent with a constant growth rate for

monthly sales. Note that we would need to confirm that the regression assumptions are satisfied before accepting the model as valid.

4. A. The plot of the series ΔUER_t seems to fluctuate around a constant mean; its volatility appears to be constant throughout the period. Our initial judgment is that the differenced series is covariance stationary.

   B. The change in the unemployment rate seems covariance stationary, so we should first estimate an AR(1) model and test to see whether the residuals from this model have significant serial correlation. If the residuals do not display significant serial correlation, we should use the AR(1) model. If the residuals do display significant serial correlation, we should try an AR(2) model and test for serial correlation of the residuals of the AR(2) model. We should continue this procedure until the errors from the final AR(p) model are serially uncorrelated.

5. The DW statistic cannot be appropriately used for a regression that has a lagged value of the dependent variable as one of the explanatory variables. To test for serial correlation, we need to examine the autocorrelations.

6. When a covariance-stationary series is at its mean-reverting level, the series will tend not to change until it receives a shock (ϵ_t). So, if the series ΔUER_t is at the mean-reverting level, $\Delta UER_t = \Delta UER_{t-1}$. This implies that $\Delta UER_t = -0.0668 - 0.2320\Delta UER_t$, so that $(1 + 0.2320)\Delta UER_t = -0.0668$ and $\Delta UER_t = -0.0668/(1 + 0.2320) = -0.0542$. The mean-reverting level is -0.0542. In an AR(1) model, the general expression for the mean-reverting level is $b_0/(1 - b_1)$.

7. A. The predicted change in the unemployment rate for next period is -7.38 percent, found by substituting 0.0300 into the forecasting model: $-0.0668 - 0.2320(0.03) = -0.0738$.

   B. If we substitute our one-period-ahead forecast of -0.0738 into the model (using the chain rule of forecasting), we get a two-period-ahead forecast of -0.0497, or -4.97 percent.

   C. The answer to Part B is quite close to the mean-reverting level of -0.0542. A stationary time series may need many periods to return to its equilibrium, mean-reverting level.

8. The forecast of sales is $13,647 million for the first quarter of 2020 and $13,800 million for the second quarter of 2002, as the following table shows.

Date	Sales ($ Millions)	Log of Sales	Actual Value of Changes in the Log of Sales $\Delta\ln(Sales_t)$	Forecast Value of Changes in the Log of Sales $\Delta\ln(Sales_t)$
1Q 2019	13,072	9.4782	0.0176	
2Q 2019	12,446	9.4292	−0.0491	
3Q 2019	12,958	9.4695	0.4030	
4Q 2019	13,428	9.5051	0.0356	
1Q 2020	13,647	9.5213		0.0162
2Q 2020	13,800	9.5324		0.0111

We find the forecasted change in the log of sales for the first quarter of 2020 by inputting the value for the change in the log of sales from the previous quarter into the equation $\Delta \ln(Sales_t) = 0.0068 + 0.2633\Delta \ln(Sales_{t-1})$. Specifically, $\Delta \ln(Sales_t) = 0.0068 + 0.2633(0.0356) = 0.0162$, which means that we forecast the log of sales in the first quarter of 2020 to be $9.5051 + 0.0162 = 9.5213$.

Next, we forecast the change in the log of sales for the second quarter of 2020 as $\Delta \ln (Sales_t) = 0.0068 + 0.2633(0.0162) = 0.0111$. Note that we have to use our first-quarter 2020 estimated value of the change in the log of sales as our input for $\Delta \ln (Sales_{t-1})$ because we are forecasting past the period for which we have actual data. With a forecasted change of 0.0111, we forecast the log of sales in the second quarter of 2020 to be $9.5213 + 0.0111 = 9.5324$.

We have forecasted the log of sales in the first and second quarters of 2020 to be 9.5213 and 9.5324, respectively. Finally, we take the antilog of our estimates of the log of sales in the first and second quarters of 2020 to get our estimates of the level of sales: $e^{9.5213} = 13,647$ and $e^{9.5324} = 13,800$, respectively, for sales of $13,647 million and $13,800 million.

9. A. The RMSE of the out-of-sample forecast errors is approximately 3.6 percent. Out-of-sample error refers to the difference between the realized value and the forecasted value of $\Delta \ln(Sales_t)$ for dates beyond the estimation period. In this case, the out-of-sample period is 1Q 2019 to 4Q 2019. These are the four quarters for which we have data that we did not use to obtain the estimated model $\Delta \ln(Sales_t) = 0.0068 + 0.2633\Delta \ln(Sales_{t-1})$.

The steps to calculate RMSE are as follows:
  i. Take the difference between the actual and the forecast values. This is the error.
  ii. Square the error.
  iii. Sum the squared errors.
  iv. Divide by the number of forecasts.
  v. Take the square root of the average.

We show the calculations for RMSE in the following table.

Actual Values of Changes in the Log of Sales $\Delta \ln(Sales_t)$	Forecast Values of Changes in the Log of Sales $\Delta \ln(Sales_t)$	Error (Column 1 – Column 2)	Squared Error (Column 3 Squared)
0.0176	0.0147	0.0029	0.0000
-0.0491	0.0107	-0.0598	0.0036
0.0403	0.0096	0.0307	0.0009
0.0356	0.0093	0.0263	0.0007
		Sum	0.0052
		Mean	0.0013
		RMSE	0.036

B. The lower the RMSE, the more accurate the forecasts of a model in forecasting. Therefore, the model with the RMSE of 2 percent has greater accuracy in forecasting than the model in Part A, which has an RMSE of 3.6 percent.

10. A. Predictions too far ahead can be nonsensical. For example, the AR(1) model we have been examining, $\Delta UER_t = -0.0405 - 0.4674\Delta UER_{t-1}$, taken at face value, predicts declining civilian unemployment into the indefinite future. Because the civilian unemployment rate will probably not go below 3% frictional unemployment and cannot go below 0 percent unemployment, this model's long-range forecasts are implausible. The model is designed for short-term forecasting, as are many time-series models.

B. Using more years of data for estimation may lead to nonstationarity even in the series of first differences in the civilian unemployment rate. As we go further back in time, we increase the risk that the underlying civilian unemployment rate series has more than one regime (or true model). If the series has more than one regime, fitting one model to the entire period would not be correct. Note that when we have good reason to believe that a time series is stationary, a longer series of data is generally desirable.

11. A. The graph of ln(Sales$_t$) appears to trend upward over time. A series that trends upward or downward over time often has a unit root and is thus not covariance stationary. Therefore, using an AR(1) regression on the undifferenced series is probably not correct. In practice, we need to examine regression statistics to confirm such visual impressions.

B. The most common way to transform a time series with a unit root into a covariance-stationary time series is to difference the data—that is, to create a new series: $\Delta \ln(Sales_t) = \ln(Sales_t) - \ln(Sales_{t-1})$.

12. The plot of the series $\Delta \ln(Sales_t)$ appears to fluctuate around a constant mean; its volatility seems constant throughout the period. Differencing the data appears to have made the time series covariance stationary.

13. A. In a correctly specified regression, the residuals must be serially uncorrelated. We have 108 observations, so the standard error of the autocorrelation is $1/\sqrt{T}$, or in this case $1/\sqrt{108} = 0.0962$. The t-statistic for each lag is significant at the 0.01 level. We would have to modify the model specification before continuing with the analysis.

B. Because the residuals from the AR(1) specification display significant serial correlation, we should estimate an AR(2) model and test for serial correlation of the residuals of the AR(2) model. If the residuals from the AR(2) model are serially uncorrelated, we should then test for seasonality and ARCH behavior. If any serial correlation remains in the residuals, we should estimate an AR(3) process and test the residuals from that specification for serial correlation. We should continue this procedure until the errors from the final AR(p) model are serially uncorrelated. When serial correlation is eliminated, we should test for seasonality and ARCH behavior.

14. A. The series has a steady upward trend of growth, suggesting an exponential growth rate. This finding suggests transforming the series by taking the natural log and differencing the data.

B. First, we should determine whether the residuals from the AR(1) specification are serially uncorrelated. If the residuals are serially correlated, then we should try an AR(2) specification and then test the residuals from the AR(2) model for serial correlation. We should continue in this fashion until the residuals are serially uncorrelated and then look for seasonality in the residuals. If seasonality is present, we should add a seasonal lag. If no seasonality is present, we should test for ARCH. If ARCH is not present, we can conclude that the model is correctly specified.

C. If the model $\Delta\ln(\text{Sales}_t) = b_0 + b_1[\Delta\ln(\text{Sales}_{t-1})] + \epsilon_t$ is correctly specified, then the series $\Delta\ln(\text{Sales}_t)$ is covariance stationary. So, this series tends to its mean-reverting level, which is $b_0/(1 - b_1)$, or $0.0661/(1 - 0.4698) = 0.1247$.

15. The quarterly sales of Avon show an upward trend and a clear seasonal pattern, as indicated by the repeated regular cycle.

16. A. A second explanatory variable, the change in the gross profit margin lagged four quarters, ΔGPM_{t-4}, was added.

   B. The model was augmented to account for seasonality in the time series (with quarterly data, significant autocorrelation at the fourth lag indicates seasonality). The standard error of the autocorrelation coefficient equals 1 divided by the square root of the number of observations: $1/\sqrt{40}$, or 0.1581. The autocorrelation at the fourth lag (0.8496) is significant: $t = 0.8496/0.1581 = 5.37$. This indicates seasonality, and accordingly we added ΔGPM_{t-4}. Note that in the augmented regression, the coefficient on ΔGPM_{t-4} is highly significant. (Although the autocorrelation at second lag is also significant, the fourth lag is more important because of the rationale of seasonality. Once the fourth lag is introduced as an independent variable, we might expect that the second lag in the residuals would not be significant.)

17. A. In order to determine whether this model is correctly specified, we need to test for serial correlation among the residuals. We want to test whether we can reject the null hypothesis that the value of each autocorrelation is 0 against the alternative hypothesis that each is not equal to 0. At the 0.05 significance level, with 68 observations and three parameters, this model has 65 degrees of freedom. The critical value of the t-statistic needed to reject the null hypothesis is thus about 2.0. The absolute value of the t-statistic for each autocorrelation is below 0.60 (less than 2.0), so we cannot reject the null hypothesis that each autocorrelation is not significantly different from 0. We have determined that the model is correctly specified.

   B. If sales grew by 1 percent last quarter and by 2 percent four quarters ago, then the model predicts that sales growth this quarter will be $0.0121 - 0.0839[\ln(1.01)] + 0.6292[\ln(1.02)] = e^{0.02372} - 1 = 2.40$ percent.

18. We should estimate the regression $\Delta\text{UER}_t = b_0 + b_1\Delta\text{UER}_{t-1} + \epsilon_t$ and save the residuals from the regression. Then we should create a new variable, $\hat{\epsilon}_t^2$, by squaring the residuals. Finally, we should estimate $\hat{\epsilon}_t^2 = a_0 + a_1\hat{\epsilon}_{t-1}^2 + u_t$ and test to see whether a_1 is statistically different from 0.

19. To determine whether we can use linear regression to model more than one time series, we should first determine whether any of the time series has a unit root. If none of the time series has a unit root, then we can safely use linear regression to test the relations between the two time series. Note that if one of the two variables has a unit root, then

our analysis would not provide valid results; if both of the variables have unit roots, then we would need to evaluate whether the variables are cointegrated.

20. C is correct. The predicted value for period t from a linear trend is calculated as $\hat{y}_t = \hat{b}_0 + \hat{b}_1(t)$.

October 2015 is the second month out of sample, or $t = 183$. So, the predicted value for October 2015 is calculated as

$$\hat{y}_t = 28.3278 + 0.4086(183) = \$103.10.$$

Therefore, the predicted WTI oil price for October 2015 based on the linear trend model is $103.10.

21. C is correct. The predicted value for period t from a log-linear trend is calculated as $\ln \hat{y}_t = \hat{b}_0 + \hat{b}_1(t)$.

September 2015 is the first month out of sample, or $t = 182$. So, the predicted value for September 2015 is calculated as follows:

$$\ln \hat{y}_t = 3.3929 + 0.0075(182).$$
$$\ln \hat{y}_t = 4.7579.$$
$$\hat{y}_t = e^{4.7579} = \$116.50.$$

Therefore, the predicted WTI oil price for September 2015, based on the log-linear trend model, is $116.50.

22. B is correct. The Durbin–Watson statistic for the linear trend model is 0.10 and for the log-linear trend model is 0.08. Both of these values are below the critical value of 1.75. Therefore, we can reject the hypothesis of no positive serial correlation in the regression errors in both the linear trend model and the log-linear trend model.

23. B is correct. There are three requirements for a time series to be covariance stationary. First, the expected value of the time series must be constant and finite in all periods. Second, the variance of the time series must be constant and finite in all periods. Third, the covariance of the time series with itself for a fixed number of periods in the past or future must be constant and finite in all periods. Martinez concludes that the mean and variance of the time series of WTI oil prices are not constant over time. Therefore, the time series is not covariance stationary.

24. B is correct. The last two observations in the WTI time series are July and August 2015, when the WTI oil price was $51.16 and $42.86, respectively. Therefore, September 2015 represents a one-period-ahead forecast. The one-period-ahead forecast from an AR(2) model is calculated as

$$\hat{x}_{t+1} = \hat{b}_0 + \hat{b}_1 x_t + \hat{b}_2 x_{t+1}.$$

So, the one-period-ahead (September 2015) forecast is calculated as

$$\hat{x}_{t+1} = 2.0017 + 1.3946(\$42.86) - 0.4249(\$51.16) = \$40.04.$$

Therefore, the September 2015 forecast based on the AR(2) model is $40.04.

25. C is correct. The standard error of the autocorrelations is calculated as $\frac{1}{\sqrt{T}}$, where T represents the number of observations used in the regression. Therefore, the standard error for each of the autocorrelations is $\frac{1}{\sqrt{180}} = 0.0745$. Martinez can conclude that the

residuals are serially correlated and are significantly different from zero because two of the four autocorrelations in Exhibit 2 have a t-statistic in absolute value that is greater than the critical value of 1.97.

Choices A and B are incorrect because two of the four autocorrelations have a t-statistic in absolute value that is greater than the critical value of the t-statistic of 1.97.

26. C is correct. The mean-reverting level from the AR(1) model is calculated as

$$\widehat{x}_t = \frac{b_0}{1 - b_1} = \frac{1.5948}{1 - 0.9767} = \$68.45.$$

Therefore, the mean-reverting WTI oil price from the AR(1) model is \$68.45. The forecasted oil price in September 2015 will likely be greater than \$42.86 because the model predicts that the price will rise in the next period from the August 2015 price of \$42.86.

27. C is correct. A random walk can be described by the equation $x_t = b_0 + b_1 x_{t-1} + \epsilon_t$, where $b_0 = 0$ and $b_1 = 1$. So $b_0 = 0$ is a characteristic of a random walk time series. A covariance-stationary series must satisfy the following three requirements:

1.   The expected value of the time series must be constant and finite in all periods.
2.   The variance of the time series must be constant and finite in all periods.
3.   The covariance of the time series with itself for a fixed number of periods in the past or future must be constant and finite in all periods.

$b_0 = 0$ does not violate any of these three requirements and is thus consistent with the properties of a covariance-stationary time series.

28. B is correct. The critical t-statistic at a 5 percent confidence level is 1.98. As a result, neither the intercept nor the coefficient on the first lag of the first-differenced exchange rate in Regression 2 differs significantly from zero. Also, the residual autocorrelations do not differ significantly from zero. As a result, Regression 2 can be reduced to $y_t = \epsilon_t$, with a mean-reverting level of $b_0/(1 - b_1) = 0/1 = 0$. Therefore, the variance of y_t in each period is $\mathrm{var}(\epsilon_t) = \sigma^2$. The fact that the residuals are not autocorrelated is consistent with the covariance of the times series with itself being constant and finite at different lags. Because the variance and the mean of y_t are constant and finite in each period, we can also conclude that y_t is covariance stationary.

29. A is correct. If the exchange rate series is a random walk, then the first-differenced series will yield $b_0 = 0$ and $b_1 = 0$ and the error terms will not be serially correlated. The data in Exhibit 1 show that this is the case: Neither the intercept nor the coefficient on the first lag of the first-differenced exchange rate in Regression 2 differs significantly from zero because the t-statistics of both coefficients are less than the critical t-statistic of 1.98. Also, the residual autocorrelations do not differ significantly from zero because the t-statistics of all autocorrelations are less than the critical t-statistic of 1.98. Therefore, because all random walks have unit roots, the exchange rate time series used to run Regression 1 has a unit root.

30. C is correct. To conduct the Dickey–Fuller test, one must subtract the independent variable, x_{t-1}, from both sides of the original AR(1) model. This results in a change of the dependent variable (from x_t to $x_t - x_{t-1}$) and a change in the regression's slope coefficient (from b_1 to $b_1 - 1$) but not a change in the independent variable.

31. C is correct. The regression output in Exhibit 2 suggests there is serial correlation in the residual errors. The fourth autocorrelation of the residual has a value of 0.6994 and a t-statistic of 4.3111, which is greater than the t-statistic critical value of 2.02. Therefore,

the null hypothesis that the fourth autocorrelation is equal to zero can be rejected. This indicates strong and significant seasonal autocorrelation, which means the Regression 3 equation is misspecified.

32. C is correct. The quarterly sales for March 2016 are calculated as follows:

$\ln \text{Sales}_t - \ln \text{Sales}_{t-1} = b_0 + b_1(\ln \text{Sales}_{t-1} - \ln \text{Sales}_{t-2}) + b_2(\ln \text{Sales}_{t-4} - \ln \text{Sales}_{t-5})$.

$\ln \text{Sales}_t - \ln 3.868 = 0.0092 - 0.1279(\ln 3.868 - \ln 3.780) + 0.7239(\ln 3.836 - \ln 3.418)$.

$\ln \text{Sales}_t - 1.35274 = 0.0092 - 0.1279(1.35274 - 1.32972) + 0.7239(1.34443 - 1.22906)$.

$\ln \text{Sales}_t = 1.35274 + 0.0092 - 0.1279(0.02301) + 0.7239(0.11538)$.

$\ln \text{Sales}_t = 1.44251$.

$\text{Sales}_t = e^{1.44251} = 4.231$.

33. B is correct. Exhibit 3 shows that the time series of the stock prices of Company 1 exhibits heteroskedasticity, as evidenced by the fact that the time series is ARCH(1). If a time series is ARCH(1), then the variance of the error in one period depends on the variance of the error in previous periods. Therefore, the variance of the errors in period $t + 1$ can be predicted in period t using the formula

$$\hat{\sigma}^2_{t+1} = \hat{a}_0 + \hat{a}_1 \hat{\epsilon}^2_t.$$

34. B is correct. When two time series have a unit root but are cointegrated, the error term in the linear regression of one time series on the other will be covariance stationary. Exhibit 5 shows that the series of stock prices of Company 2 and the oil prices both contain a unit root and the two time series are cointegrated. As a result, the regression coefficients and standard errors are consistent and can be used for hypothesis tests. Although the cointegrated regression estimates the long-term relation between the two series, it may not be the best model of the short-term relationship.

35. C is correct. As a result of the exponential trend in the time series of stock prices for Company 3, Busse would want to take the natural log of the series and then first-difference it. Because the time series also has serial correlation in the residuals from the trend model, Busse should use a more complex model, such as an autoregressive (AR) model.

CHAPTER 10

MACHINE LEARNING

SOLUTIONS

1. A is correct. The target variable (quarterly return) is continuous, hence this calls for a supervised machine learning based regression model. B is incorrect, since classification uses categorical or ordinal target variables, while in Step 1 the target variable (quarterly return) is continuous. C is incorrect, since clustering involves unsupervised machine learning so does not have a target variable.

2. B is correct. It is least appropriate because with LASSO, when $\lambda = 0$ the penalty (i.e., regularization) term reduces to zero, so there is no regularization and the regression is equivalent to an ordinary least squares (OLS) regression. A is incorrect. With classification and regression trees (CART), one way that regularization can be implemented is via pruning which will reduce the size of the regression tree—sections that provide little explanatory power are pruned (i.e., removed). C is incorrect. With LASSO, when λ is between 0.5 and 1 the relatively large penalty (i.e., regularization) term requires that a feature makes a sufficient contribution to model fit to offset the penalty from including it in the model.

3. A is correct. K-Means clustering is an unsupervised machine learning algorithm which repeatedly partitions observations into a fixed number, k, of non-overlapping clusters (i.e., groups). B is incorrect. Principal components analysis is a long-established statistical method for dimension reduction, not clustering. PCA aims to summarize or reduce highly correlated features of data into a few main, uncorrelated composite variables. C is incorrect. CART is a supervised machine learning technique that is most commonly applied to binary classification or regression.

4. C is correct. Here, 20 is a hyperparameter (in the K-Means algorithm), which is a parameter whose value must be set by the researcher before learning begins. A is incorrect, because it is not a hyperparameter. It is just the size (number of stocks) of Alef's portfolio. B is incorrect, because it is not a hyperparameter. It is just the size (number of stocks) of Alef's eligible universe.

5. B is correct. To predict which stocks are likely to become acquisition targets, the ML model would need to be trained on categorical labelled data having the following two categories: "0" for "not acquisition target," and "1" for "acquisition target." A is incorrect because the target variable is categorical, not continuous. C is incorrect because the target variable is categorical, not ordinal (i.e., 1st, 2nd, 3rd, etc.).

6. C is correct. The advantages of using CART over KNN to classify companies into two categories ("not acquisition target" and "acquisition target"), include all of the following: For CART there are no requirements to specify an initial hyperparameter (like K) or a similarity (or distance) measure as with KNN, and CART provides a visual explanation for the prediction (i.e., the feature variables and their cut-off values at each node). A is incorrect because CART provides all of the advantages indicated in Statements I, II and III. B is incorrect because CART provides all of the advantages indicated in Statements I, II and III.

7. C is correct. A fitting curve shows the trade-off between bias error and variance error for various potential models. A model with low bias error and high variance error is, by definition, overfitted. A is incorrect because there are two common methods to reduce overfitting, one of which is proper data sampling and cross—validation. K-fold cross-validation is such a method for estimating out-of-sample error directly by determining the error in validation samples. B is incorrect because there are two common methods to reduce overfitting, one of which is preventing the algorithm from getting too complex during selection and training, which requires estimating an overfitting penalty.

8. C is correct. Ensemble learning is the technique of combining the predictions from a collection of models, and it typically produces more accurate and more stable predictions than the best single model. A is incorrect because a single model will have a certain error rate and will make noisy predictions. By taking the average result of many predictions from many models (i.e., ensemble learning) one can expect to achieve a reduction in noise as the average result converges towards a more accurate prediction. B is incorrect because a single model will have a certain error rate and will make noisy predictions. By taking the average result of many predictions from many models (i.e., ensemble learning) one can expect to achieve a reduction in noise as the average result converges towards a more accurate prediction.

9. B is correct. NNs and DL are well-suited for addressing highly complex machine learning tasks, such as image classification, face recognition, speech recognition and natural language processing. These complicated tasks are characterized by non-linearities and complex interactions between large numbers of feature inputs. A is incorrect because NNs and DL are well-suited for addressing highly complex machine learning tasks, not simple single variable OLS regression models. C is incorrect because NNs and DL are well-suited for addressing highly complex machine learning tasks, not simple single variable OLS regression models.

10. A is correct. It is the least accurate answer because neural networks with many hidden layers—at least 3, but often more than 20 hidden layers—are known as deep learning nets. B is incorrect because the node's activation function operates like a light dimmer switch which decreases or increases the strength of the (total net) input. C is incorrect because the node's summation operator multiplies each (input) value by a weight and sums up the weighted values to form the total net input. The total net input is then passed to the activation function.

CHAPTER 11

BIG DATA PROJECTS

SOLUTIONS

1. B is correct. The five steps in building structured data-based ML models are: 1) conceptualization of the modeling task, 2) data collection, 3) data preparation and wrangling, 4) data exploration, and 5) model training. The five steps in building text-based ML models are: 1) text problem formulation, 2) data (text) curation, 3) text preparation and wrangling, 4) text exploration, and 5) model training. Statement 1 is incorrect: Text preparation and wrangling is the third step in building text ML models and occurs after the second data (text) curation step. Statement 2 is correct: The fourth step in building both types of models encompasses data/text exploration.

2. C is correct. Veracity relates to the credibility and reliability of different data sources. Steele is concerned about the credibility and reliability of Twitter content, noting that research suggests that as much as 10–15 percent of social media content is from fake accounts.

3. C is correct. A non-uniformity error occurs when the data are not presented in an identical format. The data in the "IPO Date" column represent the IPO date of each firm. While all rows are populated with valid dates in the IPO Date column, the dates are presented in different formats (e.g., mm/dd/yyyy, dd/mm/yyyy).

4. A is correct. There appears to be an inconsistency error in the last row (ID #4). An inconsistency error occurs when a data point conflicts with corresponding data points or reality. In the last row, the interest expense data item has a value of 1.5, and the total debt item has a value of 0.0. This appears to be an error: Firms that have interest expense are likely to have debt in their capital structure, so either the interest expense is incorrect or the total debt value is incorrect. Steele should investigate this issue by using alternative data sources to confirm the correct values for these variables.

5. A is correct. During the data preprocessing step, Steele created a new "Age" variable based on the firm's IPO date and then deleted the "IPO Date" variable from the dataset. She also created a new "Interest Coverage Ratio" variable equal to EBIT divided by interest expense. Extraction refers to a data transformation where a new variable is

extracted from a current variable for ease of analyzing and using for training an ML model, such as creating an age variable from a date variable or a ratio variable. Steele also performed a selection transformation by deleting the IPO Date variable, which refers to deleting the data columns that are not needed for the project.

6. B is correct. Steele uses normalization to scale the financial data. Normalization is the process of rescaling numeric variables in the range of [0, 1]. To normalize variable X, the minimum value (X_{min}) is subtracted from each observation (X_i), and then this value is divided by the difference between the maximum and minimum values of X ($X_{max} - X_{min}$):

$$X_{i \text{ (normalized)}} = \frac{X_i - X_{min}}{X_{max} - X_{min}}$$

The firm with ID 3 has an interest expense of 1.2. So, its normalized value is calculated as:

$$X_{i \text{ (normalized)}} = \frac{1.2 - 0.2}{12.2 - 0.2} = 0.083$$

7. B is correct. Although most punctuations are not necessary for text analysis and should be removed, some punctuations (e.g., percentage signs, currency symbols, and question marks) may be useful for ML model training. Such punctuations should be substituted with annotations (e.g., /percentSign/, /dollarSign/, and /questionMark/) to preserve their grammatical meaning in the text. Such annotations preserve the semantic meaning of important characters in the text for further text processing and analysis stages.

8. A is correct. Tokenization is the process of splitting a given text into separate tokens. This step takes place after cleansing the raw text data (removing html tags, numbers, extra white spaces, etc.). The tokens are then normalized to create the bag of words (BOW).

9. A is correct. After the cleansed text is normalized, a bag-of-words is created. A bag of words (BOW) is a collection of a distinct set of tokens from all the texts in a sample dataset.

10. B is correct. Steele wants to create a visualization for Schultz that shows the most informative words in the dataset based on their term frequency (TF, the ratio of the number of times a given token occurs in the dataset to the total number of tokens in the dataset) values. A word cloud is a common visualization when working with text data as it can be made to visualize the most informative words and their TF values. The most commonly occurring words in the dataset can be shown by varying font size, and color is used to add more dimensions, such as frequency and length of words.

11. C is correct. Frequency measures can be used for vocabulary pruning to remove noise features by filtering the tokens with very high and low TF values across all the texts. Noise features are both the most frequent and most sparse (or rare) tokens in the dataset. On one end, noise features can be stop words that are typically present frequently in all the texts across the dataset. On the other end, noise features can be sparse terms that are present in only a few text files. Text classification involves dividing text documents into assigned classes. The frequent tokens strain the ML model to choose a decision boundary among the texts as the terms are present across all the texts

(an example of underfitting). The rare tokens mislead the ML model into classifying texts containing the rare terms into a specific class (an example of overfitting). Thus, identifying and removing noise features are critical steps for text classification applications.

12. A is correct. A dataset with a small number of features may not carry all the characteristics that explain relationships between the target variable and the features. Conversely, a large number of features can complicate the model and potentially distort patterns in the data due to low degrees of freedom, causing overfitting. Therefore, appropriate feature selection is a key factor in minimizing such model overfitting. Feature engineering tends to prevent underfitting in the training of the model. New features, when engineered properly, can elevate the underlying data points that better explain the interactions of features. Thus, feature engineering can be critical to overcome underfitting.

13. A is correct. Precision, the ratio of correctly predicted positive classes (true positives) to all predicted positive classes, is calculated as:

$$\text{Precision (P)} = \text{TP}/(\text{TP} + \text{FP}) = 182/(182 + 52) = 0.7778 \ (78\%)$$

14. B is correct. The model's F1 score, which is the harmonic mean of precision and recall, is calculated as:

$$\text{F1 score} = (2 \times \text{P} \times \text{R})/(\text{P} + \text{R})$$

$$\text{F1 score} = (2 \times 0.7778 \times 0.8545)/(0.7778 + 0.8545) = 0.8143 \ (81\%)$$

15. A is correct. The model's accuracy, which is the percentage of correctly predicted classes out of total predictions, is calculated as:

$$\text{Accuracy} = (\text{TP} + \text{TN})/(\text{TP} + \text{FP} + \text{TN} + \text{FN})$$

$$\text{Accuracy} = (182 + 96)/(182 + 52 + 96 + 31) = 0.7701 \ (77\%)$$

16. B is correct. When analyzing term frequency at the corpus level, also known as collection frequency, tokens with intermediate term frequency (TF) values potentially carry important information useful for differentiating the sentiment embedded in the text. Tokens with the highest TF values are mostly stop words that do not contribute to differentiating the sentiment embedded in the text, and tokens with the lowest TF values are mostly proper nouns or sparse terms that are also not important to the meaning of the text. A is incorrect because tokens with the lowest TF values are mostly proper nouns or sparse terms (noisy terms) that are not important to the meaning of the text. C is incorrect because tokens with the highest TF values are mostly stop words (noisy terms) that do not contribute to differentiating the sentiment embedded in the text.

17. C is correct. Statement 3 is correct. TF–IDF values vary by the number of documents in the dataset, and therefore, the model performance can vary when applied to a dataset

with just a few documents. Statement 1 is incorrect because IDF is calculated as the log of the inverse, or reciprocal, of the document frequency measure. Statement 2 is incorrect because TF at the sentence (not collection) level is multiplied by IDF to calculate TF–IDF. A is incorrect because Statement 1 is incorrect. IDF is calculated as the log of the inverse, or reciprocal, of the document frequency (DF) measure. B is incorrect because Statement 2 is incorrect. TF at the sentence (not collection) level is multiplied by IDF to calculate TF–IDF.

18. A is correct; 0 percent of the master dataset of Dataset ABC should be allocated to a training subset. Dataset ABC is characterized by the absence of ground truth (i.e., no known outcome or target variable) and is therefore an unsupervised ML model. For unsupervised learning models, no splitting of the master dataset is needed, because of the absence of labeled training data. Supervised ML datasets (with labeled training data) contain ground truth, the known outcome (target variable) of each observation in the dataset.

    B is incorrect because 20 percent is the commonly recommended split for the cross-validation set and test set in supervised training ML datasets. Dataset ABC is an unsupervised ML dataset, for which no splitting (0 percent) of the master dataset is needed, because of the absence of labeled training data. In supervised ML models (which contain labeled training data), the master dataset is split into three subsets (a training set, cross-validation set, and test set), which are used for model training and testing purposes.

    C is incorrect because 60 percent is the commonly recommended split for the training set in supervised training ML datasets. Dataset ABC is an unsupervised ML dataset, for which no splitting (0 percent) of the master dataset is needed, because of the absence of labeled training data. In supervised ML models (which contain labeled training data), the master dataset is split into three subsets (a training set, cross-validation set, and test set), which are used for model training and testing purposes.

19. B is correct. F1 score is the most appropriate performance measure for Dataset XYZ. Bector gives equal weight to false positives and false negatives. Accuracy and F1 score are overall performance measures that give equal weight to false positives and false negatives. Accuracy is considered an appropriate performance measure for balanced datasets, where the number of "1" and "0" classes are equal. F1 score is considered more appropriate than accuracy when there is unequal class distribution in the dataset and it is necessary to measure the equilibrium of precision and recall. Since Dataset XYZ contains an unequal class distribution between positive and negative sentiment sentences, F1 score is the most appropriate performance measure.

    Precision is the ratio of correctly predicted positive classes to all predicted positive classes and is useful in situations where the cost of false positives or Type I errors is high. Recall is the ratio of correctly predicted positive classes to all actual positive classes and is useful in situations where the cost of false negatives or Type II errors is high.

    A is incorrect because Bector gives equal weight to false positives and false negatives. Accuracy and F1 score are overall performance measures that give equal weight to false positives and false negatives. Recall is the ratio of correctly predicted positive classes to all actual positive classes and is useful in situations where the cost of false negatives or Type II errors is high.

C is incorrect because Bector gives equal weight to false positive and false negatives. Accuracy and F1 score are overall performance measures that give equal weight to false positives and false negatives. Precision is the ratio of correctly predicted positive classes to all predicted positive classes and is useful in situations where the cost of false positives or Type-I error is high.

20. A is correct. Precision is the ratio of correctly predicted positive classes to all predicted positive classes and is useful in situations where the cost of false positives or Type I errors is high. Confusion Matrix A has the highest precision and therefore demonstrates the most favorable value of the performance metric that best addresses Azarov's concern about the cost of Type I errors. Confusion Matrix A has a precision score of 0.95, which is higher than the precision scores of Confusion Matrix B (0.93) and Confusion Matrix C (0.86).

    B is incorrect because precision, not accuracy, is the performance measure that best addresses Azarov's concern about the cost of Type I errors. Confusion Matrix B demonstrates the most favorable value for the accuracy score (0.92), which is higher than the accuracy scores of Confusion Matrix A (0.91) and Confusion Matrix C (0.91). Accuracy is a performance measure that gives equal weight to false positives and false negatives and is considered an appropriate performance measure when the class distribution in the dataset is equal (a balanced dataset). However, Azarov is most concerned with the cost of false positives, or Type I errors, and not with finding the equilibrium between precision and recall. Furthermore, Dataset XYZ has an unequal (unbalanced) class distribution between positive sentiment and negative sentiment sentences.

    C is incorrect because precision, not recall or F1 score, is the performance measure that best addresses Azarov's concern about the cost of Type I errors. Confusion Matrix C demonstrates the most favorable value for the recall score (0.97), which is higher than the recall scores of Confusion Matrix A (0.87) and Confusion Matrix B (0.90). Recall is the ratio of correctly predicted positive classes to all actual positive classes and is useful in situations where the cost of false negatives, or Type II errors, is high. However, Azarov is most concerned with the cost of Type I errors, not Type II errors.

    F1 score is more appropriate (than accuracy) when there is unequal class distribution in the dataset and it is necessary to measure the equilibrium of precision and recall. Confusion Matrix C demonstrates the most favorable value for the F1 score (0.92), which is higher than the F1 scores of Confusion Matrix A (0.91) and Confusion Matrix B (0.91). Although Dataset XYZ has an unequal class distribution between positive sentiment and negative sentiment sentences, Azarov is most concerned with the cost of false positives, or Type I errors, and not with finding the equilibrium between precision and recall.

21. B is correct. Accuracy is the percentage of correctly predicted classes out of total predictions and is calculated as (TP + TN)/(TP + FP + TN + FN). In order to obtain the values for true positive (TP), true negative (TN), false positive (FP), and false negative (FN), predicted sentiment for the positive (Class "1") and the negative (Class "0") classes are determined based on whether each individual target p-value is greater than or less than the threshold p-value of 0.65. If an individual target p-value is greater than the threshold p-value of 0.65, the predicted sentiment for that instance is positive (Class "1"). If an individual target p-value is less than the threshold p-value of 0.65, the

predicted sentiment for that instance is negative (Class "0"). Actual sentiment and predicted sentiment are then classified as follows:

Actual Sentiment	Predicted Sentiment	Classification
1	1	TP
0	1	FP
1	0	FN
0	0	TN

Exhibit 2, with added "Predicted Sentiment" and "Classification" columns, is presented below:

EXHIBIT 2   10 Sample Results of Test Data for Dataset XYZ

Sentence #	Actual Sentiment	Target p-Value	Predicted Sentiment	Classification
1	1	0.75	1	TP
2	0	0.45	0	TN
3	1	0.64	0	FN
4	1	0.81	1	TP
5	0	0.43	0	TN
6	1	0.78	1	TP
7	0	0.59	0	TN
8	1	0.60	0	FN
9	0	0.67	1	FP
10	0	0.54	0	TN

Based on the classification data obtained from Exhibit 2, a confusion matrix can be generated:

Confusion Matrix for Dataset XYZ Sample Test Data with Threshold p-Value $= 0.65$

Predicted Results	Actual Training Labels	
	Class "1"	Class "0"
Class "1"	TP = 3	FP = 1
Class "0"	FN = 2	TN = 4

Using the data in the confusion matrix above, the accuracy metric is computed as follows:

$$\text{Accuracy} = (TP + TN)/(TP + FP + TN + FN).$$
$$\text{Accuracy} = (3 + 4)/(3 + 1 + 4 + 2) = 0.70.$$

A is incorrect because 0.67 is the F1 score, not accuracy metric, for the sample of the test set for Dataset XYZ, based on Exhibit 2. To calculate the F1 score, the precision (P) and the recall (R) ratios must first be calculated. Precision and recall for the sample of the test set for Dataset XYZ, based on Exhibit 2, are calculated as follows:

$$\text{Precision } (P) = TP/(TP + FP) = 3/(3 + 1) = 0.75.$$
$$\text{Recall } (R) = TP/(TP + FN) = 3/(3 + 2) = 0.60.$$

The F1 score is calculated as follows:
$$\text{F1 score} = (2 \times P \times R)/(P + R) = (2 \times 0.75 \times 0.60)/(0.75 + 0.60)$$
$$= 0.667, \text{ or } 0.67.$$

C is incorrect because 0.75 is the precision ratio, not the accuracy metric, for the sample of the test set for Dataset XYZ, based on Exhibit 2. The precision score is calculated as follows:

$$\text{Precision } (P) = TP/(TP + FP) = 3/(3 + 1) = 0.75.$$

22. A is correct. Only Remark 1 is correct. Method selection is the first task of ML model training and is governed by the following factors: (1) supervised or unsupervised learning, (2) the type of data, and (3) the size of data. The second and third tasks of model training, respectively, are performance evaluation and tuning.
Remark 2 is incorrect because model fitting errors (bias error and variance error) are used in tuning, not performance evaluation. The techniques used in performance evaluation, which measure the goodness of fit for validation of the model, include (1) error analysis, (2) receiver operating characteristic (ROC) plots, and (3) root mean squared error (RMSE) calculations. B and C are incorrect because Remark 2 is incorrect. Model fitting errors (bias error and variance error) are used in tuning, not performance evaluation. The techniques used in performance evaluation, which measure the goodness of fit for validation of the model, include (1) error analysis, (2) receiver operating characteristic plots, and (3) root mean squared error calculations.

23. A is correct. Statement 1 is correct because some of the methods used in the fourth step of ML model building (data/text exploration) are different for structured and unstructured data, and for both structured and unstructured data, the exploration step encompasses feature selection and feature engineering. Statement 2 is incorrect because Rivera described the text preparation and wrangling step, not the text curation step. The data (text) curation step involves gathering relevant external text data via web services or programs that extract raw content from a source.
B and C are incorrect because Statement 2 is incorrect. Rivera described the text preparation and wrangling step, not the text curation step. The data (text) curation step involves gathering relevant external text data via web services or programs that extract raw content from a source.

24. B is correct. Achler uses a web spidering program that extracts unstructured raw content
      from social media webpages. Raw text data are a sequence of characters and contain
      other non-useful elements including html tags, punctuation, and white spaces
      (including tabs, line breaks, and new lines). Removing numbers is one of the basic
      operations in the text cleansing/preparation process for unstructured data. When
      numbers (or digits) are present in the text, they should be removed or substituted with
      the annotation "/number/." Lemmatization, which takes places during the text
      wrangling/preprocessing process for unstructured data, is the process of converting
      inflected forms of a word into its morphological root (known as lemma). Lemmatization
      reduces the repetition of words occurring in various forms while maintaining the
      semantic structure of the text data, thereby aiding in training less complex ML models.
      A is incorrect because although html tag removal is part of text cleansing/preparation for
      unstructured data, scaling is a data wrangling/preprocessing process applied to
      structured data. Scaling adjusts the range of a feature by shifting and changing the
      scale of data; it is performed on numeric variables, not on text data.
      C is incorrect because although raw text contains white spaces (including tabs, line
      breaks, and new lines) that need to be removed as part of the data cleansing/preparation
      process for unstructured data, winsorization is a data wrangling/preprocessing task
      performed on values of data points, not on text data. Winsorization is used for
      structured numerical data and replaces extreme values and outliers with the maximum
      (for large-value outliers) and minimum (for small-value outliers) values of data points
      that are not outliers.

25. A is correct. Data preparation and wrangling involve cleansing and organizing raw data
      into a consolidated format. Token Group 1 includes n-grams ("not_increas_market,"
      "sale_decreas") and the words that have been converted from their inflected forms into
      their base word ("increas," "decreas"), and the currency symbol has been replaced with a
      "currencysign" token. N-gram tokens are helpful for keeping negations intact in the
      text, which is vital for sentiment prediction. The process of converting inflected forms
      of a word into its base word is called stemming and helps decrease data sparseness,
      thereby aiding in training less complex ML models.
      B is incorrect because Token Group 2 includes inflected forms of words ("increased,"
      "decreased") before conversion into their base words (known as stems). Stemming
      (along with lemmatization) decreases data sparseness by aggregating many sparsely
      occurring words in relatively less sparse stems or lemmas, thereby aiding in training less
      complex ML models. C is incorrect because Token Group 3 includes inflected forms of
      words ("increased," "decreased") before conversion into their base words (known as
      stems). In addition, the "EUR" currency symbol has not been replaced with the
      "currencysign" token and the word "Sales" has not been lowercased.

26. A is correct. Achler recommends creating a word cloud, which is a common text
      visualization technique at the data exploration phase in ML model building. The most
      commonly occurring words in the dataset can be visualized by varying font size, and
      color is used to add more dimensions, such as frequency and length of words.
      B is incorrect because Achler recommends creating a word cloud and not a bag of words
      (BOW). A BOW is a collection of a distinct set of tokens from all the texts in a sample
      dataset. A BOW representation is a basic procedure used primarily to analyze text
      during Step 3 (text wrangling/preprocessing), although it may also be used in Step 4

during the feature engineering process. In contrast to a word cloud, which visually varies font size and color, BOW is simply a set of words (typically displayed in table).

C is incorrect because Achler recommends creating a word cloud and not a collection frequency. Collection frequency (or term frequency) is the ratio of the number of times a given token occurs in all the texts in the dataset to the total number of tokens in the dataset. Collection frequency can be calculated and examined to identify outlier words, but it is not a visual text representation tool.

27. C is correct. Achler should remove words that are in both Group 1 and Group 2. Term frequency values range between 0 and 1. Group 1 consists of the highest frequency values (e.g., "the" = 0.04935), and Group 2 consists of the lowest frequency values (e.g., "naval" = 1.0123e–05). Frequency analysis on the processed text data helps in filtering unnecessary tokens (or features) by quantifying how important tokens are in a sentence and in the corpus as a whole. The most frequent tokens (Group 1) strain the machine-learning model to choose a decision boundary among the texts as the terms are present across all the texts, which leads to model underfitting. The least frequent tokens (Group 2) mislead the machine-learning model into classifying texts containing the rare terms into a specific class, which leads to model overfitting. Identifying and removing noise features is critical for text classification applications.

A is incorrect because words in both Group 1 and Group 2 should be removed. The words with high term frequency value are mostly stop words, present in most sentences. Stop words do not carry a semantic meaning for the purpose of text analyses and ML training, so they do not contribute to differentiating sentiment. B is incorrect because words in both Group 1 and Group 2 should be removed. Terms with low term frequency value are mostly rare terms, ones appearing only once or twice in the data. They do not contribute to differentiating sentiment.

28. B is correct. Achler is concerned about class imbalance, which can be resolved by balancing the training data. The majority class (the failed start-up data) can be randomly undersampled, or the minority class (the successful start-up data) can be randomly oversampled.

29. B is correct. The higher the AUC, the better the model performance. For the threshold p-value of 0.79, the AUC is 91.3 percent on the training dataset and 89.7 percent on the cross-validation dataset, and the ROC curves are similar for model performance on both datasets. These findings suggest that the model performs similarly on both training and CV data and thus indicate a good fitting model. A is incorrect because for the threshold p-value of 0.57, the AUC is 56.7 percent on the training dataset and 57.3 percent on the cross-validation dataset. The AUC close to 50 percent signifies random guessing on both the training dataset and the cross-validation dataset. The implication is that for the threshold p-value of 0.57, the model is randomly guessing and is not performing well. C is incorrect because for the threshold p-value of 0.84, there is a substantial difference between the AUC on the training dataset (98.4 percent) and the AUC on the cross-validation dataset (87.1 percent). This suggests that the model performs comparatively poorly (with a higher rate of error or misclassification) on the cross-validation dataset when compared with training data. Thus, the implication is that the model is overfitted.

30. C is correct. At the threshold p-value of 0.84, the AUC is 98.4 percent for the training dataset and 87.1 percent for the cross-validation dataset, which suggests that the model is currently overfitted. Least absolute shrinkage and selection operator (LASSO)

regularization can be applied to the logistic regression to prevent overfitting of logistic regression models. A is incorrect because the higher the AUC, the better the model performance. B is incorrect because the more convex the ROC curve and the higher the AUC, the better the model performance. Adjusting model parameters with the aim of achieving lower ROC convexity would result in worse model performance on the cross-validation dataset.

31. C is correct. Slight regularization occurs when the prediction error on the training dataset is small, while the prediction error on the cross-validation data set is significantly larger. This difference in error is variance. High variance error, which typically is due to too many features and model complexity, results in model overfitting. A is incorrect. The current model has high variance which results in model overfitting, not underfitting. B is incorrect. The difference between the prediction error on the training dataset and the prediction error on the cross-validation dataset is high, which means that the current model has high variance, not low.

CHAPTER 12

USING MULTIFACTOR MODELS

SOLUTIONS

1. APT and the CAPM are both models that describe what the expected return on a risky asset should be in equilibrium given its risk. The CAPM is based on a set of assumptions including the assumption that investors' portfolio decisions can be made considering just returns' means, variances, and correlations. The APT makes three assumptions:
   1. A factor model describes asset returns.
   2. There are many assets, so investors can form well-diversified portfolios that eliminate asset-specific risk.
   3. No arbitrage opportunities exist among well-diversified portfolios.

2. In a macroeconomic factor model, the surprise in a factor equals actual value minus expected value. For the interest rate factor, the surprise was 2 percent; for the GDP factor, the surprise was –3 percent. The intercept represents expected return in this type of model. The portion of the stock's return not explained by the factor model is the model's error term.

   5% = Expected return – 1.5(Interest rate surprise) + 2(GDP surprise) + Error term

   = Expected return – 1.5(2%) + 2(–3%) + 3%

   = Expected return – 6%

   Rearranging terms, the expected return for Harry Company stock equals $5\% + 6\% = 11\%$.

3. According to the one-factor model for expected returns, the portfolio should have these expected returns if they are correctly priced in terms of their risk:

   Portfolio A. $E(R_A) = 0.10 + 0.12b_{A,1} = 0.10 + (0.12)(0.80) = 0.10 + 0.10 = 0.20$
   Portfolio B. $E(R_B) = 0.10 + 0.12b_{B,1} = 0.10 + (0.12)(1.00) = 0.10 + 0.12 = 0.22$
   Portfolio C. $E(R_C) = 0.10 + 0.12b_{C,1} = 0.10 + (0.12)(1.20) = 0.10 + 0.14 = 0.24$

In the table below, the column for expected return shows that Portfolios A and C are correctly priced but Portfolio B offers too little expected return for its risk, 0.15 or 15 percent. By shorting Portfolio B (selling an overvalued portfolio) and using the proceeds to buy a portfolio 50 percent invested in A and 50 percent invested in C with a sensitivity of 1 that matches the sensitivity of B, for each monetary unit shorted (say each euro), an arbitrage profit of 0.22 − 0.15 = 0.07 is earned.

Portfolio	Expected Return	Factor Sensitivity
A	0.20	0.80
B	0.15	1.00
C	0.24	1.20
0.5A + 0.5C	0.22	1.00

4. A fundamental factor model. Such models typically include many factors related to the company (e.g., earnings) and to valuation that are commonly used indicators of a growth orientation. A macroeconomic factor model may provide relevant information as well, but typically indirectly and in less detail.

5. This remainder of 30 basis points would be attributable to the return from factor tilts. A portfolio manager's active return is the sum of two components, factor tilts and security selection. Factor tilt is the product of the portfolio manager's higher or lower factor sensitivities relative to the benchmark's factor sensitivities and the factor returns. Security selection reflects the manager's ability to overweight securities that outperform or underweight securities that underperform.

6. A. An index fund that effectively meets its investment objective is expected to have an information ratio of zero, because its active return should be zero.

   B. The active manager may assume active factor risk and active specific risk (security selection risk) in seeking a higher information ratio.

7. This wealthy investor has a comparative advantage in bearing business cycle risk compared with the average investor who depends on income from employment. Because the average investor is sensitive to the business cycle and in particular the risk of recession, we would expect there to be a risk premium to hold recession-sensitive securities. Cyclical stocks and high-yield bonds are both very sensitive to the risk of recessions. Because the welfare of the wealthy investor is not affected by recessions, she can tilt her portfolio to include cyclical stocks and high yield bonds to attempt to capture the associated risk premiums.

8. C is correct. Arbitrage pricing theory (APT) is a framework that explains the expected return of a portfolio in equilibrium as a linear function of the risk of the portfolio with respect to a set of factors capturing systematic risk. A key assumption of APT is that, in equilibrium, there are no arbitrage opportunities.

9. C is correct. The expected return and factor sensitivities of a portfolio with a 60 percent weight in Fund A and a 40 percent weight in Fund B are calculated as weighted averages of the expected returns and factor sensitivities of Funds A and B:

   Expected return of Portfolio 60/40 = (0.60)(0.02) + (0.40)(0.04) = 0.028, or 2.8%
   Factor sensitivity of Portfolio 60/40 = (0.60)(0.5) + (0.40)(1.5) = 0.9

Fund	Expected Return	Factor Sensitivity
A	0.02	0.5
B	0.04	1.5
C	0.03	0.9
Portfolio 60/40		
60%A + 40%B	0.028	0.900
Portfolio 50/50		
50%A + 50%B	0.030	1.000

The factor sensitivity of Portfolio 60/40 is identical to that of Fund C; therefore, this strategy results in no factor risk relative to Portfolio C. However, Fund C's expected return of 3.0 percent is higher than Portfolio 60/40's expected return of 2.8 percent. This difference supports Strategy 3: buying Fund C and selling short Portfolio 60/40 to exploit the arbitrage opportunity.

10. C is correct. In a macroeconomic factor model, the factors are surprises in macroeconomic variables, such as inflation risk and GDP growth, that significantly explain returns.

11. A is correct. The macroeconomic two-factor model takes the following form:

$$R_i = a_i + b_{i1}F_{INF} + b_{i2}F_{GDP} + \epsilon_i,$$

where F_{INF} and F_{GDP} represent surprises in inflation and surprises in GDP growth, respectively, and a_i represents the expected return to asset i. Using this model and the data in Exhibit 2, the returns for Fund A and Fund C are represented by the following:

$$R_A = 0.02 + 0.5F_{INF} + 1.0F_{GDP} + \epsilon_A$$

$$R_C = 0.03 + 1.0F_{INF} + 1.1F_{GDP} + \epsilon_C$$

Surprise in a macroeconomic model is defined as actual factor minus predicted factor. The surprise in inflation is 0.2% (= 2.2% − 2.0%). The surprise in GDP growth is −0.5% (= 1.0% − 1.5%). The return for Portfolio AC, composed of a 60 percent allocation to Fund A and 40 percent allocation to Fund C, is calculated as the following:

$$R_{AC} = (0.6)(0.02) + (0.4)(0.03) + [(0.6)(0.5) + (0.4)(1.0)](0.002) + [(0.6)(1.0) + (0.4)(1.1)](-0.005) + 0.6(0) + 0.4(0)$$
$$= 2.02\%$$

12. C is correct. Surprise in a macroeconomic model is defined as actual factor minus predicted factor. For inflation, the surprise factor is 2.2% − 2.0% = 0.2%; for GDP growth, the surprise factor is 1.0% − 1.5% = −0.5%. The effect on returns is the product of the surprise and the factor sensitivity.

	Change in Portfolio Return due to Surprise in	
Fund	Inflation	GDP Growth
A	$0.5 \times 0.2\% = 0.10\%$	$1.0 \times -0.5\% = -0.50\%$
B	$1.6 \times 0.2\% = 0.32\%$	$0.0 \times -0.5\% = 0.00\%$
C	$1.0 \times 0.2\% = 0.20\%$	$1.1 \times -0.5\% = -0.55\%$

The effect of the GDP growth surprise on Fund C was the largest single-factor effect on Fund returns (−0.55 percent).

13. A is correct. The effect of the surprises in inflation and GDP growth on the returns of the three funds is calculated as the following.

	Change in Portfolio Return Because of Surprise in	
Fund	Inflation	GDP Growth
A	$0.5 \times 0.2\% = 0.10\%$	$1.0 \times -0.5\% = -0.50\%$
B	$1.6 \times 0.2\% = 0.32\%$	$0.0 \times -0.5\% = 0.00\%$
C	$1.0 \times 0.2\% = 0.20\%$	$1.1 \times -0.5\% = -0.55\%$

The combined effects for the three funds are the following.

Fund A: 0.10% + (−0.50%) = −0.40%
Fund B: 0.32% + (0.00%) = 0.32%
Fund C: 0.20% + (−0.55%) = −0.35%

Therefore, Fund A is the most sensitive to the surprises in inflation and GDP growth in Exhibit 3.

14. A is correct. When using a macroeconomic factor, the expected return is the intercept (when all model factors take on a value of zero). The intercept coefficient for Portfolio 1 in Exhibit 1 is 2.58.

15. C is correct. Active risk, also referred to as tracking risk or tracking error, is the sample standard deviation of the time series of active returns, where the active returns consist of the differences between the portfolio return and the benchmark return. Whereas GDP is the only portfolio non-zero sensitivity for Portfolio 2, the contribution to the portfolio's active return is the sum of the differences between the portfolio's and the benchmark's sensitivities multiplied by the factor return. Because all four of the factor sensitivities of Portfolio 2 are different from the factor sensitivities of the benchmark, all four factors contribute to the portfolio's active return and, therefore, to its active risk.

16. A is correct. Portfolio 1 has the highest information ratio, 1.0, and thus has the best mean active return per unit of active risk:

$$IR = \frac{\bar{R}_P - \bar{R}_B}{s(R_P - R_B)}$$

$$= \frac{1.50\%}{1.50\%}$$

$$= 1.00$$

This information ratio exceeds that of Portfolio 2 (−0.38) or Portfolio 3 (0.50).

17. C is correct. In a macroeconomic factor model, the factors are surprises in macroeconomic variables that significantly explain returns. Factor sensitivities are generally specified first in fundamental factor models, whereas factor sensitivities are estimated last in macroeconomic factor models.

18. B is correct. An advantage of statistical factor models is that they make minimal assumptions. However, the interpretation of statistical factors is generally more difficult than the interpretation of macroeconomic and fundamental factor models.

19. B is correct. Analysts can use multifactor models in passively managed portfolios to replicate an index fund's factor exposures.

CHAPTER 13

MEASURING AND MANAGING MARKET RISK

SOLUTIONS

1. B is correct. Duration is a measure of interest rate risk. To reduce risk in anticipation of an increase in interest rates, Montes would seek to shorten the portfolio's duration. He is limited, however, in the amount he can shift from P_2 to P_1. Selling $15 million of P_2 reduces that portfolio to the lower end of the permitted 40 percent to 60 percent range. By reinvesting the proceeds at the shortest maturities allowed, Montes substantially reduces the portfolio duration.

2. B is correct. An index-tracking portfolio without options has a delta of 1. To achieve a delta of 0.9, the delta of the options position must be negative. Of the three choices, only short calls have a negative delta. Long call options have deltas ranging from 0 to 1. Short calls, therefore, have deltas ranging from 0 to −1. The short call position lowers the portfolio's overall delta as desired.

3. B is correct. VaR measures the frequency of losses of a given minimum magnitude. Here the VaR indicates that on 5 percent of trading days, the portfolio will experience a loss of at least $6.5 million. (Although C may appear to say the same thing as B, it actually implies that the portfolio will experience a loss on 95 percent of trading days.) The correct interpretation is that returns will be equal to or greater than −$6.5 million on 95 percent of trading days; those returns include gains as well as losses.

4. A is correct. The bank policy requires the addition of forward-looking risk assessments, and management is focused on tail risk. Conditional VaR measures tail risk, and stress tests and scenario analysis subject current portfolio holdings to historical or hypothetical stress events.

5. A is correct. VaR measures do *not* capture liquidity risk. "If some assets in a portfolio are relatively illiquid, VaR could be understated, even under normal market conditions. Additionally, liquidity squeezes are frequently associated with tail events and major market downturns, thereby exacerbating the risk."

6. C is correct. The Monte Carlo simulation method can accommodate virtually any distribution, an important factor given the increased frequency of large daily losses. This method can also more easily accommodate the large number of portfolio holdings. The Monte Carlo method allows the user to develop her own forward-looking assumptions about the portfolio's risk and return characteristics, unlike the historical simulation method, which uses the current portfolio and re-prices it using the actual historical changes in the key factors experienced during the lookback period. Given the limited return history for infrastructure investments and Hamilton's expectations for higher-than-normal volatility, the historical simulation method would be a suboptimal choice.

7. C is correct. Conditional VaR is a measure of tail risk that provides an estimate of the average loss that would be incurred if the VaR cutoff is exceeded.

8. C is correct. A hypothetical scenario analysis allows the risk manager to estimate the likely effect of the scenario on a range of portfolio risk factors. A sovereign ratings downgrade would affect Hiram's India equity and corporate bond exposures as well as the government bond exposure. In addition, the assumptions used in constructing the scenario analysis can specifically address the effect of a need to sell large position sizes under decreased liquidity conditions resulting from a ratings downgrade. VaR alone does not accurately reflect the risk of large position sizes, which may be difficult to trade.

9. C is correct. A hypothetical scenario analysis allows Hamilton to estimate the direct effect of a ratings downgrade on the portfolio's government bond holdings and the resulting need to sell a number of the portfolio's holdings because they no longer meet the ratings guidelines. VaR alone does not accurately reflect the risk of large position sizes, which may be difficult to trade. The hypothetical scenario analysis will also highlight the effect of increased economic turmoil on all of the portfolio's exposures, not only the government bond exposures.

10. B is correct. The VaR is derived as follows:

$$VaR = \{[E(Rp) - 2.33\sigma_p](-1)\}(\text{Portfolio value}),$$

where

$E(R_p)$ = Annualized daily return = $(0.00026 \times 250) = 0.065$

250 = Number of trading days annually

2.33 = Number of standard deviations to attain 1% VaR

σ_p = Annualized standard deviation = $(0.00501 \times \sqrt{250}) = 0.079215$

Portfolio value = CAD260,000,000

$VaR = -(0.065 - 0.184571) \times CAD260,000,000$

$= CAD31,088,460.$

11. B is correct. Given the large fixed-income exposure in the LICIA portfolio, examining the portfolio duration more closely would be prudent. Duration is the primary sensitivity exposure measure for fixed-income investments.

12. B is correct. VaR is the minimum loss that would be expected a certain percentage of the time over a specified period of time given the assumed market conditions. A 5 percent VaR is often expressed as its complement—a 95 percent level of confidence. Therefore, the monthly VaR in Exhibit 5 indicates that $5.37 million is the minimum loss that would be expected to occur over one month 5 percent of the time.

Alternatively, 95 percent of the time, a loss of more than $5.37 million would not be expected.

13. C is correct. Flusk experienced zero daily VaR breaches over the last year yet incurred a substantial loss. A limitation of VaR is its vulnerability to different volatility regimes. A portfolio might remain under its VaR limit every day but lose an amount approaching this limit each day. If market volatility during the last year is lower than in the lookback period, the portfolio could accumulate a substantial loss without technically breaching the VaR constraint.

    A is incorrect because VaR was calculated using historical simulation, so the distribution used was based on actual historical changes in the key risk factors experienced during the lookback period. Thus, the distribution is not characterized using estimates of the mean return, the standard deviation, or the correlations among the risk factors in the portfolio. In contrast, the parametric method of estimating VaR generally assumes that the distribution of returns for the risk factors is normal.

    B is incorrect because a specification with a higher confidence level will produce a higher VaR. If a 99 percent confidence interval was used to calculate historical VaR, the VaR would be larger (larger expected minimum loss). During the last year, none of Flusk's losses were substantial enough to breach the 5 percent VaR number (95 percent confidence interval); therefore, if McKee used a 1 percent VaR (99 percent confidence interval), the number of VaR breaches would not change.

14. B is correct. In order to simulate the impact of the latest financial crisis on the current bond portfolio holdings, McKee's valuation model for bonds should use the historical yields of bonds with similar maturity. Historical yields drive the pricing of bonds more than the price history or the current duration. Historical prices for the fixed-income positions currently held in the portfolio may not exist, and even when historical prices do exist, they may not be relevant to the current characteristics (e.g., maturity) of the instrument. Even if the same bonds existed at the time of the latest financial crisis, their durations would change because of the passage of time.

    A is incorrect because using a bond's past price history would mischaracterize the risk of the current portfolio holdings. For this reason, the historical yields are more important in explaining the risks. Historical prices for the fixed-income positions currently held in the portfolio may not exist, and even when historical prices do exist, they may not be relevant to the current characteristics (e.g., maturity) of the instrument.

    C is incorrect because historical bond durations would not capture the current characteristics of the bonds in the portfolio. Duration is a sensitivity measure and is the weighted-average time to maturity of a bond. Even if the same bonds existed at the time of the latest financial crisis, their remaining time to maturity and durations would change because of the passage of time.

15. C is correct. Ming suggested in Analysis 1 to use a historical scenario that measures the hypothetical portfolio return that would result from a repeat of a particular period of financial market history. Historical scenarios are complementary to VaR but are not going to happen in exactly the same way again, and they require additional measures to overcome the shortcomings of the VaR.

16. B is correct. Analysis 2 describes surplus at risk. Surplus at risk is an application of VaR; it estimates how much the assets might underperform the liabilities with a given confidence level, usually over a year.

17. B is correct. Incremental VaR measures the change in a portfolio's VaR as a result of adding or removing a position from the portfolio or if a position size is changed relative to the remaining positions.

18. B is correct. McKee suggests running a stress test using a historical scenario specific to emerging markets that includes an extreme change in credit spreads. Stress tests, which apply extreme negative stress to a particular portfolio exposure, are closely related to scenario risk measures. A scenario risk measure estimates the portfolio return that would result from a hypothetical change in markets (hypothetical scenario) or a repeat of a historical event (historical scenario). When the historical simulation fully revalues securities under rate and price changes that occurred during the scenario period, the results should be highly accurate.

     A is incorrect because marginal VaR measures the change in portfolio VaR given a very small change in a portfolio position (e.g., change in VaR for a $1 or 1 percent change in the position). Therefore, marginal VaR would not allow McKee to estimate how much the value of the option-embedded bonds would change under an extreme change in credit spreads.

     C is incorrect because sensitivity risk measures use sensitivity exposure measures, such as first-order (delta, duration) and second-order (gamma, convexity) sensitivity, to assess the change in the value of a financial instrument. Although gamma and convexity can be used with delta and duration to estimate the impact of extreme market movements, they are not suited for scenario analysis related to option-embedded bonds.

19. A is correct. VaR has emerged as one of the most popular risk measures because global banking regulators require or encourage the use of it. VaR is also frequently found in annual reports of financial firms and can be used for comparisons.

20. A is correct. VaR is an estimate of the loss that is expected to be exceeded with a given level of probability over a specified time period. The parametric method typically assumes that the return distributions for the risk factors in the portfolio are normal. It then uses the expected return and standard deviation of return for each risk factor and correlations to estimate VaR.

21. B is correct. Value at risk is the minimum loss that would be expected a certain percentage of the time over a certain period of time. Statement 2 implies that there is a 5 percent chance the portfolio will fall in value by $90,000 (= $6,000,000 × 1.5%) or more in a single day. If VaR is measured on a daily basis and a typical month has 20–22 business days, then 5 percent of the days equates to about 1 day per month or once in 20 trading days.

22. A is correct. Statement 2 indicates that the Equity Opportunities Fund reported a daily VaR value. One of the limitations of VaR is that it focuses so heavily on left-tail events (the losses) that right-tail events (potential gains) are often ignored.

     B is incorrect because VaR is viewed as forward looking in that it uses the current portfolio holdings and measures its potential loss. The Sharpe ratio represents a backward-looking, return-based measure and is used to assess the skill of the manager.

     C is incorrect because VaR does not provide an accurate risk estimate in either trending or volatile regimes. A portfolio might remain under its VaR limit every day but lose an amount approaching this limit each day. Under such circumstances, the portfolio could accumulate substantial losses without technically breaching the VaR constraint. Also, during periods of low volatility, VaR will appear quite low, underestimating the losses that could occur when the environment returns to a normal level of volatility.

23. C is correct. Measuring VaR at a 5 percent threshold produces an estimated value at risk of 2.69 percent. From Exhibit 6, the expected annual portfolio return is 14.1 percent and the standard deviation is 26.3 percent. Annual values need to be adjusted to get their daily counterparts. Assuming 250 trading days in a year, the expected annual return is adjusted by dividing by 250 and the standard deviation is adjusted by dividing by the square root of 250. Thus, the daily expected return is $0.141/250 = 0.000564$, and volatility is $0.263/\sqrt{250} = 0.016634$. 5 percent daily VaR $= E(R_p) - 1.65\sigma_p = 0.000564 - 1.65(0.016634) = -0.026882$. The portfolio is expected to experience a potential minimum loss in percentage terms of 2.69 percent on 5 percent of trading days.

24. C is correct. The change in value of a bond is inversely related to a change in yield. Given a bond priced at B with duration D and yield change of Δy, the rate of return or percentage price change for the bond is approximately given as follows: $\Delta B/B \approx -D\Delta y/(1 + y)$. Under Scenario 3, interest rates decrease by 20 bps. In an environment of decreasing interest rates, the bond with the highest duration will have the greatest positive return. Bond 3 has a duration of 10.2, which is greater than that of both Bond 1 (duration = 1.3) and Bond 2 (duration = 3.7).

25. C is correct. A traditional asset manager uses *ex post* tracking error when analyzing backward-looking returns. The Diversified Fixed-Income Fund prospectus stipulates a target benchmark deviation of no more than 5 bps. Tracking error is a measure of the degree to which the performance of a given investment deviates from its benchmark.

26. B is correct. Position limits are limits on the market value of any given investment; they are excellent controls on overconcentration. Position limits can be expressed in currency units or as a percentage of net assets. The Alpha Core Equity Fund restricts the exposure of individual securities to 1.75 percent of the total portfolio.

CHAPTER 14

BACKTESTING AND SIMULATION

SOLUTIONS

1. A is correct. The analyst assumes a reporting lag of four months, which can introduce stale information even though it can significantly reduce look-ahead bias. C is incorrect because Ruckey has accounted for survivorship bias in backtesting by using point-in-time index constituent stocks, and not just the current survivors.

2. B is correct. Factor Strategy 2's signal provides the strongest predictive power in the long term because the Spearman rank IC for the first month is positive and the decay speed is slow.

   A is incorrect because Factor Strategy 1 has the highest 30-year average signal autocorrelation of the three strategies, which indicates that portfolios formed using this factor experience the lowest turnover. All else being equal, factors with low turnover, indicated by a high autocorrelation, are preferred because such factors lead to lower portfolio turnover, lower transaction costs, and therefore higher after-cost cumulative performance.

   C is incorrect because Factor Strategy 3 has the lowest Spearman rank IC for Month 1, indicating the weakest predictive power in the first month. The higher the average IC, the higher the factor's predictive power for subsequent returns.

3. A is correct. A risk parity multifactor model is constructed by equally weighting the risk contribution of each factor. B is incorrect because Statement 2 is incorrect. The process for creating multifactor portfolios by equally weighting all factors and equal-weighting the risk contribution of all factors requires a second rolling-window procedure in order to avoid look-ahead bias, not model selection bias. C is incorrect because Statement 1 is correct but Statement 2 is incorrect. The process for creating multifactor portfolios by equally weighting all factors and equal-weighting the risk contribution of all factors requires a second rolling-window procedure in order to avoid look-ahead bias, not model selection bias.

4. C is correct. Approach 1 is a historical simulation and assumes that past asset returns provide sufficient guidance about future asset returns. A is incorrect because both approaches are non-deterministic and random in nature. Approach 1 is a historical simulation and Approach 2 is a Monte Carlo simulation. B is incorrect because Approach 1 is a historical simulation and each random variable of interest (key driver and/or decision variable) is randomly drawn from historical data. A functional form of the statistical distribution of returns for each decision variable needs to be specified for a Monte Carlo simulation, which is Approach 2.

5. C is correct. Approach 2 is a Monte Carlo simulation. The returns of Portfolios A and B are driven by the returns of the nine underlying factor portfolios (based on nine common growth factors). In the case of asset or factor allocation strategies, the returns from six of the nine factors are clearly correlated, and therefore it is necessary to specify a multivariate distribution rather than modeling each factor or asset on a standalone basis. In the context of a multivariate normal distribution with nine random variables, nine randomly generated numbers from the uniform distribution are mapped onto a point on the joint cumulative probability distribution function.

    A is incorrect because Approach 2 is a Monte Carlo simulation to generate investment performance data for the nine underlying factor portfolios. The returns of six of the nine factors are clearly correlated, which means specifying a multivariate distribution rather than modeling each factor or asset on a standalone basis.

    B is incorrect because the analyst should calculate the elements of the covariance matrix for all factors, not only the correlated factors. Doing so entails calculating 36, not 15, elements of the covariance matrix. Approach 2 is a Monte Carlo simulation using the factor allocation strategies for Portfolios A and B for the nine factor portfolios, the returns of which are clearly correlated, which means specifying a multivariate distribution. To calibrate the model, a few key parameters need to be calculated: the mean, the standard deviation, and the covariance matrix. For 9 assets, we need to estimate 9 mean returns, 9 standard deviations, and $\frac{9 \times (9-1)}{2} = 36$ elements of the covariance matrix. Assuming just the 6 correlated assets, the calculation is: $\frac{6 \times (6-1)}{2} = 15$.

6. B is correct. The distribution of Factor 1 returns exhibits excess kurtosis and negative skewness. The excess kurtosis implies that these strategies are more likely to generate surprises, meaning extreme returns, whereas the negative skewness suggests those surprises are more likely to be negative (than positive). A is incorrect because risk-averse investors are more likely to prefer distribution properties such as positive skew (higher probability of positive returns) and lower to moderate kurtosis (lower probability of extreme negative surprises). The distribution of Factor 1 returns exhibits excess kurtosis and negative skewness. C is incorrect because the distribution of Factor 1 returns exhibits excess kurtosis and negative skewness. The joint distribution of such returns is rarely multivariate normal—so, typically the means and variances of these returns and the correlations between them are insufficient to describe the joint return distribution. In other words, the return data do not line up tightly around a trend line because of fat tails and outliers.

7. B is correct. Random sampling with replacement, also known as bootstrapping, is often used in historical simulations because the number of simulations needed is often larger than the size of the historical dataset. Because Approach 1 is a historical simulation and

Concern 3 notes that the number of simulations needed is larger than the size of the historical dataset, bootstrapping should be used.

A is incorrect because although bootstrapping (random sampling with replacement) would address the concern that the number of simulations needed is larger than the size of the historical dataset, a walk-forward framework is used for backtesting as a proxy for actual investing, not for bootstrapping. For historical simulation, researchers typically use a rolling window (also called walk-forward) framework to rebalance the portfolio periodically and then track the performance over time.

C is incorrect because choosing the multivariate normal distribution as the initial functional form is typically done in a Monte Carlo simulation (Approach 2), not in a historical simulation (Approach 1). Historical simulation randomly samples from the historical dataset by drawing a number from a uniform distribution so that there is equal probability of being selected. Choice of distribution would not address the concern about the size of the dataset.

8. B is correct. Sensitivity analysis can be implemented to help managers understand how the target variable (portfolio returns) and risk profiles are affected by changes in input variables. Approach 2 is a Monte Carlo simulation, and the results depend on whether the multivariate normal distribution is the correct functional form or a reasonable proxy for the true distribution. Because this information is almost never known, sensitivity analysis using a multivariate skewed Student's t-distribution helps to account for empirical properties such as the skewness and the excess kurtosis observed in the underlying factor return data.

A is incorrect because Ruckey is describing sensitivity analysis, not data snooping. Data snooping is the subconscious or conscious manipulation of data in a way that produces a statistically significant result (i.e., a p-value that is sufficiently small or a t-statistic that is sufficiently large to indicate statistically significance).

C is incorrect because Ruckey is describing sensitivity analysis, not inverse transformation. The inverse transformation method is the process of converting a randomly generated number into a simulated value of a random variable.

9. A is correct. Statement 1 is correct because the main objective of backtesting is to understand the risk–return tradeoff of an investment strategy by approximating the real-life investment process. B is incorrect because Statement 2 is not accurate. Although backtesting fits quantitative and systematic investment styles more naturally, it has also been heavily used by fundamental managers. C is incorrect because Statement 2 is not accurate. Backtesting is used in quantitative and systematic investment styles and is also heavily used by fundamental managers.

10. A is correct. A number of key parameters need to be specified when backtesting an investment strategy, including the investment universe, stock returns, frequency of rebalancing, and start and end dates. Because Galic has specified his desire to use only domestic (Canadian) equities, the MSCI World equity index and currency hedging of equity returns should not be used. Therefore, a key parameter to be incorporated into the analysis of Value Portfolio I is the frequency of rebalancing. Practitioners typically use monthly returns and monthly rebalancing.

11. B is correct. Backtesting typically follows the three steps of (1) strategy design, (2) historical investment simulation, and (3) analysis of backtesting output. Analysis of backtesting output encompasses the calculation of portfolio performance statistics and

other key metrics such as turnover, the Sharpe ratio, the information ratio, and the Sortino ratio. Galic's apprehension about the long–short hedged portfolio approach relate primarily to issues (e.g., loss of interest income, transaction costs, turnover) that could negatively affect his risk-adjusted performance. Therefore, his statement expresses the most concern with matters measured in Step 3: analysis of backtesting output.

12. B is correct. The alternative approach to the long–short hedged portfolio method is to use an information coefficient (IC). The Spearman rank IC is the correlation between the prior-period ranked factor scores and the ranked current-period returns.

A is incorrect because the Pearson IC is the simple correlation coefficient between the factor scores for the prior period for all stocks in the investment universe under consideration and the current period's stock returns.

C is incorrect because, although a cross-sectional (univariate) regression approach may use returns at time t and factor scores at time $t - 1$, it does not use the correlation between the prior-period ranked factor scores and the ranked current-period returns, whereas the Spearman Rank IC does. A univariate regression's inference centers on whether or not the fitted factor return is statistically significant. Because the regression coefficient and the Pearson IC [i.e., $Corr(r_t, f_{t-1})$] always have the same sign, they typically produce similar results.

13. C is correct. The statistical study performed by GWP on the relationship between value and momentum factors found that the joint distribution between the returns for the factors had two peaks in the tails and that the peaks were higher than that from a normal distribution. This result implies a higher probability of positive co-movements in the tails of the two variables, relative to that from a normal distribution. Because the tail dependence coefficient focuses on the correlation in the tails of two random variables, the tail dependence coefficient in the study is most likely high and positive.

14. C is correct. Exhibit 1 presents three downside risk measures: VaR, CVaR, and maximum drawdown. Conditional VaR is defined as the weighted average of all loss outcomes in the return distribution that exceed the VaR loss. Thus, CVaR is a more comprehensive measure of tail loss than VaR. Based on Exhibit 1, the factor with the smallest downside risk based on CVaR is Factor 3.

15. B is correct. The fact that the two firms' investment performance results differ over similar time horizons using the same data and factors may be the result of selection bias. Data snooping is a type of selection bias. Fastlane Wealth Managers is most likely selecting the best-performing modeling approach and publishing its results. A is incorrect because risk parity is a portfolio construction technique that accounts for the volatility of each factor and the correlations of returns among all factors to be combined in the portfolio. It is not regarded as selection bias. C is incorrect because cross-validation is a technique used in the machine learning field to partition data for model training and testing. It is not considered selection bias.

16. A is correct. Using the Sharpe ratio, the best risk-adjusted relative performance can be determined by comparing the sensitivity of the two strategies under differing macroeconomic regimes: recession versus non-recession and high volatility versus low volatility. The best risk-adjusted return will exhibit the highest Sharpe ratio. Strategy II demonstrates higher risk-adjusted returns compared with Strategy I under all four

macroeconomic conditions, particularly in periods of low volatility, when the Sharpe ratio outperformance is 0.96, and recessions, when the Sharpe ratio outperformance is 1.56.

Scenario Analysis Using Sharpe Ratio

Strategy/Regime	High Volatility	Low Volatility	Recession	Non-recession
Strategy I	0.88	0.64	0.20	1.00
Strategy II	1.56	1.60	1.76	1.52
Difference (II – I)	0.68	0.96	1.56	0.52

 CFA Institute

ABOUT THE CFA PROGRAM

If the subject matter of this book interests you, and you are not already a CFA Charterholder, we hope you will consider registering for the CFA Program and starting progress toward earning the Chartered Financial Analyst designation. The CFA designation is a globally recognized standard of excellence for measuring the competence and integrity of investment professionals. To earn the CFA charter, candidates must successfully complete the CFA Program, a global graduate-level self-study program that combines a broad curriculum with professional conduct requirements as preparation for a career as an investment professional.

Anchored by a practice-based curriculum, the CFA Program body of knowledge reflects the knowledge, skills, and abilities identified by professionals as essential to the investment decision-making process. This body of knowledge maintains its relevance through a regular, extensive survey of practicing CFA charterholders across the globe. The curriculum covers 10 general topic areas, ranging from equity and fixed-income analysis to portfolio management to corporate finance—all with a heavy emphasis on the application of ethics in professional practice. Known for its rigor and breadth, the CFA Program curriculum highlights principles common to every market so that professionals who earn the CFA designation have a thoroughly global investment perspective and a profound understanding of the global marketplace.

www.cfainstitute.org